The story goes...

Nico ter Linden was born in 1936 and studied theology in the Netherlands and the United States. After working as a prison chaplain in Alkmaar and a hospital chaplain in Nijmegen, in 1977 he became minister of the Westerkerk in Amsterdam, where he remained until 1995. His biblical sermons brought him fame, and he became a newspaper columnist and a television broadcaster as well as writing many books. In 1995 he retired to devote himself to full-time writing and began on *The story goes...*, which became a bestseller on publication in the Netherlands in 1997. More than 150,000 copies of the first volume, on the stories of the Torah, have been sold, and 80,000 of the second volume, on the Gospels of Matthew and Mark, which appeared in 1998. Both are available in English. Three more volumes are planned and will appear in English versions. Volume 3, on the 'Former and Latter Prophets', the historical and prophetic books of the Old Testament, is due in 1999; volumes on the 'Writings', including Job, Proverbs and the Psalms, and on the works attributed to Luke (the Gospels and Acts) and John (the Gospel and the Book of Revelation) will appear by 2002.

Nico ter Linden

The
story
goes...

1

THE STORIES
OF THE TORAH

SCM PRESS

222.1
LIND

Translated by John Bowden from the Dutch *Het verhaal gaat... 1. De verhalen van de Thora*, published 1996 by Uitgeverij Balans, Amsterdam.

© Uitgeverij Balans, Amsterdam and Nico ter Linden 1998

Translation © John Bowden 1999

500 410217
2221/LIND

0 334 02764 0

This edition first published 1999 by
SCM Press
9–17 St Albans Place London N1 0NX

SCM Press is a division of SCM–Canterbury Press Ltd

Typeset by Regent Typesetting, London
Printed in Great Britain by
Biddles Ltd, Guildford and King's Lynn

CONTENTS

Please note

The asterisks in the text refer to the list of sources and quotations at the back of the book.

In five volumes I shall be retelling and explaining the stories of the Bible.

This volume is about the Torah, the first five books of the Old Testament. The New Testament cannot be understood without the Old Testament, but the Old Testament can be understood without the New Testament.

In retelling the New Testament I shall constantly have to keep referring back to the Old Testament. In retelling the Old Testament, now and then I take the liberty of looking forward to the New Testament. In doing so I hope to draw the attention of readers to words and images that the New Testament authors took from their Bible.

1

IN THE BEGINNING

GENESIS 1.1

The story goes that in the beginning God created heaven and earth.

It's a story from Israel, and it's said to have been written down some twenty-six centuries ago, when the Israelites were in exile, prisoners by the rivers of Babylon. They were far from home. And it's often when you're far from home that the big questions arise. How did everything get to be the way it is? Where do we come from, and where are we going? Is there a God who willed and made us? Why are we on this earth, which is sometimes such a paradise and sometimes so barren and empty? We're exiles, refugees with no refuge, and misfortune is our lot. Is there a God who sees this, or are we left helpless to fate, to sun and moon and stars? We can barely keep our heads above water, the breath is knocked out of us; is there any hope left? Is there no one who, in God's name, can throw some light on our darkness?

Hush, Israel is telling a story. A priest of Israel is telling a story. He's a priest without a temple. He, too, is far from home. The people can no longer bring their young rams or doves to him for sacrifice. But they can bring him their questions. And the priest becomes a storyteller. Some of his sources are centuries old; some are those of his day. That's how this story was born, this story with which he comforts his people: *In the beginning God created the heavens and the earth...*

Don't suppose that this priest is talking about the beginning of the world. He knows nothing about that, nor is he interested in it. He isn't giving a lecture on *how* the world came to be; he's singing a song of faith about *why* it is. In this way the priest is answering a question which doesn't really have an answer. However, the question never goes away, so he ventures an answer.

So the priest isn't out to provide his despairing people with a geological explanation of how God began the heavens and the earth. He wouldn't try to comfort them with that, even if he knew. No, he's telling them – theologically, and to the best of his ability – what God was doing when he began on heaven and earth, what God set out to do *in principle*. People in Israel had already been reflecting on this enormous question for centuries. And certainly now, in exile, the people are reflecting on it, just as their neighbours, the Egyptians and the Babylonians, reflected on it. The priest offers the exiles the good ideas that he has gathered from here and there and from then and now in the form of a song. It's an educational poem. In Israel, teachings are never abstract. They're always turned into stories and parables and songs.

In the beginning... Bereshit in Hebrew.

But what was there before the beginning?

Israel's rabbis wondered about that too. After all, there's no end to the questions you can ask about the beginning! But, the rabbis said, there's a reason why the Bible starts with the letter *Beth*. In Hebrew, which is read from right to left, the letter looks like this:

Scripture begins with this *Beth*, the rabbis said, so that we don't ask what's above, below or behind us, but listen to what's coming. Israel has no story about the birth or origin of God. God is the wholly Other. Unlike the heavens and the earth which he created, God stands above creation. Hence that mysterious *Beth* at the beginning.

That *Beth* looks just like a little house, and that's exactly what it means in Hebrew: house. The rabbis were very well aware of that: 'My child, we may be in a strange land, but we have firm ground under our feet and a roof over our heads; we've a shelter behind us and we have a future before us. There are those who say that we're ruled by mysterious forces. Others say there's nothing at all, only emptiness. Don't believe it, my child. Always remember the first letter of our great Book; that's the whole of our faith.'

In the beginning God created the heavens and the earth.

The heavens and the *erets*. That word *erets* is impossible to translate, for it means both the earth in its entirety and the land of Israel, *erets Yisrael.*

That has to do with the faith of the Israelites. They began to suspect that *in* Israel God is concerned with the *whole* earth. Israel is God's chosen people. But (except at unguarded moments) Israel doesn't see itself *just* as having been chosen by God. In its finest moments, Israel sees itself as having been chosen by God *for service,* for service to the world of the nations. Historically, Israel is an insignificant little people, but in the Bible it stands for no less than all of humankind. Geographically, Israel is an insignificant little country, but in the stories of faith which it tells, this little *erets* is no less than a testing ground for the whole *erets.* So the history-in-miniature of God's involvement with this people stands for the history of the world as a whole. Non-Jews, the Gentiles, those who belong to the peoples, the *goyim,* are invited to take part in that history. In fact, that's the only reason why we're sitting by the rivers of Babylon at the feet of this priest, who is about to tell his story. Just imagine! What if there in Israel they really were on the track of the Creator of heaven and earth!

In the beginning God created the heavens and the earth.
    Heaven and earth are to be the stage on which the history of God and humankind will soon unfold. Heaven and earth belong together, just as God and human beings belong together. The storyteller can be brief about heaven, because that's God's place. He prefers to turn to the earth.
    And the earth was waste and desolate, and darkness lay upon the flood.
    The Israelites, driven from their homes and exhausted, captives by the rivers of Babylon while their distant *erets Yisrael* lies in ruins, know what this means. Life is waste and desolate. *Tohu wabohu,* as they say in Hebrew. No words could better evoke the bitter life of the exile. The primal flood all around. Who will divide the floods? Who can walk on the waters?
    Hush, the priest is telling his story.
    The spirit moves him, and he tells it.
    And the Spirit of God hovered over the waters. Like an eagle poised quivering, almost motionless in the air, above its nest of young, so God's spirit hovered over the primal flood. When one of its young spreads its wings for the first time and seems about to fall, the eagle swoops, bears up the eaglet on its wings and brings it back to the safety of the nest. Protective, watchful, caring, the eagle hovers above the nest which contains its young. So God's breath hovers over the dark waters, brooding on a plan.

And God said...

Who says that God says anything? What are we to imagine by 'God speaking'? After all, this can happen only 'after a manner of speaking'.

I was about to give my first Bible lesson in a village school north of Amsterdam. 'And God said...,' I remarked, but I never got round to what God said, because immediately a little boy raised his hand: 'Does God still say things?'

I've never forgotten that boy. What a splendid question! He wanted to know exactly what kind of story I was going to tell. Growing up in the Dutch countryside, he had never come across a talking God. Had this teacher met one? How was this boy to imagine such a talking God? Or could it be that God used to speak, but at some point stopped? Or was it all fantasy?

I can't remember what answer I gave at the time. Today I would say this: 'Of course it's a fantasy, Israel's fantasy about God. No one has ever seen God or spoken with him. There is a veil of cloud between where we live and where God lives, just as a curtain hangs in the temple between the holy place where people come to pray and the Holy of Holies, where God is enthroned between the cherubim. We can only have fantasies about God. We project our images of God, our notions of God, on to the veil of cloud, the screen that hangs between heaven and earth: Mother, Father, Creator, Perfecter, Eagle, King, Judge, Shepherd, Old Man with a Beard. They're all images taken from *our* reality; where else could we get them from?'

Does this mean that God is merely the result of our projections? Wouldn't it be better, rather than saying 'God created human beings', to say that human beings created God? Who can guarantee that there's a grain of truth in these projections? Maybe there's nothing on the other side of the veil but empty space!

That's could be. But it could also be that God lives on the far side of the clouds, above the ceiling of our thought, the same God who made us beings capable of projection. All talk about 'up there' comes from down here; there are no two ways about it.* Israel's experience was that human beings on earth could catch a glimpse of heaven every now and then, and they turned these divine encounters into stories. Of course God is completely different from those who fantasize about him. Nevertheless, they boldly believe that one day, when they see him face to face on the other side of the curtain, their thoughts and dreams and fantasies will prove to be not far off the mark.

Every people on earth has projected its thoughts of God on to the veil of clouds. But has any people ever done so as beautifully and as profoundly as the people of Israel? Is this perhaps why God chose this people? Was it God's will to reveal himself on our *erets* by way of the *erets Yisrael*?

And God said... , says the priest.

Here he is trying to describe something about God, and about himself. What he means to say is, 'I imagine God as someone who said...' And whenever the spirit of God moved them, before, during and after their exile, the children of Israel heard these stories and told them and retold them, wrote them down and rewrote them, and finally gathered the fruits of their labours into a book. In turn, Israel gave to the peoples, the *goyim*, what they had been given: a godsend.

And God said...

Let me interrupt the priest one last time, with a little Hasidic legend about Rabbi Susya.* Susya was a disciple of the great Rebbe of Mezritch, but he never passed on a single word of his master to his followers. That was because he had never listened to any of his master's teaching all the way through. At the beginning of his discourse, when he was about to read the portion of scripture that he wished to expound, the Rebbe would always start with the words 'And God said...'. No sooner had these great words passed his lips than Susya was overcome and went into a rapture. The other disciples had to drag him to the woodshed. There he could be heard pounding on the walls, wailing, 'And God said... And God said...'. What God said, Rabbi Susya never heard from his master's lips. Only that God was speaking.

2

AND GOD SAID

GENESIS 1-2.4A

God said, 'Let there be light.' And there was light.

Every year on Simchat Torah, the feast of Joy in the Law, these words from 'In the beginning' resound in the synagogue. And all the children of Israel sense that this is about the *tohu wabohu* of their own lives and the belief that the last word has not been spoken about them. *Let there be light! And there was light.*

For the God of Israel, saying and doing are one and the same. In the beginning was the word, and the word is immediately also deed. God calls for light, and light is there.

This isn't the light of sun and moon. That light was kindled only on the fourth day. It's the light that shines in the darkness and that the darkness cannot quench. It's the light that comes from what God says, and as long as God continues to speak, it will never be dark again. It's the light that so enraptured Rabbi Susya in the dark woodshed: we aren't floating unnoticed and unloved through a silent universe; no, God speaks, and for the people walking in darkness a light dawns. *And God saw that the light was good.*

And God divided the light from the darkness. And God called the light day, and the darkness he called night. Then there was evening and there was morning, the first day.

God divided the light from the darkness, and so came into being a time which he protected. God called the light day. It was good of God to give the light a name and thus a purpose. What's the point of being there if you don't know what you have to do? The light looked questioningly at God: 'What must I do?'

'Be day,' God said. 'Day's your name, day's your nature.' The light is to be daylight for God and human beings.

'You're night,' said God to the darkness. 'And let's agree that every morning you give way to the light of day.'

God has made time. Now for space.

And God said, 'Let there be a firmament in the midst of the waters, and let it divide the waters from the waters.' And God divided the waters under the firmament from the waters above the firmament. And God called the firmament heaven. Then there was evening and there was morning, the second day.

God divided the waters from the waters, making a space which he protected. 'You're heaven,' said God to the firmament. 'You keep the waters in check.'

So the priest sings his song, seeing before him the world-view of those days: the earth a flat surface, above it a heavenly firmament resting on pillars, and below it the underworld, the whole surrounded by the waters of the primal ocean. He sings his song for all he's worth. The people can barely keep their heads above water, there by the rivers of Babylon. That's not good. But the priest assures his people that ultimately they have nothing to fear from the waters of death: our God, who once spoke the first word, will one day also have the last word. It's a vision, a dream about a new heaven and a new earth, spoken of on the last page of the Bible as well: *and the sea was no more.**

There's time, there's space, but there's still no solid ground.

And God said, 'Let the waters under the heavens be gathered together into one place, and let the dry land appear.'

'You're earth,' God says to the dry land. 'And you're the seas,' he says to the waters. God knows the mighty primal ocean, the waters of the terrifying floods, like the back of his hand; he talks to them in an intimate way, puts them in their place: 'Be sea, and no more!' And God saw that it was good.

However, the earth wasn't yet completely good, for the earth is only really good when it's green earth, with plants that yield seed after their kind and fruit trees that bear fruit after their kind. *And the earth put forth vegetation, plants yielding seed after their kind, and trees bearing fruit after their kind, and God saw that it was good. Then there was evening and there was morning, the third day.*

And God said, 'Let there be lights in the firmament of heaven to divide the day from the night, to indicate the fixed times of days and years, and to give light upon the earth.' And it was so. And God made the two great lights, the greater light to rule the day, and the lesser light to rule the night. And with his fingers God also made the stars. God saw that it was good. Then there was evening and there was morning, the fourth day.

The Sun and the Moon, the gods before whom Babylon bows, aren't these the powers that rule people's characters, their fate and lives? Isn't everything written in the stars?

'Don't believe it,' proclaims the priest of Israel. 'These are no gods.' He doesn't even call the sun and moon by name; as far as he's concerned, they have no name. They're mere lanterns, lamps, good for warmth and light and good for the calendar. Little lights. Pretty and useful little lights, nothing more.

What a bold priest he is! He's de-mystifying the cosmos. He isn't giving a lecture on how the world began. He's confessing what he believes: behind this world, above this world, is God. The Eternal One is our partner. He gave us light to live by, room to breathe, a habitable earth. Chaos, death, darkness, the wilderness, God has opposed them from the start and will continue to do so. All will be well and all will be well. Don't be afraid. The earth is land to live on; the sea is water to sail on; the heavenly bodies are lamps to work by; and the darkness is time to rest. God has given these things to human beings, as their partners.

This is how, by the rivers of Babylon, the priest comforts and encourages his errant people: with a song against fear, a song of faith in seven stanzas.

The fifth stanza: *God created the birds of the air after their kind. God created the fishes of the sea after their kind. And God saw that it was good. And there was evening and there was morning, the fifth day.*

And God made the wild animals after their kind, and the cattle after its kind, and all that creeps upon the earth after its kind.

What is it that distinguishes one animal from the other? Its species, its kind.

God saw that it was good.

Good for God's purposes. We mustn't forget to add that, for there are a few things in creation that by God we can hardly call good. But in Israel, they believe that before God it was good. That also makes this creation good in *their* eyes.

And God said, 'Let us make human beings...'

The heavenly court holds its breath. What's God up to now... ? He seems to have something special in mind. God doesn't come up in the same breath with a powerful new word of creation: *Let there be human beings, and there they were human beings.* No, it's as though the work of creation pauses for a moment. God is reflecting. You can hear him thinking. Hush, something's about to happen... God hasn't spent the last few days creating the universe for nothing. God has created the heaven and the earth. He's made time and space and solid ground and the trees and the animals. And he's done all of that for the sake of the creature that is now to be created. God is now going to put the crown on his creation: *Let us make human beings, after their kind.*

No, that's not what it says. The trees, the birds, the fish, the cattle and the wild animals were all created *after their kind.* But human beings are created differently: *Let us make humankind in our image, after our likeness, so that they rule over the fish and the birds and the cattle and the earth. And God created humankind in his own image, in the image of God he created them: male and female he created them. And God blessed humankind. 'Be fruitful,' said God to humankind, 'be numerous, fill the earth and rule over it, and over the fish, the birds and the cattle.' And God saw everything that he had made, and look, it was very good. Then there was evening and there was morning, the sixth day.*

God blesses humankind. God calls humankind, and from now on humankind must observe its calling. Human beings are to rule over the earth and over the animals. God has his will done in heaven, humankind is to see to it that his will is also done on earth. As bearer of God's image, humankind is given the task of taking good care of the earth and the animals. And the second task of human beings, male and female, is to be fruitful. Fathering and giving birth are to be the order of the day. That is what the rest of this first book of the Bible is all about.

Thus the heavens and the earth were completed. When on the seventh day God had completed his work which he had done, he rested on the seventh day and hallowed it, because on that day he rested from all his work which he had done in creation.

The sabbath, Israel's gift to the world. Also a godsend. The priest has composed his hymn in seven stanzas in tune with it. In the midst of a pagan world he maintains that human beings do not live to work, but work to live. A person must know when to stop. Moreover that's precisely what *shabbat* means, to stop. On the sabbath you celebrate your freedom. And not only you, but also your manservant and your maid-servant are to share in this joy. And your ox and your ass, the animals, created on the same day as you. On the seventh day all creation is free. God created the first day, and the last day is also God's. The sabbath is the herald of eternal rest, of the eternal light that God has promised.

Moreover the seventh day doesn't end. We don't read, *and there was evening and there was morning, the seventh day.*

The seventh day is an endless day.

3

THE BREATH OF LIFE

GENESIS 2.4B-17

These are the generations of the heavens and the earth, when they were created.

A strange sentence, which we shall be hearing often, since the narrator joins the stories of Genesis together with the word *generations*. Heaven and earth form the scenery against which human history is to be played out. That scenery is constructed in six days; every day some pieces of the set are added. The question now is: what will they produce, heaven and earth? What will come forth?

Humankind. Humankind appears on the stage. Heaven and earth have been created in the service of humankind. Moreover the narrator will continue his story by telling us about the generations of humankind. For it is the calling of humankind, in the image of God, under heaven and upon earth, to be fruitful, to father children, to give birth. Our narrator has umpteen stories about this.

But first of all he has something else, something different to tell us. Precisely what was God's intention in creating humankind? And what happened to humankind? Humankind, called to be a humankind *before* God, began to behave *like* God. The narrator knows a number of other stories about this, different from the hymn of creation with which he has just begun the Bible. Only now does he want to let us hear these stories. For he wants us to be well aware what the holy theatre of the *erets Yisrael* will be about: it will be about humankind, humankind upon earth, humankind and its God, humankind – man and woman, man and his brothers. After that he will tell us the story of the generations of humankind.

God made heaven and earth, but no green plant was yet to be seen on earth, for God had not yet caused it to rain and there was still no human being to cultivate the earth. A vapour arose and moistened the earth, and God formed the human being from the earth and breathed the breath of life into his nostrils.

So this is another creation story. It isn't like the Babylonian story about sun and moon and stars; no, this is nearer to home and closer to the ground. All attention is immediately focussed on the human being, *adam* in Hebrew: taken from the earth, the *adama*. He is carefully formed by God himself, with God's own hands: the man of the soil.

However, without moisture and without *adam* the earth cannot be a field, *adama*. Moisture makes the *adam*a a land for living beings. And God's breath brings the *adam* to life. Breath shoots into the lungs of a human child at birth. Where does it come from? Surely, from God. Breath leaves a human being at death. Where does it go to? Surely, to God.

God's breath brings the man of the soil to life. The *adam* is dust, and to dust he will return. But as long as he lives, he breathes by the grace of God, and is called to cultivate the *adama*.

And what did Rabbi Bunam, the great Hasidic teacher, say? A human being must always carry two bags on his shoulders, so that if need be he can reach into one or the other. In the right-hand bag is the saying 'For my sake the world has been made'. In the left-hand bag is the saying 'I am dust and ashes'.*

God planted a garden in Eden, in the East, and in it he put the adam *whom he had formed. Four streams flowed from the river which watered the garden in Eden: the Pishon, which flows round the land of Havilah, where there is gold and bdellium and onyx; the Gihon, which encircles the whole land of Cush; the Tigris, which flows east of Assyria; and the fourth river is the Euphrates.*

The garden lies in the East, the origin of light and life. Precisely where? Four branches of the river of paradise flow round the garden. Far, far from here must the Pishon, the *Springing-up*, flow: in the golden land of Havilah, they say. Close by flows the Gihon, the *Bubbling-up*, in the land of Cush, somewhere to the south of Egypt. With the third river we are on more familiar ground: the Tigris, which flows to the east of Assyria. *And the fourth river is the Euphrates.* So the garden is here! The land where the Euphrates flows is the land in which we are living; from here we have a view of the whole world. And this place is good. As good as the gold of Havilah.

So the garden is none other than our own human world. And in the garden is little *adam*, called to cultivate and to look after the *adama*. The field is the world. *Adam* is Everyman. *Adam* represents all human beings.

The garden, God's garden, has to be looked after by the human being. That means that he must keep the commandments there. So alongside the tree of life, in the midst of the garden, stands the tree of the knowledge of good and evil. *And God commanded the* adam: '*Of all the trees in the garden you may eat freely, but of the tree of the knowledge of good and evil you may not eat. On the day that you eat of it, you shall surely die.*'

What kind of tree is that? It stands in the middle, in the heart of the garden. It embodies the heart of all the commandments: you must let God be God. You may eat of all the trees in the garden. Have a happy life there. Love God and do what you want. But keep your hands off this one tree: you mustn't begin to play God. A comprehensive knowledge of life is reserved for God alone. There's a limit beyond which human beings must not go, for beyond this limit there's a gaping abyss. This tree is a boundary marker, a touchstone, which shows whether we recognize that our world is God's world and that our lives aren't just ours. If the *adam* begins to live for himself and departs from God, he will perish. Then the *adama* will again become *tohu wabohu*.

The garden is a pleasure garden, but if the *adam* wants to lord it there instead of serving, he will again become what he was before God brought him to life with a kiss: a lifeless lump of mud. 'Of the tree of the knowledge of good and evil you shall not eat. It is my garden. It is not your garden. So there is this one tree in it, to remind you that I was the one who gave you this place to look after. You don't own it. So don't behave as if you did. I'm entrusting my royal garden to you. Be a good steward.'

4

HUMANKIND: MALE AND FEMALE

GENESIS 2.18-25

And God said: it is not good…

Up to now God has said seven times that everything is good, indeed very good. What now is suddenly not good? *It is not good for the* adam *to be alone; I will make a helper for him, as his partner.*

So God still has something to make good, for the *adam* is lonely. He's discovered from the animals that he's lonely. *God formed the beasts of the field and the birds of the air from the adama, and he brought them to the* adam *to see what he would call them, and whatever the adam called every living creature, that was its name.*

We can just imagine it: the *adam* alone and lonely amongst the trees and the animals. It makes his head spin, since he doesn't yet have a word for tree, let alone for oak and lime. And what's that up above and below and around him, swimming and flying and creeping and grazing and trotting and crowing? Nothing has a name yet, so the *adam* can't get a grip on anything. Which are bats and which are cats? Do bats purr and cats squeak? As long as nothing has a name, nothing has a place yet.

But listen, the *adam* is beginning to name the animals as he finds them, just as a small child on the beach brings order out of chaos by sorting its shells into different kinds. 'You're a bat and you're a cat: you have wings and hang from the trees; you have paws and prowl under them.'

But it's very complicated, for there is more to it than that. There's a big cat which isn't by itself; alongside it is another which is the same and yet different. 'You're a lion,' says the *adam* to one, and 'You're a lioness,' he says to the other; no sooner has he said this than the lion and the lioness lope off together into the bushes. A peacock struts proudly, while under a tree a peahen is clearly brooding on something. 'But there's only one of me,' thinks the *adam*, and suddenly he feels so alone. He has no one who can think and talk as he does; no one with a name who can ask what *his* name is; no one who knows that all other creatures are in pairs and he is all alone.

Fortunately God was well aware of this. And God thought that it was *not good*: *I will make a helper for him, as his partner.*

The *adam* needs a helper in this life who at the same time is also his partner. He would be unhappy with only a partner as a companion for life, and he would also be unhappy with only a helper.

The *adam* was tired of his solitary existence. He fell asleep and dreamed. What did he dream of? Not a woman, since as yet he had no picture of one. Or had he?

That night God created the woman from a rib which he had taken from the *adam*, from one of his sides. Alone, you're one-sided. With another, a helper as your partner, you're akin, you're close, you're whole. God created the woman from one of the *adam*'s sides. Without the other, the *adam* is only half there. Human beings must have another half, something or someone to whom they can give themselves: a man, a woman, a friend, a vocation, a task to which they can devote themselves, a partner to keep them up to the mark, a person to love and to comfort and to be loved and comforted by. The rabbis acutely observed that God did not create the woman from the man's head, so that she wouldn't feel superior to him. Nor did God create the woman from the man's feet, so that she wouldn't feel subordinate to him. That night the woman was taken from the *adam*'s rib, so that they should be equals.

And when the *adam* awoke… yes, what always happens when life wakes someone up, when a boy or a girl wakes up? The *adam* doesn't know what's happening to him when there in this green pleasure garden he perceives the glorious figure of a woman. God gave him his beloved in sleep. '*Are you there at last?*', he stammers. '*This is it! Flesh of my flesh, bone of my bone.* You shall be called *Issha*, wo-man human being, because you have been taken from *Ish*, man human being. At last you're there, my other self, my other half, beloved figure from the wound of my heart. How I've longed for you! How overjoyed I am! I suddenly feel *so good*. I feel another person. Now I feel human, and together we're human.'

The *adam* doesn't know what's happening to him; it's too marvellous to understand; he can't grasp it properly.

That's right. He wasn't even there. He was in a deep sleep. It's a great mystery and remains hidden from his eyes.

So God didn't create *Ish* and *Issha* in one day. Male and female bats and cats and lions and peacocks were created on one day, but not man and woman. God drew breath between them. Human beings are different.

When the *adam* awoke... And so it will continue, from generation to generation, when a man and a woman awaken in the garden of life and find each other. *Then they shall leave their father and mother and cling to each other, and they shall become one person.*

Quite often it's a complicated business to detach ourselves from those from whom we were born. But we have to break with our fathers and mothers. Often, too, it's a way which brings much loneliness. But it's the way that has to be taken.

Let's just take another look at *Ish* and *Issha*. See how innocently they play in the garden! They're naked. But they aren't ashamed. Why should they be?

And God saw that it was good.

5

HUMANKIND AS GOD

GENESIS 3

Prisoners by the rivers of Babylon, the exiles dream of the good land of Canaan, lost Canaan. One of the exiles speaks. He tells a story. He dreams of paradise, lost paradise. It was good there, he says; it was very good.

But what happened then? What did humankind do with God's goodness? What is it about the *adam* that he always causes problems? What do *Ish* and *Issha* do with God's goodness, that things go so badly for them? Is it because humankind, which is called to live *from* God and *for* God, cannot resist living *like* God?

Our narrator has reflected on this question, and he turns his thoughts into a story. Remember that this is a story. We mustn't turn it into history and claim that in the beginning everything was good until the first human couple spoilt things for ever. The world has never been 'good' in a different way from the way in which it is 'good' now. Suffering and death are embedded in creation. That's a bitter enigma, and no one knows the answer to it. God knows about evil. The snake is also one of God's creatures. But *Ish* and *Issha* aren't victims with no will of their own. In the narrator's eyes they aren't tragic figures who have unjustly been kept out of 'the garden of the gods'. They're responsible; they shouldn't have listened to the snake.

The snake is cunning. And plausible: *God has probably told you that you may not eat of all the trees in the garden.*

Typical of God, says that poisonous creature. Don't I know God! God doesn't let you do anything! Hands off everything, don't touch!

But God hasn't said that. God has said that they may eat of all the trees but one: the tree of the knowledge of good and evil. Well, the snake concludes: that means that you can't eat from all the trees. God might have expressed himself rather more precisely. 'God is just intimidating you when he says that you'll die. He grudges you your independence. God wants to keep comprehensive knowledge to himself. He wants to reserve this tree for himself. Don't you think it's a lovely tree? Don't listen to God. Take a good look at this tree. Don't listen, but look! Seeing is knowing. Take, eat, your eyes will be opened and you'll be like God.'

The tree is indeed a delight to the eyes. And the thought of being like God is just as tempting. *Issha* stretches out her hand and takes some of the fruit.

Couldn't it just as well have been *Ish's* hand? After all, the two are one, so isn't the deed a joint one? *Ish* is the silent, assenting witness to what *Issha* does: *Issha took the fruit and ate and she also gave it to her man, who was with her, and he ate.*

Or is there a deeper significance in the fact that *Issha* was the first to hear the snake's voice? Could it be that *Ish* and *Issha* depict the male and the female in every human being? Since time immemorial, a predominance of mind, reason, has been regarded as quintessentially 'masculine', and a predominance of feeling, of a bond with nature, has been regarded as typically 'feminine'. Is that why *Issha* was the first to be captivated by the tempting fruit? She feels a desire; she doesn't just want to see but also to touch and possess. The mind, reason, must restrain this feeling. But what if *Ish* stands aside, remains passive? Then the human being falls. Then there is one fall after another.

'Take, eat, your eyes will be opened and you will be like God.'

Issha took and ate, and *Ish* took and ate, and then indeed their eyes were opened. What do they see? Not that they're like God, as the cunning snake had promised. They see that they're naked. This is no longer an innocent nakedness. They've lost their innocence. Earlier they had nothing to hide from each other. Now they become strangers to each other. And in order not to see each other naked any longer, they stitch fig leaves together and make skirts.

They're also ashamed before the Eternal One. For no sooner have they heard the sound of God walking through the garden in the cool of the evening than they hide in the undergrowth. *Ish* and *Issha* haven't just become strangers to each other; they've also become strangers before God. Scared to death, they take refuge in the bushes.

'*Adam*, where are you?'

'When I heard you in the garden I was afraid, because I'm naked.'

'How do you know that you're naked? Have you eaten from the tree of knowledge?'

'The woman you gave me, she gave me some of the fruit.'

'Is that so?,' God asks the woman.

'The snake led me astray, and then I ate.'

Ish hides behind *Issha,* and *Issha* hides behind the snake.

God doesn't engage in discussion with the snake. 'You're cursed. On your belly you shall go and dust shall you eat as long as you live. There will be enmity between your offspring and the offspring of the woman. Finally your head will be shattered.'

'You shall bear children in pain,' God says to the woman; 'you will desire your husband, and he will rule over you.'

'Because of you the ground is cursed,' God says to the man. 'You shall eat bread in the sweat of your brow until you, *adam,* return to the *adama* from which you've been taken. For dust you are and to dust you will return.'

That's what life comes to look like for the human being who wants to be like God: alienation develops between man and woman, between humankind and animals, and between humankind and the earth. Those who divinize themselves dehumanize themselves.

Israel calls humankind to account. Our fate isn't written in the stars. We aren't the plaything of the snake or of the powers of fate. Human beings have responsibility, and therefore are creatures who mustn't look up in surprise when God reminds them of their responsibility as they evade it: '*Adam,* where are you?'

Why does a pig have a curly tail, and why does a zebra have stripes?

People have always told attractive stories by way of explanation.

Why does a snake creep on its belly, why is childbirth so painful, why is (was) the woman subordinate to the man, why must the man toil so hard on the land among the thistles in the heat of the day? And why must human beings die?

Israel tells an attractive story by way of explanation: human beings want to be more than human beings. A split has developed between God and human beings. We no longer live in paradise. We've been driven out of it.

But that's not the end of the story told by the priest in exile. All isn't up with fallen human beings. An old legend relates that when God told the man that he would eat bread in the sweat of his brow, the man said to his wife, 'Do you hear that, wife? At least we'll get bread.' And that when God told the woman that she would bear children in pain, the woman said to her husband, 'Do your hear that, husband? We'll have children.'

Despite everything, God continues his experiment with human beings, and moreover the *adam* gratefully resumes his old role of giving names. '*You're Eve,*' he says to his wife. *The mother of all living beings.*

So life goes on. Dying isn't the last word, but living. There will be abiding hostility between the snake and human beings. But one day the snake's head will be shattered. Then paradise will once again await human beings.

And God made for the human beings garments of skins, and clothed them.

God the tailor. The human beings could cover their nakedness before each other by themselves, but their nakedness before God has to be covered by God. With garments which he himself has made God takes away their nakedness and their anxiety about appearing before his face. Love covers all.

Meanwhile the tree of life has been standing in the heart of the garden alongside the tree of the knowledge of good and evil. We've heard nothing of it for a long time, but now it comes back into the picture. For what if human beings also stretch out their hands towards this tree? Wouldn't it be safer if God put this tree beyond human grasp? Wouldn't it be better if the human beings went to live elsewhere? *Then God drove the* adam *out of the garden, to cultivate the* adama *from which he had been taken. East of the garden of Eden God placed the cherubim with a flaming sword, to guard the tree of life.*

That's what human beings were to do in the first place, to look after and guard the garden. All right, now the cherubim do it. They're heavenly beings, a mixture, with the wings of eagles, the claws of lions and a human head. The picture of speed, power and intelligence: God's guard.

The *adam* is driven eastwards, the priest goes on. The exiles of Israel, driven eastwards, understand who is being talking about.

A Hasidic legend tells us about a rabbi who was imprisoned in Cracow.* He was thought to be a danger to the state. The gaoler was a typical rationalist: 'If your God knows everything, why did he ask, '*Adam,* where are you?'

'God didn't mean that in the way that you think,' said the rabbi in reply. 'At that time *Adam* was just forty-two. God was really asking him, 'Now you're forty-two, but where are you in your life?'

The gaoler became afraid.

He was forty-two.

6

THE MAN AND HIS BROTHER

GENESIS 4

Being human is being human together, we've been told in the story about the man and woman human beings. The narrator could also have illustrated this thought with a story about human beings as brothers. Suppose Eve bore two sons...

Now the adam *had intercourse with Eve, his wife, and she became pregnant and bore Cain. 'I have brought forth a man,' said Eve, 'with God's help.'*

It's good Jewish practice to add that this happened with God's help. In Israel things weren't as they were among the *goyim*: there was no fathering and no giving birth without God's involvement. Our narrator will return to that at length, soon, when he begins to tell of the generations of humankind and of Israel's matriarchs, who are barren and thus wholly dependent on God.

Then Eve bore his brother Abel.

His name means *vapour*. So Abel is a brother who is almost nameless. He's thin air, mist, no more than a breath. He's born noiselessly. Will he also die noiselessly?

Cain is the oldest, the first. *Creature* is his name. He takes over the role of the *adam*: he becomes a farmer. Like his father he will cultivate the land, the *adama*. Abel becomes a shepherd.

Cain and Abel each offer a sacrifice. Cain offers the firstfruits of the land, Abel a firstborn from his sheep. That's also good Jewish practice. For the land isn't their land; it's *God's* land. They're merely stewards. Really the whole harvest and the whole flock belong to God. As a sign of this, Cain and Abel bring the first produce before God's throne, a part for the whole. 'For all is yours, and of your own we give you.'

And God looked upon Abel and his gift, but he did not look upon Cain and his gift.

As earlier in the garden, the Eternal One is present 'bodily'; he comes there to receive the first produce. And he looks on the younger brother. In the end you can look only in one direction at a time. We aren't told that the smoke of Abel's sacrifice rose to heaven and that the smoke of Cain's sacrifice didn't. Nor are we told that Abel offered a better sacrifice than Cain. All we're told is that God looked upon the younger brother and not on the older.

It's always like this in Israel's stories: the first becomes the last and the last the first. Israel's God keeps reversing the roles: not Ishmael but Isaac is the first; not Esau but Jacob; not Manasseh but Ephraim. Not the oldest of Jesse's seven sons, but the eighth, who wasn't counted to begin with, the youngest, David. Not the rich man but the poor Lazarus. Not the oldest son but the prodigal son. God has a weakness for the weak, for people in the shadows and in the darkness, for the virtually nameless who are disregarded by the great names.

It's 'unnatural' for God to act like this, and difficult for a human being to understand. Is that why this theme is constantly repeated in the Bible?

God looked first at the last, at Abel. And if only Cain had looked with God, he would have seen his brother standing there. Then he would have been truly devout in offering his sacrifice. You can't appear before God's face without having an eye for your neighbour. Those who can't say *our* Father with all their hearts can't enter the world of prayer.

God looked on Abel, but Cain didn't look with God. *He looked down.*

Encounters are always face to face. Cain looks down. Cain was evil. He didn't want to look at his brother. Nor did he look up to heaven. He looked at the ground. Thus he broke off not only his relationship with his brother but also his relationship with God. He looked down.

'*Why are you so angry, Cain? Why have you looked down?*'

Cain didn't reply. God was no concern of his. Nor was his brother. Cain is ready to bring his offering to God, he's a religious man – but religion must remain religion. God mustn't begin to ask inconvenient questions. Religion must sanction the existing order and not turn things upside down. God mustn't suddenly ask about his brother.

'*Cain, why are you so angry?*'

Would God be silent when Cain silenced Abel? Would Cain be redeemed by God if he was redeemed by his brother?

And when they were in the field, far from where people live, Cain rose up against his brother and killed him.

Premeditated murder. The first human being born of a woman becomes a murderer. The first death among human beings was a murder: a murdered brother.

'Cain, where is Abel, your brother?'

'I do not know. Am I my brother's keeper?'

What are you saying, Cain? What are you saying? You are your brother's keeper. And you know very well that you were. But you refused. *Listen, your brother's blood is crying to me from the* adama. The field is crying it out; the good earth has become red earth. Can you hear how its lament is crying to heaven? *Cain, where is your brother?*

'Adam, where are you?' was God's first question. This is his second question: 'Cain, where is your brother?' Everything always turns on these two questions: 'Human being, creature, how do you stand towards God and how do you stand towards your neighbour?'

Cain has silenced Abel. At least, he wanted to. But the frail Abel has never called louder than after his death. *'Listen, your brother's blood is calling to me from the* adama. What you did to this least brother, Cain, you did to me. The *adama* which I created to open itself to the seed from the sower's hand has had to open itself to the blood that flowed through your murderer's hand. You are cursed from the *adama*. Whenever you cultivate the *adama*, it will no longer give you its full harvest. *You shall be a fugitive and a wanderer on the earth.'*

Now God had two lost sons. He lost one to death, the other to life.

'O God, my guilt is too great to bear. Away from the face of the adama *and away from your face I shall be a fugitive and a wanderer on earth, and whoever finds me will kill me.'*

'Not at all, Cain; anyone who kills you, vengeance shall be taken upon him sevenfold.'

Just as surprisingly as God first looked on Abel, now he looks to Cain. However, that isn't really so surprising. For true to himself, God now opts for the weak, the least, for the person in the darkness, for the creature in the shadow of death. *'Not at all, Cain; anyone who kills you shall repent for it sevenfold.'*

And God put a sign on Cain that no one should kill him. Then Cain went *far from the face of God and went to dwell in the land of Nod, east of Eden.*

The one who according to the law of blood vengeance should have been killed may remain alive. God accuses the sinner, but also intervenes personally for him. '*Adam, where are you?*' calls God, but then he makes garments for the naked human beings. '*Cain, where is your brother?*' calls God, but even the defenceless Cain may count on his protection. East of Eden he receives the mark of Cain. It isn't a sign which puts him permanently in the pillory and brands him a criminal. It's a sign of the mercy of God who doesn't let him go even now, precisely now. God appears as the protector of the wicked.

> He dwells, his exit permit stamped by God,
> close to paradise, in the land of Nod.*

Nod. The one who has strayed goes to live in the *land of error.*

But how is the human race going to go on now? A *wanderer* who *settles* – isn't that ambiguous? What if this ambiguity continues?

And Cain had intercourse with his wife; she became pregnant and bore Enoch. Cain became the builder of a city.

There you have it. He builds a city. It sounds ominous. For the narrator, the city is little more than a godless mass of wickedness and misery. Cain has lost his way again.

Enoch fathered Irad, Irad fathered Mehujael, Mehujael fathered Methushael, Methushael fathered Lamech. Lamech took two wives, Adah and Zillah. Brightness and Shadow.

Yet more ambiguity. Who will Brightness and Shadow bear?

Brightness bore Jabal; he fathered all those who dwell in tents and have cattle. She also bore Jubal, the father of all those who play the harp and flute.

Shadow bore Tubal-Cain, who fathered all those who work with copper and iron. She also bore Naamah, Tubal-Cain's sister.

Tubal-Cain – his name reeks of murder and death. He is the patron of the smiths, those itinerant types who could produce ploughshares but could also make swords, depending on the need. And his sister is called Naamah, *sweetheart.* A wandering sweetheart. Oh yes, those sweethearts are always wandering round, on the shadow side of life.

In other words, here we find them amazingly mixed up: city-dwellers, tent-dwellers and vagrants, musicians, iron workers, and women of pleasure. It's a confusing mixture of harmony and discord in the land of Nod, a puzzling chiaroscuro of brightness and shadow. Where is all this leading?

And Lamech said to Adah and Zillah, his wives: 'Hear my voice. I have killed a man for wounding me, a child for striking me. For Cain was avenged seven-fold, but Lamech seven and seventy-fold.'

So that's where it leads. That's how the godless person rants and roars. By the mouth of Cain's seventh son, a cruel avenger, a Cain seven times over, from time immemorial the embodiment of unbridled revenge.

Is that it, then? Does the trail end here?

In a sense, it does. Lamech's way is a dead end. Cain's family isn't given any future in this story. It disappears from the scene. Over and out.

Fortunately a new human being later sees the light, and hope gleams again. *And Adam* – as *adam* he was the representative of the whole human race; as *Adam* he's the father of the son who is now born – *and Adam again had intercourse with his wife; she bore a son and called his name Seth. Another seed.*

There is still hope. A son is born who may take the place of the murdered Abel. In Seth Abel rises again from the dead.

A son is also born to Seth. Enosh. *Human.* The namesake of Adam, *human being.* So there's a new beginning.

Then they began to call on the name of the Lord.

Thank God, we can expect salvation. Israel knows a secret. The story goes on.

7

THE GENERATIONS
OF HUMANKIND

GENESIS 5

This is the book of the generations of Adam.

The narrator takes up the thread of the story again with the word *generations*, which by now is familiar to us. He had begun with the creation of heaven and earth and with the generations of heaven and earth: humankind, man and woman, man and his brother. Now it's high time to continue the story with *the generations of the adam*. For that is the calling of humankind: to be fruitful, to father children and to give birth.

On the day that God created humankind, he made them in his own likeness, man and woman created he them. And he blessed them and he called them 'humankind' the day that they were created.

In Israel, a story about a person's birth doesn't end when the first breath is taken, but always with the naming of the name. Only when your name has been spoken over you, only when the name by which you are called has sounded out, are you there. The name by which you're called reveals your calling. Without a calling there's no life. *'Human being, you must be human.'*

So we aren't just born human beings. We have to become human beings. A fish is a fish, but human beings can also be inhuman, for example when they want to be like God. We've just heard about the disasters to which that leads. No, human beings must be human before God: they must serve the earth as good stewards, be fruitful, father children and give birth.

When Adam had lived for one hundred and thirty years he fathered a son and called him Seth. And the days of Adam after he had fathered Seth were eight hundred years, and he had sons and daughters. Thus all the days of Adam that he lived were nine hundred and thirty years. And he died.

When Seth had lived for one hundred and five years, he fathered Enosh. And after he had fathered Enosh, Seth lived for eight hundred and seven years, and he had sons and daughters. Thus all the days of Seth were nine hundred and twelve years. And he died.

So it goes on: ten generations in a row. Is it a genealogy? No, it's not that. In a genealogy you look back, from the present as far as possible into the past. But our narrator is looking in precisely the opposite direction: his gaze is focussed on the future. Look who surprisingly enters history, hear who is born next!

Here special attention is paid to the fathering and birth of the firstborn. For it is the firstborn who represents the whole family in the absence of the father, just as the people of Israel, God's firstborn, represents the whole human family on the *erets*. As the firstborn among many brothers and sisters, Israel is the one who brings blessing in the midst of the people. In this one who is blessed, all shall be blessed.

These are the generations of...

Ten times we hear these words in the first book of the Bible, just as ten words of creation rang out, and just as in a little while, after the ten plagues which scourge Egypt, ten commandments will be given. Ten is the number of the acts of God. Moreover there is a good reason why the list of generations which now follows contains ten names, from Adam up to and including Noah. And from Noah up to and including Abraham beyond doubt another ten generations will appear, which you can count on the fingers of two hands.

These are the generations of Adam: people appear on the scene – Adam and sons. And always the firstborn is special. In a little while the name of Israel will resound. A special people.

Adam fathered Seth, had sons and daughters, and died at the age of nine hundred and thirty. Seth died at the age of nine hundred and twelve. Enosh died at the age of nine hundred and five.

A long life was regarded in Israel as a favour from God, a sign of his goodness (if you add up all these ages you will arrive at almost six thousand years, which according to the Jewish reckoning separate us from the creation). But clearly something went wrong between God and human beings, since the lives of the patriarchs steadily decrease in length. Evidently something has happened to human beings for the life force to have been attacked like this.

Enosh fathered Kenan, Kenan fathered Mahalalel, Mahalalel fathered Jared, Jared fathered Enoch.

  When Enoch had lived sixty-five years, he fathered Methuselah. And Enoch walked with God after the birth of Methuselah, three hundred years, and he had sons and daughters. Thus all the days of Enoch were three hundred and sixty-five years. And Enoch walked with God, and he was no more, for God had taken him.

Ten men in a row. How does it go with them? How does it go with men? They're fathered, they themselves become fathers, and they die. Men, women, children, they come, they live and then they die. That's how it's been from time immemorial.

There's something very sad about this. Human beings are born, they marry, have children, but the end is always death. *And he died.*

But there's an exception. Of one person it is said that God took him. That is told of the seventh son, of Enoch. It doesn't say that he died. God took him to himself. So you can even look death in the face.

The seventh son is Enoch. A man of the sabbath, initiated into God's mysteries. Moreover that's the precise meaning of his name: *the initiate.* For earthly mortals a distant prospect opens up every seventh day. From sabbath to sabbath Enoch was initiated into the mystery of life and into the mystery of death. He walked with God and he did not see death, as is written so nicely elsewhere in the Bible. Of course that happened because in life and in death he always kept his gaze on that distant view. Then one doesn't see death.

Among God's first ten, both hands full of strange characters, is Enoch the initiate, *the* model of the true man of the sabbath, man number seven. In the midst of the time in which earthly mortals have so much enjoyment, but in which they also suffer so much, as a result of one another and of death, this sabbath child, this initiate into God's mysteries, seems to want to free them from their fear of death. 'Walk with God,' he says. 'Those who walk with God will never see death.'

He himself walked with God for three hundred and sixty-five years. As many years as there are days in the year. So Enoch lived, from sabbath to sabbath, from day to day, walking with God, until, full of days, he was taken by God. It happened quite unobtrusively, as though he could just keep walking.

A Sunday school child once told the story like this:* 'Enoch walked with God and they were so deep in conversation, they were talking and walking, that they forgot the time. They had so much to tell each other that they didn't notice how far they had come from Enoch's house. Then, suddenly, they got to God's house. Enoch was afraid, 'God, I've got to get back.' 'Well,' said God, 'now you've got this far, you must come in.'

They were good friends, those two. They walked together. Gradually God revealed himself to his creature. Gradually the creature entrusted himself to God.

Methuselah fathered Lamech and died, nine hundred and ninety-six years old. We already heard the name of Lamech earlier: he was the seventh of Cain's sons, a cruel brute, who preached boundless vengeance. He swore that he would wreak bloody vengeance seventy-seven times, although it was on a defenceless child, and although it was simply for a blow. But this Lamech is dead and his generation has died out.

Here we have another Lamech, the father of a son to whom he gives the name Noah, '*for out of the* adama *which God cursed this one shall comfort us in our work and in the work of our hands*'. With Noah God will very soon make a new beginning. Where the first Lamech barred the way to a hopeful future, the second Lamech holds the future open in faith. This Lamech lived to the age of seven hundred and seventy-seven. Not as old as Methuselah. But what a blessed life!

Centuries later a prophet was to arise from his seed in Israel who preached boundless forgiveness: seventy times seven.*

8

NOAH

And Lamech fathered his firstborn son and gave him the name Noah. After Noah he had other sons and daughters.

Time and again the story revolves around the firstborn son among other *sons* and daughters, the firstborn of the family, who represents the whole clan. Generation after generation, things revolve around this one son, and *in* this one son around the one who will soon be called Abraham, and after that Isaac, and after that Jacob/Israel. If you want to know what is going on with all of them, and what is in store for the whole human family, keep an eye on the one around whom everything revolves.

But isn't there something to say about the others, apart from this one? Don't those other sons and daughters also make history?

Indeed they do, but it's a dubious history. Take those daughters. From the age-old tradition, we can't tell exactly what they were up to but this much is clear: God's distinction between heaven and earth, which had been drawn so carefully, wasn't respected by the daughters of men; they broke all the rules, knew no bounds, coupled with sons of gods and bore giants. No, things aren't going well down on earth: borders are becoming blurred, the sons of gods get human urges and the daughters of men deify their passions. 'After us the deluge!' As though they already sense that this calamity is on its way! As though, deep down, they realize that this humanization of the gods and this deification of human beings must end in catastrophe.

With tears in his eyes, God sees the sad scene from the heights of heaven: mortals of flesh and blood are inflating themselves to become superhuman giants and bearing monsters. He truly regrets having made humankind. (Later the Eternal One would come to regret his regret; there's nothing more changeable than God!) God was sorry that he had ever created human beings. He suddenly remembered how his holy angels had stood with bated breath on that sixth day: what had their Lord begun now...?

If only I could make a new beginning with humankind, God thought to himself. What if I let the waters, which I divided and limited so carefully in the beginning, cover the earth again? What if I were to release a great flood in which all humankind died, except for some good and righteous person? Then I could make a new start with these human beings. God immediately thought of Noah, who, just like Enoch, was so fond of walking with him on the earth. God thought of Noah and Noah's wife. What if he were to spare those two, along with their children? And a male and female of every species of animal? What if he were to allow Noah and his family, along with the animals, to escape the flood in a huge ark? And then just start all over again? Wouldn't that be a good idea?

A question arises. What kind of God is this, to come up with such ideas, and to be ready to fight the violence on earth with violence of his own?

It's the God of the storyteller. In fact, he didn't make up the story himself: from Tibet to Mexico, from Sulawesi to Wales, the world is full of flood legends. For all over the world people found the fossils of sea creatures far inland, and this led them to fantasize about a huge flood which, whether or not provoked by the gods, must once have covered the earth. At every place, in every age, people have felt threatened by possible catastrophes and have allayed their fears with stories about rescue from disaster. Besides, the exiles in Babylon knew better than anyone else about the floodwater of history that swamps people in a moment, the waves of hatred in which they get submerged.

The storyteller clearly has no qualms about a God who opens the windows of heaven. Today, we tend to sympathize more with Yiska, the beloved of Noah's son Ham, as portrayed in a story of our own day.* She refuses to board the ark. 'Ham, I'm not going to go on that ark and sit there in state with God's elite, while everything and everyone I care about drowns. Your God clearly wants tears; fine. Your father Noah and his family can float on tears as far as I'm concerned. Count me out. '

Does our storyteller attribute the disaster that overcomes humankind to God as boldly as the old Dutch farmer who after the great flood of 1953 said, 'Pastor, it was no stranger who did this to us'? Or does he see the flood more as a disaster that humankind brought upon itself? Does it seem to him that God in the end had finally told the constantly rebellious inhabitants of the earth, 'All right, then, your will be done'?

Or doesn't the storyteller ask himself this bitter question at all, since he is concentrating on a compassionate God who wants to spare his good earth any more misery, wishing ultimately not to lay it waste but to preserve it? Isn't this story above all the story of the preservation of Noah?

These are the generations of Noah. Noah was a righteous man, a man of integrity, who walked with God. And Noah was the father of three sons: Shem, Ham, and Japheth. And God said to Noah, 'I am going to bring a flood upon the earth, and everything that lives will perish in the waves. Make yourself an ark of gopher wood and cover it from within with pitch. Bring into it the animals, two by two: the birds, the cattle, those that creep and the beasts of the field. You and your wife and your sons and their wives must go into the ark. You I shall spare. The ark must be three hundred cubits long, fifty cubits broad and thirty cubits high.'

Noah has to make an ark, a huge crate. Noah and his family and the animals are all to be shipped in a larger version of the pitch-smeared basket in which the little Moses would one day be entrusted to the waters, so that he, too, would escape death.

Noah chops and planes and hammers and saws. 'As if your life depended on it,' the neighbours mock.

'You've said it,' Noah replies.

He hammers. The bulky barge grows slowly on his premises, a madman's dream. It's a sermon in wood, three hundred cubits long, fifty cubits wide, thirty cubits high, Noah's testimony to the impending inundation of a culture. It's a misunderstood, silent protest, because not a man alive comprehends this tightly-crafted prophecy of doom; they only laugh in scorn: 'Noah, what are you doing? Going sailing?'

Noah hammers. Even at night the blows of his hammer ring through the sleeping village, as if he were almost in a hurry. The fool! One day, Jesus will think back on this: *'It is as in the days of Noah: before the flood they were eating and drinking, marrying* and *giving in marriage, and they noticed nothing. Until the flood came.'**

Only Noah noticed anything. Because Noah walked with God. He could tell from God that something was happening. God clearly regretted having begun on humankind in the first beginning.

Noah hammered on, building his big rudderless barge, that stumpy black monstrosity in the middle of his land, right there on dry land. There was no water for miles around. The sons and daughters of humankind made fun of the industrious Noah. 'How will you get your boat into the water?'

'This boat doesn't have to get to the water,' Noah said. 'The water will get to the boat.'

9

THE FLOOD

GENESIS 7, 8 AND 9

The water *did* get to the boat. For forty days and forty nights the earth was pounded by heavy downpours, rivers overflowed their banks, seas swelled, for Someone had opened the floodgates of heaven. '*Didn't it rain, oh, didn't it rain, children of my Lord?*'

Noah brought the animals into the ark, two by two, and finally went on board himself with Mrs Noah, their three sons and their wives.

And the Lord shut the door behind them.

So tender. Suddenly God is very different. God is now like a mother who tucks her child up in bed, kisses it goodnight and then quietly closes the door. 'Sleep tight. Don't be afraid, soon it'll be light again.'

The water surged, the flood rose, the great deluge. The earth again became *tohu wa bohu*, and darkness lay over the waters, as if God had never proclaimed '*Let there be light*'. The first to die were the creeping things, then the cattle, and after that the people. When the water had reached the treetops, the squirrels and birds finally drowned, too. The fish, as usual, were the only ones who noticed nothing strange. Silence reigned everywhere.

Deathly silence. No sign of life anywhere, except in that clumsy crate heaving on the dark waves. Noah bobbed along on the floodwater, only a thin wall between him and death. But he felt borne up.

Is this a story to make mortals tossing around believe that God will bear them up, carry them right through death? Is this what the people of Israel were dreaming of as they drifted over the world sea, far from home, that one day God would bring them home from exile?

For one hundred and fifty days Noah sailed on the waters with his floating zoo. Then spring came. *And God remembered Noah, and all the animals and all the cattle that were with him. And God made his breath blow over the earth, and the waters subsided, and the ark came to rest upon the mountains of Ararat.*

The storyteller thinks that Ararat is the highest mountain in the world. So don't go off piously on an expedition in search of this ark; you'd have a better chance of finding Hansel and Gretel's gingerbread house in Mother Goose Land.

Noah opened the window of the ark and sent a raven out on reconnaissance.

The raven is a wild bird, a scavenger. The bird kept flying back and forth, and Noah was none the wiser.

Seven days later he sent out a dove, a bird that prefers to nest in human habitations. But nowhere did the bird of peace find a perch; the waters still covered the whole earth. Noah stuck his hand out of the window and brought the dove safely back on board.

After another seven days, Noah released the bird again. In the evening the dove returned with an olive branch in its beak, the first greeting from paradise regained, the promise of a new garden.

Again Noah waited seven days. The godly captain clearly reckoned from sabbath to sabbath. He counted the days out from God, and back again. Then he released the dove for the third time. That evening the dove didn't return. Peace returned.

Noah and his family left the ark, along with the animals. On dry land he built an altar on which to offer a burnt offering, to thank God for their rescue, for their safe voyage and for this new beginning.

God smelled the savour of the burnt offering, and God smelled that it was good. And God spoke quietly to himself, but fortunately loud enough for our storyteller to hear: 'Although the human heart is evil from his youth, never again will I curse the *adama* because of *adam*. From now on, seedtime and harvest, cold and heat, summer and winter, day and night, shall never cease.'

God blessed Noah and his sons: 'Be fruitful, become numerous, fill the earth. Look, I am establishing my covenant with you and with your descendants and with the birds, the cattle, and the wild beasts. No life shall ever again be swallowed up by the waters of a flood. This is the sign of the covenant that I make between me and you and every living creature, for always: the rainbow in the clouds. When dark clouds gather above you, lift up your eyes to heaven. When the bow which binds heaven and earth appears in the clouds, know that I am remembering my covenant. Don't be afraid.'

Be fruitful, become numerous, fill the earth. As Adam once stood among the animals, so now Noah stood among them, and he heard the very words that Adam heard then. God was making a new beginning.

Noah offered a sacrifice. Devout as ever, he thanked God. The great flood hadn't changed him noticeably. Fortunately, however, God had changed in the meantime. 'I shall never do it again,' said God.

High above Noah curved a bow of sevenfold light, as wide as the world.

And Noah planted a vineyard.

Noah's seen and drunk enough water for the time being. After all he's been through, a glass of grape juice will do him good. *Lechayim!* He cheerfully broaches the cask. To life!

His cup runs over. But he doesn't yet know that grape juice can just turn into wine, and so the world's first vintner also becomes the world's first drunkard. He had no idea what came over him. Dead drunk and naked he lay in his tent, sleeping it off. Ham saw it. But instead of protecting his defenceless father and keeping it quiet, he spread the news around. Ham gleefully told everyone something that he should have kept quiet about: 'Just look, father's drunk!'

However, Shem and Japheth weren't amused. Walking backwards diffidently, so as not to see their father in his nakedness, they entered Noah's tent. They covered him with a cloak of love.

Sooner or later children discover the vulnerability and limitations of their fathers. So what do we do with the drunken sailor? Shem and Japheth continue to respect him. Ham abandons him. Ham, *the father of Canaan.* Pagan Canaan, where in Israel's eyes the religion leads to immorality and shameless acts. Israel feels that no attitude towards it can be too hostile. Ham is cursed.

A tragic story.

10

THE TOWER OF BABEL

GENESIS 10 AND 11

These are the generations of Noah's sons Shem, Ham and Japheth, after the flood...

Seventy sons have been fathered. They represent the seventy peoples of the world. The *goyim* see the light of day. And God makes a covenant with all these seventy peoples. The seven-coloured rainbow high in the sky enfolds them all. Together they form one great human family.

Only Israel is still lacking. But in the midst of all the brother and sister peoples the people of God too will soon appear on stage. Israel isn't the firstborn; it's a latecomer into the world of the peoples. But Israel is the firstfruit. Israel isn't there before the peoples; Israel is there for the peoples. First the *goyim* are there and then the people of the covenant appear, in the figure of the patriarch Abraham, to bear witness to that covenant in word and deed in the world of the *goyim*. Abraham's children thought that that was God's intention: *'In you, Abraham, shall all generations of the earth be blessed.'* In a little while Israel, too, will see the light of day. In a little while Abraham will appear.

And about time, too, since things aren't going well with the *goyim*. The sons and daughters of man are getting completely out of hand.

We've already heard how the *daughters* didn't respect the frontiers between heaven and earth and allowed themselves to become pregnant by sons of gods. They gave birth to giants. That happened before the flood. Did they bring the flood upon themselves by doing this?

How the great human family has lost the way can also be illustrated by the *sons*. And by now it's well after the flood! In other words, history teaches that we don't learn from history. 'After us the deluge,' exclaimed the people before the flood, and after the flood people went cheerfully on with what they had been doing before the flood, again exclaiming, 'After us the deluge!' If it was first the daughters of man, now it's the sons who don't respect the frontiers between heaven and earth and are guilty of a fatal transgression of these frontiers: '*Come, let us make a name for ourselves. Come, let us build a city with a tower the top of which reaches to heaven, so that we are not scattered over the earth. Let us make bricks and bake them thoroughly.*'

The sons are afraid of being scattered over the earth, whereas now it is precisely God's intention that the peoples shall disperse over the earth, to clear it and cultivate it and make it habitable. But the sons daren't accept this freedom; they prefer to shut themselves up in a city with walls and a tower.

In those days the sons of man still had one language and one speech.

We can hear nostalgia here and a longing for the days of old. Once upon a time... But something went wrong. What? The sons of man got above themselves. They stormed heaven and reached for God's crown. *Come, let us...* In their arrogance fed by anxiety they no longer wanted to be before God; they wanted to be like God. They built *Babel, God's Gate* in Babylonian. Their city was to be the centre of the earth, the heart of the universe. And in the heart of their city a temple was to rise as high as heaven. Before long they would be able to step in through the gate of heaven. They would be like God.

From above God looked with regret at the anxiety, the presumption and the crazy arrogance of the sons of men. All trust, all respect, all devotion had gone. 'And this is only the beginning!' thought God. 'They really will stop at nothing, these children of men. They're actually still coming up... *Come, let us go down and confuse their language, so that they no longer understand one another.*'

That's witty of God. '*Come, let us...*' God can also do a good imitation of human beings. 'Come, let us go down, so that I can take a close look at their building.'

Of course the gigantic project of human self-glorification could hardly be seen from the heights of heaven. God has to go down to see what is going on. And God went down and *confused* their language. In Babylonian, Babel may mean *God's Gate,* but to Israelite ears it sounded like the word *confusion.* 'God's Gate? Sounds a mess to me,' mocked the exiles when they heard the story. Confusion, rabble-babble.

The children of Israel aren't impressed by Babylon's great religious buildings, since they know that these are jerry-building by a robber state which made peace by enslaving peoples and created unity by smothering the opposition in blood. It's impossible for this to be a state, a city of the kind that the Creator had envisaged when he made Adam and Eve and when once again he gave Noah and companions firm ground under their feet.

'Come, let us go down and confuse their language, so that they no longer understand one another.' And they stopped building the city and were dispersed from there over the whole earth.

What they so feared happened: the human beings were dispersed, scattered over the field of the world. Farewell Babylon! Once again they turned round. There lies their city. There stands their incompleted project, silhouetted majestically yet sadly against the azure sky.

'It's a sin,' says a stone-cutter to a brick-baker.

The brick-baker makes a helpless gesture with his arms. 'Can't understand,' he says.

How good it would be if now a son arose among human beings who didn't shut himself up and was willing to follow the call of God's voice! Someone who would leave his city in faith and who, living in tents and travelling from one stopping place to another, was willing to travel towards the unknown, in hope of blessing.

11

ABRAM MAKES AN APPEARANCE

GENESIS 11.10-32; 12.1-9

These are the generations of Terah...

Now at last we've reached the point when *Israel* is going to appear in the midst of the *goyim*. At long last God's firstborn sees the light of day, in the form of the patriarch Abraham, Terah's firstborn. However, originally he wasn't called Abraham. He has yet to become Abraham. At first he was called Abram.

Terah was the father of Abram, Nahor and Haran.

Haran died and Abram took pity on his son Lot. Perhaps Lot would later become his heir, since Sarah, Abram's wife, was barren. However, originally she wasn't called Sarah. She has yet to become Sarah. At first she was called Sarai.

They lived in Ur of the Chaldaeans, in the land of Babylon. But Terah wanted to go away from there. Why? He wanted to go to the land of Canaan. Why? What kind of unrest was there in his soul that he no longer wanted to live in Babylon?

Terah set out with his two sons and with Lot, the son of the dead Haran. They set out for Canaan, but Terah stopped in Haran; he pitched his tents still within the frontiers of Mesopotamia. Terah didn't go further. Why did he give up his destination? Was Canaan too far for him? Was he afraid of getting outside the sphere of power of his gods? Did Haran, the name of this place, revive his grief over Haran, his dead son, and fix him there?

How will the story of the generations continue now? Sarah is barren; *she has no little child*, as the narrator says with some tenderness. How will things go on now, there in Haran, with the stranded Terah, with Abram and Sarai and their nephew Lot?

God said to Abram: 'Go from your country, from your family, from your father's house, to the land that I shall show you. I shall make you a great

people; I shall bless you and I shall make your name great. Be then a blessing.
I shall bless those who bless you, and those who curse you I shall curse. And
all families on earth shall be blessed in you.'

Abram went. And Lot went with him.

Why does God want Abram to depart from Haran? Haran is the heart of a highly-developed culture, the cradle of our civilization: this is where writing was invented, and the first cities were built here. Why does Abram want to go away from here?

Abram has heard a Voice, and a strange restlessness has come over him. He can no longer believe in life as an eternal cycle of rising, shining and setting. It's as if Someone is calling him out of this circle in which existence is enclosed and where essentially nothing new is to be expected, because everything comes as it must, and everything goes as it goes.

Terah had already been restless for a while: 'Abram, do you still believe in our gods?'

'I'm sorry, father, but I don't think so.'

The rabbis tell a nice story about this. Terah is a sculptor who makes statues of the gods, and Abram has to sell them in the market. But he's a bad salesman, since he no longer believes in his own trade. People crowd in front of his stall, hunger in their hearts. Abram can become very rich if he is ready to exploit their sorrow and their longing. Instead of this he stands in the market-place and loudly proclaims how worthless his stuff is. 'It's all junk,' says Abram, and finally he destroys the statues with his own hands. 'They weren't gods. My father made them himself. I'm going in search of the God who made my father.'

Abram is in search of another God. Not the God of fertility and innate power, who simply moves in the rhythm of the seasons, the annual cycle. No, this is a God who has to be sought before the beginning and after the end of all existence. This isn't a God of whom you can make a statue to put in a niche. If Abram's God is God, then he can't be put or fixed anywhere. This God is a God who goes with people through time and through countries.

What is happening here is completely new. On the one hand it's a non-event: a nomad sheikh saddles his camel because he has a strange itch and wants to get away. But the moment the little caravan sets off, in the heights of heaven God and his holy angels hold their breath a second time, for down there is a human being who is the first to have an inkling that life isn't an endless cycle, an eternal circle. Down there a man is breaking with the cyclical thought of centuries. Now history begins. 'I see something that you don't see,' says Abram; 'I believe that we must see life as a line, as a way.' And he ventures along this way.

So this way can't be indicated on a map. The way that Abram goes is the way of faith. It's the way that the people of Israel went, and still goes, since hearing God's Voice. We aren't talking about the adventures of a nomad sheikh who is travelling from A to B; no, in telling about Abram, Abram's children are relating the fortunes of their own faith. The Abram stories don't form some man's biography. They form Israel's autobiography. Ask Israel where human beings come from and what their destiny is, and you will be told the story of Abram's origin and destiny.

And God said: 'Abram, go from your country...'

What an invasion of his life! Away from his land, his family, his house. All the certainties of life are taken from him. And where must he go? To a land that God will show him. He doesn't know more. And he's also told that his descendants will be numerous. He, a childless man, married to a barren woman... Abram has to believe the unbelievable!

He saddled his camel. Since he'd heard the voice, he'd become a stranger in his own land. He went.

'Are you going on a journey, Abram?'

'Yes, I'm going on a journey.'

'And where are you going to, Abram?'

'I'm going to Canaan.'

'When do you think you'll be back?'

'I don't know whether I shall ever be back.'

There's a discussion about it at the city gate. 'Abram's going to leave us. What's up with the man?'

'Oh, he's special. He hears voices and suchlike. There's something about him. He's got something...'

Yes, Abram has got something.

But suppose he really has *it!*

12

ABRAM GOES DOWN TO EGYPT

GENESIS 12.10-20

Through the night the quiet camels glide like shadows. At the front we can make out the figure of Abram, rocking high in the caravan, the man who is steering this dream ship. Above him the countless stars, behind him the land of the Euphrates and the Tigris, before him the wilderness, an undiscovered world. A land that God is to show him must lie beyond every horizon!

'*Abram, go from your country... I shall make you a great people; I shall bless those who bless you, and those who curse you I shall curse. And in you all generations on earth shall be blessed.*'

Words of love. A love song for the chosen one: 'I love you, I will remain with you, and whoever raises his hands against you raises them against me.'

Abram went.

He trusts that God will show him a land and give him a son. That's a very human longing: a place where you feel at home and someone to live for. But here this dream means infinitely more, for if it's all true, it means salvation and blessing for all people of all times.

Abram went. Mr Lackland. Mr Lackson. And Lot went with him.

They came to the land of Canaan. *But,* says the narrator laconically, *the Canaanite was in the land.* There you are then. You enter the promised land but there's already a people there, and there they'll stay. Abram will have to be content with the promise all his life, and when he dies, a grave will be all of that land that he possesses.

The Canaanite was in the land. They certainly weren't sitting there waiting for Abram. But despite the threat posed by the Canaanites, Abram builds an altar to his God. Isn't this the promised land?

He builds that altar in Shechem, in the north, in a Canaanite place of worship, next to their holy oak. Fanaticism is alien to Abram. He doesn't

44

declare a religious war; he doesn't cut down this tree; he doesn't curse their gods. Unobtrusively and silently Abram confesses his God.

He builds a second altar between Bethel in the west and Ai in the east, precisely in the centre of the land. Then Abram goes south, for there too he wants to set up an altar to his God.

That's a special act of faith. In the understanding of those days, by doing this he's claiming the land for his God. He proclaims the name of God over the land, like a herald who proclaims the name of his ruler over a conquered city. Abram believes that this is the land in which his seed will dwell. The altars are signs of God's presence, meeting places for God and human beings. 'O Lord, I thank you for this land. I shall never forget that you gave it to us. Sarai, our help is in the name of the Lord who has made heaven and the *erets*.'

Abram travels south, but before he can build his third altar there, a famine breaks out. Nice of God! He didn't say a word about this when Abram prepared to leave Haran. This is a bitter disappointment. Or was the Voice a figment of his imagination? Is it of his own making, just like the statues of the gods made by his father Terah?

How terrible! This man set out full of trust, but now doubt also seems to have accompanied him. What a torture that is for faith: one moment you feel close to God and secure, and the next moment you suddenly can't understand it and feel abandoned by God! Why does God make it so difficult to believe in him all along the line?

There was a great famine in the land. Then Abram went down to Egypt to live as a stranger there.

He went down. The narrator always talks of travelling from Canaan to Egypt as going down. And travelling from Egypt towards the promised land is always going up. Of course that has to do with the geographical situation of the two countries, but at the same time it has to do with something far more important, with descending below the level of faith. Israel isn't relating a 'biblical history' to be illustrated with pictures from a 'Bible atlas'. No, the narrators aren't concerned with geography but with theology. They illustrate how things go between God and human beings.

And how are things going now between Abram and God?

Not so well. Abram's faith is slipping badly. He abandons God. Didn't God also abandon him? Abram will have to look after himself, then. So he lands up in Egypt.

Abram has gone in the wrong direction, since in this story Egypt stands for a world which is below the level of true humanity. Having set out so bravely not long ago, Abram has lost his way as hunger confuses him. He's left the land of God and gone down to the pagan world. There's bread there.

But of course the pagan world remains the pagan world, and the further Abram goes down and approaches the frontier of that rock-bottom Egypt, the more anxious he becomes. For as he sees Sarai sitting there, gracefully swaying on her camel... she really is a jewel of a woman. And you know what pagans are: they respect neither God nor commandments. Soon the Pharaoh will want to have this attractive Sarai in his harem. And to achieve that, the man won't hesitate to do away with Abram.

'Sarai.'

'Yes, Abram.'

'Sarai, if they ask you whether you're my wife, tell them that you're my sister, otherwise they'll kill me. *Say that you are my sister, so that things go well with me.*'

Sarai is silent.

What is she to say? Doesn't Abram care at all about her? She can disappear into the harem as Abram's widow or as Abram's sister, but into the harem she will disappear. Sarai is silent. She embodies the fate of the oppressed wife. What voice does she have in such a man's world?

No sooner have they arrived in Egypt than Sarai is summoned to the palace and taken into the Pharaoh's harem.

At the crucial moment Abram is a coward. He's been promised a land and a son and what does he do? He goes away from the land and he abandons his wife. And why? The motive is always the same: *that things may go well with me.* The father of believers, who not so long ago in distant Haran preferred the uncertain to the certain, now prefers the certain to the uncertain. Things can change. Not long ago, 'Go, Abram.' And he went, full of trust. But now? Now there is no God. Abram has begun to go his own way. A bit of independence. And we also see him become prosperous: slaves, sheep, oxen and camels. The attractive Sarai has done well for him.

How Sarai fares in that harem the story doesn't tell. But things go well with Abram.

Not, however, with the Pharaoh.

Suddenly he's troubled by all kinds of unpleasant things: one plague after another happens to him and his house. One of his illustrious successors will soon have to cope with ten of these plagues; this seems to be a prelude. The question arises at court what this disaster means. Why is this happening to the Pharaoh?

That's always the question when people are in distress: why? We're inclined to be restrained in our explanations, but in those days they didn't believe so quickly in chance: some god or other had to be behind this evil and was calling for satisfaction. Those who invade anything holy, whether consciously or unconsciously, bring disaster upon themselves. Whose God can be at work here? Can it be Sarai's?

It could well be. Isn't he the God who hears the cry of the voiceless and who wants to be a helper for those who have no helper?

The Pharaoh summons Abram and the deception comes out. 'A regrettable story,' says the king. 'Why didn't you say anything? It's especially sad that things have turned out like this, both for you and for me. And also, of course, for your wife. Here she is. Take her, and go.'

Now it is Abram who remains silent. Hadn't God too already said 'Go'? A so-called believer is put to shame by a so-called blind pagan.

Again Abram saddles his mount, now to go up out of Egypt. Servants of the king courteously escort him away. He's allowed to keep the sheep, oxen, asses, men and women slaves, she-asses and camels which he'd received in exchange for Sarai. The one who is to be a blessing for the *goyim* receives the blessing from a *goy*. The father of believers has to be made wise by hurt and shame. Abram too had ups and downs along his way.

13

ABRAM AND LOT

GENESIS 13

Abram went up out of Egypt. He's become a prosperous man there. Having left the promised land because there was a *great* famine, now he returns *great with cattle, silver and gold.*

Once again Abram enters the land of Canaan. And he can be said truly to retrace his steps, for his first journey is to the altars which he built there earlier, in the north and in the centre of the land. He goes there to pray. He takes up the threads again and once more reports to his God. 'Here I am, Lord, back from being away. I thank you that we may stand here again. Sarai, our help is in the name of the Lord who has made heaven and the *erets.'*

Abram went away from Haran. *And Lot went with him.*

Abram went up out of Egypt. *And Lot went with him.*

Lot was Abram's nephew, son of his dead brother. He was a 'hanger-on'. Whenever Abram goes on a journey he does so *as the Lord has told him,* but Lot doesn't go *as the Lord has told him.* Unlike Abram, Lot isn't driven, called, a man with a mission. No, he follows Abram: it seems, like his shadow. Yes, that's a good description of Lot: he's Abram's shadow.

The narrator often contrasts two types of being human, two types of faith. Canaan and Egypt form counterparts, just like Cain and Abel. And it's just like the two women in the detergent advertisements: one's washing is shining white and the other can't get the stains out.

In our story Abram and Lot are contrasted. Abram plays the role of the one who is called, the believer, the 'true Israelite', and Lot illustrates how a pagan, the average *goy,* thinks and acts. Through Lot it becomes clear who Abram is.

Abram went away from Haran. *And Lot with him.*

Abram went up from Egypt. *And Lot with him.*

Do they go hand in hand?

No, they don't. *For their possessions were great.* Abram's shepherds quarrel with Lot's shepherds over the scarce wells. The conflict was a familiar one in those days. It's a conflict of all times: a feud over the wells.

It begins with small acts of provocation: at night the servants of the one sneak over to the camp of the other and loosen the tent pegs – even then a favourite trick when camping. But after that things get completely out of hand, and soon there's war.

Abram takes Lot with him up a hill. He wants to avoid violence and bloodshed. He feels that Lot and he must go different ways, but he wants to part in peace. *'After all, we are brother men!'*

They begin to orientate themselves – the word says it all – standing with their faces to the east. On the left promised land, on the right promised land. 'You may choose,' says Abram. 'If you want to go left, then I shall go right. If you want to go right, then I shall go left. Let there be no dispute between you and me.'

Lot looks. But he doesn't look right, nor does he look left. Lot looks straight ahead, to the land of the river Jordan. Fertile land. Lovely land. Yes, for (as the narrator subtly adds) Sodom and Gomorrah hadn't yet been destroyed... It's a really pleasant place there. Like the garden of Eden. Like the land of Egypt. River country. Lot looks. It seems tempting.

This story is somewhat reminiscent of another story that also takes place on a mountain: Jesus, who sees all the kingdoms of the earth lying at his feet while a seductive voice says to him, 'This is for you, you can have it all. You only need to kneel down.'

Lot too is tempted. For there lie Sodom and Gomorrah, and of course things aren't as good as they might be there; it's better not to ask how the people there achieved all this prosperity. However, there's something you don't like everywhere, and it's none of your business. Or is Lot so naïve that he really doesn't know what kind of a land this is? Be that as it may: 'Abram,' says Lot, 'I think that I shall opt for the land of the Jordan.'

Lot pitched his tents near Sodom. Having accompanied Abram without being called, he now parts company with him of his own free will. Lot has no eye for the promised land. He turns his back on that land.

It's a matter of perspectives.

Lot simply sees what's there. And he wants to grab it. That's how it is with the *goyim*.

Abram sees more. *'Lift up your eyes, Abram, and look towards the land that I shall give you and your seed for ever. Look!'*

And what does he see? Abram sees what he also saw *before* he went down to Egypt: an arid plain! There isn't much to see. But he doesn't just see what is there. He also sees what he heard at his call. This land is a land full of promise. Abram looks with the eyes of faith. Those who do, always see more.

Lot prefers the visible to the invisible and goes to live in the land by the Jordan. Abram pitches his tents in the land where he is dependent on the rain and on God. He believes that there he is closer to paradise. That's his place. God has said that there Sarai and he will be fruitful. And he gently sings the old song about the desert that will blossom like a rose.

'What kind of a song is that?,' Sarai asks.

'Oh,' says Abram, 'just a song.'

Together they enter the land of Canaan.

'Abram, go through the length and breadth of the land, for to you I shall give it.'

He goes there, with the step of a man surveying a property that he's just acquired. As yet Abram may not call even a square inch of this land his own, but he anticipates the fulfilment of the promise. God has promised it to him, and there he stops. There's nothing to be seen yet. But he can imagine it clearly.

Again Abram builds an altar, and so the story ends as it began. It's his third altar. It's the altar in the south, which he had wanted to build earlier, but didn't get round to it because he had gone down to Egypt. Now, at long last, this altar is also built. So Abram has built altars in three strategically important points of Canaan, and in so doing has declared that the whole of this land is God's land. 'Sarai, our help is in the name of the Lord, who has made heaven and the *erets.*'

So the story goes. The story of a man of God. They call him the father of believers. The forefather of a man of God who said on a mountain, 'Blessed are the meek, for they shall inherit the earth.'

14

ABRAM AND MELCHIZEDEK

GENESIS 14.1-24

Abram and Lot have parted company. Abram pitched his tents near the trees of Mamre. Lot went to live in Sodom. *It had not yet been destroyed.* From outside it may look like paradise, but inside it's a mess. Disaster is already rumbling in the distance.

Suddenly this disaster comes close: wars and rumours of wars, kings rise up against kings, plundering and deportations – it's the same old story.

And it happened that in the days that Augustus was emperor and Quirinius ... No, wait, that's Luke. That story comes later; it's a different story. *And it happened in those days that Amraphel was king of Shinar and Arioch king of Ellasar...* In short, not to name them all, all these great warlords with their great names, nine in number, go out to wage war, five against four, since they have grudges against one another. We know that. It happened and it still happens. It's impossible to count the dead, and it's difficult to imagine them unless the camera focusses on a battlefield. One hungry child showing us a world of hunger. One Anne Frank looking at us with a friendly smile. One bewildered girl hit by napalm.

The camera zooms in on one of the victims of this war: Lot. *Lot who dwelt in Sodom.*

There's dwelling and dwelling in the Bible. Abram dwells under the trees of Mamre, but he doesn't really *dwell* there. He hasn't settled there, because he's a wanderer here below, an alien. His home isn't in this time.

Lot's dwelling is a quite different type of dwelling. Lot dwells in Sodom, and he really lives there; he's settled there and become part of the city. All his possessions are there. So when he's suddenly led away prisoner from Sodom by the armies of these kings, he suddenly no longer has anything. He loses all he has. That's your Lot!

A messenger comes to bring Abram the bad news about his nephew Lot. But that's not quite what it says. What it says is: Lot, his *brother*. For Lot is in distress, and in that case Abram is his brother's keeper.

Immediately Abram goes to war. This is kingly. He goes to war to free Lot. He doesn't say, 'Well, nephew, that's what comes of living in the land of the "haves"; the "haves" attract greedy kings and then they must take what comes.' Nor does he say, 'I'm terribly sorry, Lot, but I can't help you. What can I do with a few men and a couple of camels?'

No, Lot his brother is in need and Abram sets out to rescue him. Our patriarch may not yet be able to call any piece of ground his own, but here the spirit of the promised land is already at work. And although Abram and his men are only a handful, they're able to cause such confusion in the camp that the enemy takes flight in panic and the prisoners of war can be freed.

In those days... kings... five against four... wars and rumours of war. Is that what always happens, everywhere? Is that the only history that there is?

No, thank God, there's something else: Abram is there with his handful of *trained* men.

Trained in what? We aren't told – which always suggested to rabbis that they were trained in the Torah. That's what the Ten Words of the Torah teach us: not to live greedily but to be there for one another, even for our debtors. Abram and his men were trained in these thoughts.

They win the battle.

Now they ride back. Back home: Abram and Lot, his nephew who was his brother. Don Quixote and Sancho Panza. Don Quixote, the wandering knight who preferred the uncertain to the certain. And Sancho Panza, the squire who opts for possessions, who loves peace and security rather than adventure. We know them well. They always travel together. There's always room in the one person for the other. They belong together. Our story tells us that they're family: Abram the wanderer and Lot with his possessions.

Now it's significant that the name of Baal, the God of Canaan, is written with the letters of the word 'having', and that in Hebrew you write the holy name of God with the word 'being'.

It all turns on this.

They ride back. Back home. Lot to Sodom, Abram to... Yes, where to? Here he isn't looking for 'an abiding city'; he's looking for a city the foundations of which the Lord measures out in heaven.* He hasn't seen a stone of it yet, but that doesn't bother him; he isn't a man of possessions, he's a man of God. When the kings offer him part of the booty, he doesn't want any of it: not a penny, not a thread, not a shoelace. He wants to remain independent and not to tie himself to the king of Sodom by accepting gifts. They say cynically that everyone has a price, but Abram isn't for sale. During the occupation the Nazis quite often offered presents, but the good people always knew that it was better to endure misery than to become dependent on another lord than the Lord of Israel, whose name isn't written with the letters of 'having' but of 'being'. No one can serve two masters.

'Nothing for me,' says Abram. 'However,' he adds considerately, pointing to his men, 'perhaps they would like it.'

Abram doesn't exercise any tyranny over the consciences of others. Although he doesn't take any of the booty himself, he doesn't want to dictate to others. Abram isn't the pious type who burdens others with his own piety.

Silently, high in the saddle, they ride on.

Then something marvellous happens on the way. The troop goes through a valley. Above them, on a hill, lies a city, Salem. In a thousand years the great king David will found here the city of his dreams: Jeru-Salem. You can hear the word *shalom*, peace, in it.

Something marvellous happens. It's as if the promise is being greeted with fulfilment. Jerusalem, the city in which Abram's seed, yet unborn, will dwell, won't rise here for centuries. But it's as if now already Amen is being said from on high to the hunger of his heart. For out of the blue a silent figure suddenly descends. A king, the king of Salem. The tenth king, Melchizedek, *king of righteousness*. And of course he's the real king: we can count that on our ten fingers. He comes afterwards, and unexpectedly, but *he* is the only one who is rightly called king.

We often find this in the Bible. They write 'And it happened...' and we hear great names of great men, Amraphel and Chedorlaomer, Augustus and Quirinius, and the whole world that has to be registered for the 'haves' – and then suddenly the camera pans to something that also happens in this great history. Then we hear of the true king, who unexpectedly comes out of the blue. At first he's left out of the count, but wait – *he* will write the true history.

Melchizedek, king and priest of Shalom City, has heard how Abram has rushed to meet his brother Lot in a royal and priestly way, without selfishness or vain pursuit of honour. Melchizedek sees him as a kindred spirit and knows that he wants to meet *this* man: this man has it. He's the one. So Melchizedek appears out of the blue to greet him and to say to him, 'What you've done, Abram, is what the world is waiting for.' '*Blessed are you by the Most High God, creator of heaven and earth, and blessed is the Most High God who has given the enemy into your hand.*'

Who is the Most High God of the Canaanite king? Can Abram let himself be blessed by a Canaanite deity?

Yes, he can. Abram accepts Melchizedek's blessing. Someone who doesn't belong with Abram and his followers can still be a servant of the God of Abram and his followers. Abram must be a blessing to the *goyim*, but this priestly man among the *goyim*, this king of righteousness, is a blessing to Abram.

There are kings who have and kings who are, kings who take and kings who give. Melchizedek comes down the mountain as a king who wants to give; as one who serves, in his hands he carries bread and wine. He's a messianic manifestation, a Davidic figure. What the nine kings do is to wage war, *lacham* in Hebrew. The tenth king comes with bread, *lechem*. In a world which hungers and thirsts for having, Melchizedek offers bread and wine to Abram. 'Take, eat, Abram. You must be hungry and thirsty, you must be tired; it was a long, heavy night. Let's pray together, Abram, to the God on whose track we both are, you as a Hebrew, I as a Canaanite. O Lord, creator of heaven and earth, bless this food and drink. And one day bring this brave warrior home to your holy city. Amen.'

Melchizedek disappeared again as unexpectedly as he had appeared. We've only just met him. Who was he? No one knows. The rest is fantasy. But it's attractive fantasy. He was a man without father, without mother, without ancestors; without beginning of days or end of life. A priest who just came down from heaven. As if God himself was involved. Such stories go the rounds about Jesus, David's son.

It's marvellous how these stories fit! Close to the place where Melchizedek gave Abram the blessing, just outside Jerusalem, centuries later there stood the cross of the vagrant of whom everyone also said, as they did of Abram, 'This man is chasing fantasies.'

But just as he gives up his life a figure suddenly appears, a Gentile, who says, 'Truly this man was a son of God. *He's* the one.'

15

ABRAM DESPAIRS

GENESIS 15.1-6

It's night. Abram is lying in his tent. He can't get to sleep. He's been promised a land and a son. Will anything come of that? Is there anything still to hope for? A man wants to live somewhere, he wants to be fruitful, to do something, to devote himself to something. Is that still possible? Can he still expect? He's afraid he can't.

Abram, the one who has been called, has lost his calling. His hope is dimmed, his expectations are dulled. That can suddenly happen. It's dark around him. It's night.

We all know about the dark night of the soul. Like this priest in Amsterdam: 'I'm not sure. It may be to do with my faith, but things aren't going well for me. I tell you, my birth was a mistake. I shouldn't been here. I'm beginning to wonder whether it wouldn't be better for me not to be here any more.'

No ground under his feet. *Spiritually homeless.* And as for his fruitfulness: 'Whatever I do goes wrong.'

Of course this priest was right: it is to do with his faith, with his vocation. Am I wanted, desired, loved? With this sorry life-story he can't believe that he is. Now and then, let it be said in love, that unbelief also works well for him, because it sanctions his idleness and spares him the pain of change. But at the same time he does want to believe again. 'And I also *preach* faith, I preach it to the church people and to myself. "Don't worry," I proclaim to the congregation below. "It is accomplished." And of course what I preach is true, honestly, it's really true. But...'

'But you would so like to *feel* that it's true. Now you're probably engaged in wishful thinking rather than drawing on your own experience.'

'Yes,' he says. 'You're right.'

So we all have our own stories. The story of the dark night of the soul Many believers can talk about that, beginning with the father of believers. He's lying in his tent. It's night. He's lost his vision.

That happens to all the patriarchs. They're seers, but sometimes they no longer see. Isaac will go blind. Jacob wrestles in the dark for the blessing. It's always at night that things are worst. It's all very well for God to assure him, '*Fear not, Abram, I am your shield; your reward shall be very great,*' but what is Abram to make of that? What's the use of it if he has to live and die without a land and without a son? '*O Lord, please fulfil your promise. If you give me this, you give me everything; if you do not, you give me nothing. Then I shall depart childless. Then all my possessions will go to Eliezer, that man from Damascus.*'

Eliezer, Abram's major-domo. Abram is so bitter. What can he still expect? Soon he will die childless and all his possessions will go to this man from Damascus. If things go on like that, soon not Jerusalem but Damascus will be the capital of a people. Of course Eliezer has been his faithful and devoted servant for years, but he's a foreigner and always will be. Abram vents all his anger and wrath on Eliezer's innocent head.

It's night. Abram can't sleep. He's too sad and too cross. And so unspeakably alone. Sarai lies beside him. He knows that she's awake too. And alone. And they can't comfort each other.

Abram stirs, gets up and goes outside. Or has God provoked him, just as not long ago Abram was provoking God with his audacious questions? Does God want Abram to be like this, defiant, militant, not resigned but fighting for the blessing?

Abram gets up and goes outside. It's very still. He looks up to the stars. Countless immortal stars above his mortal head.* Who could have devised and made these stars? What lies beyond them? Who lies beyond them? What a wonderful world which stretches over us so majestically and with such a shining light!

Abram isn't looking at the Great Bear and the Little Bear. Abram looks with other eyes. He doesn't give the stars names; the stars tell *him* something. Abram looks as you might look at the birds of the air or the lilies of the field, at a rock or a bush. By looking in this way you don't take possession of something. You yourself are possessed. Abram looks with the eyes of faith.

Where does he suddenly get his faith from?

Don't ask how, but that night a light dawned in Abram. The riddle of his destiny deepened into mystery. The despair which resounded in his audacious complaint disappeared. Once again he heard his name being called: '*Abram, Abram, look up. Look at the work of my fingers, the stars which I made and which I put in place. Can you count them? I promise you, your descendants shall be as numerous. Eliezer will not be your heir. Abram, your own seed shall inherit from you. Believe me.*'

'Where were you?,' asked Sarai.

'I've just been outside. I was looking at the stars.'

'What is there to see in them?'

'Everything, Sarai, everything. They tell of God. We mustn't be anxious. God will not abandon what his hand has begun. I truly believe that. Sleep well, Sarai.'

'Sleep well, Abram.'

He put his arm around her. And so they went to sleep. Comforted.

Above the stars God smiled. Abram trusted in God, and God reckoned it to him for righteousness.

16

ABRAM FIGHTS

GENESIS 15.6-20

Again it's night.

Yes. Sadly enough, Abram hasn't been able to cling on to the vision of that shining starry sky. Things keep going wrong with his faith; there's much that he's afraid of, and the way is long.

But surely Abram trusted in God? And God reckoned that to him for righteousness? Yes, but faith doesn't come on a plate. It's always vulnerable. Then night comes again. Then Abram is right back at the beginning.

Again he lies tossing in his tent. 'Try to sleep,' says Sarai. Abram is silent. If he said anything now, he would say too much. He keeps quiet. It's also quiet in heaven. An angel flying by thinks that God could have made a better choice of a true believer. Not one who keeps losing his dreams and coming up with new questions. Listen, there he goes again: *'Lord God, how shall I know that I will inherit the land?'*

Abram so wants to have a guarantee, and one can hardly blame him. A promise is fine, but it would be so good if there was something in black and white. 'Lord God, how shall I know? I think that all will turn out well; you've promised and I believe you; truly, I believe you. But couldn't you have give me a little more assurance? Something in writing? Then I could keep it somewhere and be certain.'

As soon as the sun appears over the horizon, Abram gets up and prepares to depart. 'I think I shall be gone a while,' he tells Sarai.

What's he up to? What has come over him? 'I'll see you when you get back,' she says, as naturally as she can.

Abram sets off. With a cow, a goat, a ram, a turtledove and a pigeon. At a flat rock he stops. What's he doing now? What's Abram doing? He is cutting the animals in half. One by one. The cow. The goat. The ram. But not the turtledove and the pigeon. What does this mean?

It's an age-old ritual. When two people want to make an agreement, conclude a covenant, they take one or more animals, cut these down the middle and separate the halves, putting them opposite each other. Then the two partners in the covenant walk through that street of blood between the animals, and swear a solemn oath to each other: 'As the two halves of these animals belong together and the turtledove to the pigeon, so we belong together. There is a bond of blood which binds us together from now on. If one of the two of us breaks the word that is given here, may he perish like these sacrificial animals. May he be food for the vultures.'

Sarai is sitting at home. Where can Abram be? In her mind she keeps seeing him, going off with his animals. Did he go to conclude a covenant? But with whom?

'Isn't the master here?' asks Eliezer.

'No, he isn't here.'

Sarai is glad that Eliezer doesn't ask any more questions.

High up on the bare rock Abram has chopped his animals down the middle. He paces to and fro between the blood like one possessed. Solitary. A desperate man who wants certainty. If the Voice wasn't imagination, if God is there on the other side, then he must come now. Abram refuses to be alone any longer. Surely love can't always come only from one side?

All his weariness and distress is unloaded in this bloody ritual of despair, this challenge to the Other from beyond the stars finally to establish his vague promise in something tangible on earth. 'Come, for all is prepared.'

Abram is there. The waiting is for God, for a sign from the other side that he isn't crazy to believe that salvation is on the way. That there's a real reason to hope and to go on hoping. That God hears our prayers. That faith isn't imaginary, the delusion of a faint-hearted man.

There was a Jewish girl in my class, shortly after the war. She had prayed like this when one day she was in hiding all by herself. But there was no answer. Were her father and mother still alive? And her little sister? One night, in despair, she thought, 'I'll try just once more.' 'Dear Lord, while

I'm asleep tonight will you please just turn this matchbox over? You needn't do more. Just turn this matchbox over. Then I shall know that you're there and care for us. Will you do it?'

The next day she'd forgotten which side of the matchbox had been on top.

That's what Abram does, but in a grown-up way. Slaving away and following the custom of the land, he lays out the red carpet. 'Dear Lord, please, I believe; help my unbelief.'

But who will come? One party for the covenant is present, but he cannot begin until the Other is there, and the Other hasn't arrived.

God doesn't come. Only the vultures come. When the temperature rises, the corpses stink to heaven and the vultures attack. Abram sees them coming, chases them away, waves his staff around, shouts himself hoarse. The birds of prey keep flying around, swooping on their prey and mocking Abram to his face: 'Give it up, man! You're crazy. You can't conclude a covenant on your own.'

However, Abram doesn't give an inch. We never surrender what we hold sacred. He stubbornly keeps up his fight with the birds flying to and fro, circling round his head. Or are they circling *in* his head? How long can a man keep this up?

Night falls. Sarai doesn't understand where Abram is. She's getting anxious. It's so dark outside. Where can he be?

'Isn't the master back yet?'

'No, Eliezer, he's not back yet.'

Out of weariness Abram has fallen into a deep sleep. Worn out. In a sweat. Covered in blood. He has lost.

Abram dreams. He dreams of a people to be born from his seed. He dreams of the suffering that awaits this people. Abram sees boundless torment for his people in the distance, a nightmare.

But Abram sees more. Yes, he sees it clearly: he sees smoke and fire. Flames flicker above the blood; a fiery torch goes between the parts of the sacrifice. God has come! Smoke. Light. Tongues of fire. God has come!

Strange. When Abram wants to make an appointment, the Lord God isn't there, and when the Lord God comes, Abram is asleep. It seems that that covenant is firm only from his side. The promise doesn't depend on

Abram's faithfulness. Nor can Abram force God to come. God makes his gift to his beloved when they are sleeping. But could God have given it had not his beloved fought until he could fight no longer?

When the sun had risen, Abram returned home. With new hope. Don't ask precisely what happened. It's a mystery. Abram was the first to be initiated into this mystery, the first of many who have encountered God in the dark night of the soul. They all always stammer something about smoke and fire, about warmth and light. Their weariness and distress seem to rise to heaven. And although they remain ordinary, vulnerable mortals who don't know whether they were waking or dreaming, and who also sense that suffering awaits them, they continue the journey and feel themselves called to spread warmth and light in a world which so longs for them.

'I'm so glad you're back,' said Sarai. 'I was worried.'

'I saw a wonderful sight,' said Abram.

17

ABRAM AND HAGAR

GENESIS 16

Abram trusted in God.

But only, of course, until the trust ran out again. For it goes on and on, and Abram's life is just as barren as Sarai's. In wondrous nights he's seen visions of a shining starry heaven and he's heard God's voice ardently promising him that his seed will be as numerous as the stars. But didn't he imagine all that? Nothing has happened. No baby has announced itself. The generations since Adam are clearly coming to an end with Abram. It's a dead end. In order to spare himself yet more pain and disillusionment, Abram finally opts to go on possessing his soul in patience. After a fruitless life he will die fruitlessly. So be it.

'Abram, are you asleep?'

'No, I'm awake. What is it?'

'I won't be able to give you a child, Abram. It didn't happen before, but now that things are no longer with me after the way of women, it's completely impossible.'

Sarai is barren. So will Rebecca be, later. And Rachel. Israel's matriarchs are all barren. That's strange. It seems to be a hereditary disease. Why does the narrator tell it like this? What's behind it, for heaven's sake?

Behind it is the thought that Israel exists for heaven's sake. Looking back, Israel can only see its birth in the midst of the *goyim* as a miracle. The children of Israel don't owe their life to their own fertility and potency; no, they're there by the grace of God.

So we aren't talking about biology but about theology; we aren't talking about the secrets of the bedroom but about the mysteries of faith. Ask godparents where their godchild comes from and they will confide something in you, not about the bedroom but from the inner room of their faith. 'God,' they stammer, for they can only see the child as a gift of God, put into the womb. Made in heaven.

Sarai, Rebecca, Rachel are barren. In other words, the way of Israel keeps leading to a dead end unless from on high God himself puts new life into a barren womb. Later Samson will be born from a barren woman: the time of the judges is there. Later still, Samuel will be born from a barren woman: the time of the kings will dawn.

And when later still history again reaches a turning point and the birth of Jesus has to be related, then in this narrative tradition we inevitably expect to hear that his mother was barren.

But that's not what we're told. The narrator opts to have Jesus born of a virgin. Why? Well, that's a well-known story among the *goyim*. The evangelist can't find a better illustration for his *goyse* readers than that this human child is a gift from the beyond. For that's how he began to see the child of Joseph and Mary: as a godsend. Made in heaven.

But it's a pity that the quintessentially Jewish motif of the barren woman has got completely lost in the story of Jesus' birth. Unless our narrator can also bring a barren woman of Israel on the stage at this pivotal moment in Israel's history... But look, he creates her in the figure of Elizabeth, the mother of John the Baptist. It is from the initially barren womb of this Sarai figure that Jesus' forerunner sees the light of day.*

'Abram, are you asleep?'

'No, I'm awake. What is it?'

'Abram, God has closed my womb. So I want you to father a child by Hagar, my slave girl. Take Hagar, Abram. Let her bear a child for me.'

It wasn't unusual in those days to have a slave girl as a surrogate mother. Sarai (her name means princess) has a serf, so it's possible for the body of the slave girl to bear a child for the princess: Hagar the surrogate mother, Sarai's slave girl from Egypt.

Sarai's plan isn't so strange. They could wait until it finally pleased God, but there's something to be said for lending God a hand. And after all, the child will be from the seed of Abram.

Yes, that's true.

But it's also true – and that is the narrator's concern here – that there's a temptation to go faster than God. Certainly a child will soon be born, but with it will come a good deal of misery and sorrow.

Abram listened to Sarai's voice.

Abram enters Hagar and she becomes pregnant. And she knows that now she will bear Abram's firstborn. God smiles on her, not on Sarai. Actually, Hagar is the princess now. And as the child grows in her womb, so too does her contempt for her mistress. She feels superior to the unhappy Sarai, and she lets Sarai know it. From that moment on, relations between them break down completely. All those involved suddenly become displaced. In everyday life a husband, a wife, a slave girl do what is expected of them – they all play their roles and all get their shares. However, here the distribution of roles is thoroughly confused: no one knows their place, and peace is far away. As Abram sits more often with Hagar in the tent, Sarai sits alone, and when Abram gets back, everything is quite different from before. They can't even talk about it, and that too is different from before. Things have gone very wrong between Hagar and Sarai. The slave girl, who now has power at last, is proud as a peacock with the fruit of her womb. She says nothing, but her eyes! The child is far from being born, but she acts as though she were the queen mother. *She looked with contempt upon Sarai.*

'Hagar, will you leave my tent immediately!'

'Why, madam, I'm not doing anything. Have I said something?'

No, she hasn't said anything. But the way she looks!

That's written in a prayer of Israel: *'O Lord, let me find favour in your eyes.'* And what does Sarai find in Hagar's eyes? What does she read in that ruthless gaze? That she's a nonentity. Not a wife, not a mother, but a nonentity. She's an outcast, at a dead end. *'Abram, this woman must leave. I'm contemptible in her eyes. The way she looks at me, I never want to see her again.'*

The triangular relationship upsets everyone. We see the slave girl, the oppressed one, freed and beginning to oppress in her turn. We also know that Sarai, the princess, suddenly feels inferior and gets an irresistible urge to humiliate the one who has been exalted. And Abram is just as upset: as the servant of two mistresses we see him playing a dubious role in the family drama. The seed bore fruit where it shouldn't have done, and that produced not only a child but also a good deal of trouble. Abram senses that he won't get out of this unscathed, but he tries to limit the damage as much as possible.

'*Abram, that woman's eyes! She has to go!*'

Is Sarai contemptible only in Hagar's eyes, or is she also perhaps contemptible in her own eyes?

'Calm down, Sarai! Who is the mistress of the house? Aren't you? *So do what is good in your eyes.*'

Now it's Sarai who may do something with her eyes. After all, she's still the mistress.

Again it's clear that Abram isn't playing a heroic role. He leaves the decision to Sarai. He continues to sit tight and doesn't lift a finger. He lies low.

Yes, and then Sarai's eyes get to work, and the vulnerable Hagar in turn can't bear Sarai's humiliating gaze. Pregnant though she is, she takes flight, in the direction of Egypt. That's where she originally came from. By a spring in the wilderness she tries to get some rest.

We shall soon hear of Israel's exile in Egypt. Hagar's history is the mirror image of this: it's the story of the exile of an Egyptian in Israel. And just as God soon notices Israel's fate, so now he notices Hagar's fate. God doesn't lose sight of Hagar. She's precious in his eyes, as is also the fruit of her womb. God immediately sends an angel down to her. The story doesn't tell us whether this was a male angel or a female angel, but in any case it's someone who takes pity on her and asks: '*Hagar, slave girl of Sarai, where have you come from and where are you going?*'

That was a customary greeting in those parts. But …! These two simple questions are at the same time the great questions of anyone's life: '*Where are you from? Where are you going?*'

'*From Sarai, my mistress.*'

Hagar is well aware of where she is coming from. She doesn't say where she's going. She doesn't know. Desperate people never do.

'*Hagar, slave girl of Sarai…*'

Alas, that '*slave girl*' implies that her flight goes against all the old rules. After all, Hagar is Sarai's slave girl. Furthermore, we hear the angel say '*Go back.*' Hagar must comply with the existing order. She must return. But not just her. Abram and Sarai must also change. 'For this Hagar,' says God, 'is above all *my* serf. If you harm her you harm me. And if you harm her child, you also harm me.'

He should never have been conceived, this calculated child, but now that he's there, there he may be. God looks after him. *He will be a wild ass of a man.* Not a farmer. He will live on the edge of the arable land. 'But his name and mine shall be linked for ever. Ishmael shall be his name. *God hears.* For, Hagar, I have heard you in your humiliation.'

In the story of the Exodus we hear how God saw the oppression with which the Egyptians oppressed Israel.

In the story of Hagar we hear how God has seen the oppression with which Israel oppresses an Egyptian.

God makes no distinctions here. God also looks upon Hagar. Grateful and overawed, she names the spring in the wilderness Lachai-roi, *Spring of the Living One who looks upon me.* Spring of God in whose eyes she has found grace.

Hagar returned and bore Abram a son.

Abram gave him the name Ishmael.

Abram was eighty-six when Hagar gave birth to Ishmael.

18

ABRAM AND SARAI GET NEW NAMES

GENESIS 17

Abram is now ninety-nine. Ninety-nine! Another year and he'll get into the newspapers. And it's virtually certain that this won't be in the birth announcements: 'To Abram and Sarai... a son...' No, that won't appear.

'Abram.'

'Yes, Lord.'

'Abram, I will increase you more and more. You shall be father of a host of peoples. Therefore your name shall no longer be Abram. Your name shall be Abraham, *father of a host of peoples.* I shall establish my covenant between me and you and your descendants. All who are born of the male gender need to be circumcised on the eighth day, as a sign of this covenant.'

Originally circumcision was an initiation rite before marriage. Later it became the sign of Israel's covenant, by which the newly born were accepted into the people of God. On the eighth day. A strange number. We count seven days and then we begin again. The eighth day is the day which transcends the ordinary course of time. On the eighth day another reality dawns, of a higher order than we naturally know. On the eighth day ordinary life becomes a life with God.

'Abram, your name shall be Abraham, *Father of a host of peoples.*' And Sarai? Kings of many peoples shall be born from her. Sarai's name from now on will be Sarah, *Princess of Israel.*

Here Abram and Sarai both get the letter H, the fifth letter of the alphabet. Or, better, the number five is added to both their names, for as in Latin, in Hebrew letters are also figures. The number five stands for Israel: four plus one. Four stands for the world with its four points of the compass, and one is God. *Hear, Israel, the Lord is our God, the Lord is one.* Therefore the five stands for Israel, for Israel is called to honour the name of the One God all over the world. That is what is written in the five books of Israel's Torah. Abraham and Sarah are to be the father and the mother of that Israel. They're called to this task with new names. This one H makes a world of difference.

'Abraham, didn't I promise you that Sarah would give you a son?'

'Yes, Lord, but that was long ago. I suggest that we don't mention it again. You'll understand that I...'

'It's going to happen now, Abraham. I don't let any of my words fail. I do what I've promised. Don't you know that?'

Abraham laughs. 'Lord God, don't tell me that Sarah at ninety and I at a hundred... Don't make me laugh.'

Abraham laughs. He can't believe it, and he doesn't want to believe it. Please don't let God arouse any more expectations. It only leads to disappointment.

Tragic, certainly. A lifelong desire seems finally to be about to fulfilled, but for Abraham it's too late. He's too old, too tired, too cross; he refuses to allow his dashed hope to be revived by God. He laughs. It isn't a liberating laugh but a bitter laugh, the laugh of someone being teased: 'God, may I ask you something? You mean well. I don't doubt it for a moment. But is it really necessary? *Let Ishmael live before your face!* I mean, why shouldn't we stop at Ishmael? Look, if only you had come earlier. But now that Ishmael's there, let him be the one. Yes, I know that by firstborn you understand something different from what actually came first in fruitful nature. But to be frank, you're so late, and honestly I'm done for. Do you know how old I am? You mustn't be offended, but I'd rather not believe it; I don't want the heights of the promise again. Things are all right as they are.'

'No, Abraham, they aren't. I am a God who does not leave unfinished what his hand has begun. A promise is a promise, Abraham. I am who I am. Why aren't you what you must be? Why are you opting out? Why don't you have any trust or any guts? Why do you laugh like that? We aren't yet at the end of the road, Abraham, there's still a stretch to go. And he who laughs last, laughs longest. Sarah will bring a son into the world. And you will call his name Isaac. *Yitzhak! He laughs.* The name of your unbelief, Abraham, *Yitzhak.* Whenever you call your Yitzhak, his name will peal over the fields. With him I shall establish my covenant, for ever, for his descendants. As for Ishmael, I shall bless him, too, Abraham, I shall increase him, too, more and more. He shall be the father of a great people. But I make my covenant with Isaac, whom Sarah will bear to you next year.'

Abraham couldn't believe it.

19

ABRAHAM HAS AN IMPORTANT VISIT

GENESIS 18.1-15

It's high summer, and the hottest time of the day. The burning sun is high in the sky, scorching the earth. The green of spring has disappeared, the crops are in, the fields lie brown and withered. That's also how Abraham sees his own life: barren and dry. For him too the spring has passed, for good.

> *My days are past and my thoughts*
> *in this old body are shapeless and barren.*
> *He sleeps in me, so painfully awaited,*
> *my son, my son, who never will be born.* *

There he sits, old Abraham, by the oaks of Mamre, taking a nap beneath the canopy at the opening of his tent. He's dozed off.

And he lifted up his eyes and saw three men standing there. Abraham was startled, and hurried to meet them: 'I'm sorry, I didn't see you coming. You seem to have dropped out of thin air.'

Abraham is so wrapped up in the customary courtesies shown to strangers that he fails to notice how the three turn and exchange sly winks. Dropping out of thin air is precisely what they've done: no less than God himself has looked in – accompanied by two of his angels. Incognito on a working visit to Mamre, God seeks the shade of Abraham's oaks. Just when Abraham was having a siesta. God gives it to his beloved in sleep.

Where else do we find such bold imagery to describe how God shows himself to human beings? Here is no dream in the night, with only the moon and stars as witnesses. Far less is there a vision in smoke and fire. No, here in broad daylight we see God paying a visit like anyone else. What could be more normal and everyday?

'You'll stay for something to eat, I hope?'

'Kind of you to offer.'

'Do sit down. What would you like to drink?'

God drops in. It's almost blasphemous of Israel to speak of the Eternal One in such ordinary terms. But it's precisely this ordinary touch that reveals the extraordinary. For it isn't as if God has so to speak just left heaven. The angels up there aren't just sitting waiting until He gets back. As a psalm puts it, *'He who is seated on high, sees to the depths.'** God wants to meet people as informally as he meets Abraham here, like someone visiting a friend who is feeling low. Like a mother appearing out of the blue when she knows that her child is feeling unhappy and lonely.

'You'll stay for something to eat, I hope?'

'Kind of you to offer.'

Abraham makes a point of giving his guests a royal welcome, and offers them all kinds of delicacies: cakes made of fine flour, butter and milk; indeed, he even kills a fatted calf. It's as though his prodigal son had come home at last. And of course there's a grain of truth in that.

'And who might this be?' God asks.

A small boy is crossing the yard, armed with bow and arrow.

'Ishmael, come over here and introduce yourself to our guests,' Abraham says.

'What do you want to be when you grow up?' God asks.

'An archer, sir. An archer in the desert.'

'That's good. And do I understand that you're called Ishmael? That's a good name. Do you know what it means?'

'I've forgotten, sir.'

'Come now, you haven't forgotten,' says Abraham. 'Your name means *God hears*. Surely you know that.'

'Now I remember,' says Ishmael.

God has to smile, but Abraham is still perturbed: 'Our Ishmael can never remember. I don't know why.'

'Oh well,' says God, smiling again, 'it *is* difficult to remember, isn't it, Abraham?'

Meanwhile, Abraham's guests enjoy the food and drink which Abraham has set before them so hospitably.

'I've been meaning to ask you, Abraham, Where's your wife Sarah?'

'My wife Sarah is in her tent, sir.'

'Abraham, I've come to tell you that one year from now she will bear a son.'

Sarah hears this. Hidden behind the curtains of the women's quarters, she hasn't missed a single word of the conversation. But are her ears playing tricks on her? Is she going to make love again in her old age? She's withered, and Abraham is old. Is this stranger claiming that she will yet have a child? She expects nothing in this life; is she to become an expectant mother? Don't make me laugh, Sarah thinks to herself, and laughs. This is ridiculous. The stranger must have drunk too much wine! A son? In her womb? Impossible! What a laugh!

'Why is Sarah laughing?' the stranger asks.

Of all creation, human beings are the only creatures capable of laughter. Not a single animal can laugh, that's a human privilege. What a great moment it is for a father and mother when their child laughs for the first time!

But the worst is the corruption of the best. There's a laugh that heals, but there's also a laugh that destroys; there's easy laughter and forced laughter, a liberating laugh and a mocking laugh, healthy laughter and sick laughter. There's resentment in Sarah's laughter, as there had been earlier in Abraham's laughter. Sarah's laughter is somewhat manic. Or should we call it pagan laughter, because it's a mockery of God?

'Why is Sarah laughing?' the stranger asks.

Why indeed? After all, God had promised! Would anything be too miraculous for him? Isn't God's word as good as his deed? Later on, when the child is born, the storyteller will repeat three times: 'and the Lord visited Sarah, *as he had spoken,* and the Lord did to Sarah as *he had spoken,* and Sarah became pregnant and bore Abraham a son at the time *of which he had spoken*'.

'Sarah, why are you laughing?'

Now she has to show her face. But she's frightened, and can only retreat into denial: 'I wasn't laughing, sir, truly, I...'

'Sarah, you did laugh. But you're forgiven. It's just as difficult for you not to laugh as it is for Ishmael to remember the meaning of his name. But think about this later, when you become a mother. The mother of Isaac. *Isaac. The child brought by laughter.*

'You're an angel,' Sarah said.

Now it was God's turn to laugh. 'I think you're a bit confused.'

'Who would have thought it,' the woman next door says. 'A son!'

By dusk she had no longer been able to contain her curiosity. She had seen the three visitors that noon and wanted to hear all about it. And Abraham and Sarah were bursting to tell their news. The whole thing had only just started to dawn on them.

'And have you already thought of a name for the baby?'

'*Yitzhak*,' said Abraham.

The woman next door thought it a ridiculous name, but didn't dare say so. An uncomfortable silence followed.

'Yes,' said Sarah, 'we're going to call him *Yitzhak*, aren't we, Abraham?'

And they looked at each other so mysteriously, the two of them, that the woman next door began to feel that she was in the way. 'I think I'll be off,' she said, 'it's getting late.'

'I'll explain it to you some other time,' Sarah called after her.

'Yes,' said Abraham, 'Sarah will explain it to you some other time.'

The woman next door had gone. Abraham remained standing in the door of the tent for a while. Night fell quickly. An unforgettable day was coming to an end. Abraham looked up. God was just turning the lights on, one by one. So many stars! Abraham couldn't count them.

He heard Sarah singing inside. It was a song that he didn't know. But it sounded good in this silent, holy night. A song about a woman as humble as Israel itself, barren and without hope. And about the Spirit of God that began to move and overshadowed her and caused new life to awaken in her barren womb. A real woman's song.

It was a new song. One day, Rebecca and Rachel would also sing this song. Later Hannah would join in with these matriarchs, and later still, mother Mary would add her voice to the choir:

> *My soul magnifies the Lord,*
> *And my spirit has rejoiced in God my Saviour.*
> *for he has looked upon the lowly state of his handmaiden.*
> *For see, from henceforth all generations shall call me blessed,*
> *because he that is mighty has done great things to me.* *

Only when the song was finished did Abraham dare to go back into the tent.

'Sarah, can I help you with anything?'

'Am I hearing things?' Sarah asked in amazement. 'Did you just ask if you could help me with anything?'

'Yes, that's what I just asked,' said Abraham.

He had just heard how highly God thought of her, and now he wanted to show his best side.

'It's good of you to ask, Abraham, but tomorrow's another day,' said Sarah wisely. 'Shall we go to bed?'

I think that Abraham and Sarah made love that night. But the Bible doesn't say that. Not out of prudishness; that foolishness only came much later. I think that it doesn't say anything about it because what God does here is what really matters.

'Are you asleep?,' Sarah whispered.

'No, I'm still awake.'

'I was just wondering why you told the woman next door that *I* would explain to her later why we're going to call *Yitzhak Yitzhak*. Why don't you explain it to her yourself?'

'Because you were the one who laughed about it.'

'Are you trying to say that you didn't?'

Abraham wasn't quite sure what to say to that.

'You're right,' said Abraham. 'I'd forgotten.'

Sarah snuggled up a bit closer.

20

ABRAHAM PLEADS FOR
SODOM AND GOMORRAH

GENESIS 18.16-33

It's a sinister landscape, by the Dead Sea, where the Salt Mountains lie. Thousands of years ago, long before human beings appeared on earth, this barren wilderness arose from the depths in a powerful earthquake and everything is still as it was then. Nothing can live in this region: it's *tohu wabohu* here, waste and desolate. No creature makes its lair here; no bird sings its song; no tree, no flower, no blade of grass will grow here. No trace of human civilization has ever been found here.

It's an awesome place, and when people arrived there for the first time, in their imaginations they immediately looked for an answer to the question how such a godforsaken place could ever have come into being. Such a place calls for a story. It's as if God's judgment had been passed on it.

'Father, what sort of a place is this? Why won't anything grow here? Why does no one live here?'

'I'll tell you, my child. It's a terrible story. I heard it from my father and he heard it from his father. A long time ago there must have been two cities here, Sodom and Gomorrah. No, you won't find any trace of them. They've perished. Because of God's wrath. Sodom and Gomorrah. God wiped them out. God couldn't bear to look on them any longer. 'Out of my sight,' said God. They say that that happened long ago, in the time of father Abraham. Shall I tell you the story?'

What kind of a story is the father going to tell his child?

He's going to tell a saga. He won't say anything about history or geology; he won't give some scientific explanation of a bizarre natural phenomenon. The father puts his imagination, his intelligence, his faith, to work. He tells a story.

If we were to make an excursion to the Salt Mountains and wanted to know how in the world this ghostly landscape could arise in primaeval times, and we had with us a geologist and a theologian, then we would naturally turn to the geologist for an explanation. We're modern men and women, and we no longer attribute natural disasters to God's judgment. We find that primitive. Are we right?

One day I met a man who immediately told me that he'd received a warning from God. What do you say to that? You say nothing. You nod – God attracts crazy people, as we well know – and you wait patiently until this man begins to tell you what really happened. But don't get it wrong, this man thinks that he's already told you what really happened. He's already told you what in his eyes is the most important thing.

Returning on his motor-cycle from a senseless party, typical of his senseless life, he skidded on a bend and crashed into a canal – he went under the ice. His life passed before him in a flash, and he knew better than ever before that he hadn't made much of life; he'd made very little of it. 'O God, not yet, not yet; for heaven's sake give me another chance' – and suddenly he found a hole in the ice; he could only regard that as a miracle. Chilled to the bone and more dead than alive he clambered on to the canal bank. 'Thank you, God. I've got the message.'

'Yes,' he said, 'I made a mess of it. I totally ruined things, and God must have thought: pity about that man. It was really good of God to think of me like that. Clearly he still sees something in me. Then he took hold of me and threatened to bring down the curtain.'

What's going on? Is this man thinking primitively? Is such an interpretation stupidity? Or is it wisdom?

And the story that the father tells his child about Sodom and Gomorrah, about Abraham and Lot and God, is that primitive too? Does it bear witness in a naïve way to views that enlightened spirits have left miles behind them? Or are we blind? Must we hope that one day we will regain such an insight?

It must have happened long ago, my child, in the time of our father Abraham. I'll tell you and then you can pass it on later.

You'll remember the story of God who with two angels came to visit Abraham to tell him that he would have a son. You know that Sarah had to laugh behind the curtain of the tent because she couldn't believe it.

Abraham was very hospitable to the important visitors. It was a good meeting, quite exceptional, and Abraham was sad when God said that they must leave.

'I'm so grateful that you came,' said Abraham, as he saw his distinguished guests out.

Outside, by the fence, God seemed to linger a moment. 'You go ahead,' he said to the two angels.

God seemed somewhat indecisive. He looked towards Sodom. He looked at Abraham. He looked again at the tent where Sarah was no longer laughing, but weeping quietly for happiness.

God was delighted that he'd been able to bring her this good news. Sarah was to become a mother, a mother of a great and powerful people. And not just any people, but God's firstborn, called to be transparent to God in the midst of the peoples and to follow the way of the Lord by acting in justice and righteousness. 'But,' thought God, 'in that case I must no longer have any secrets from the father of that people. In that case I must let Abraham into my plans.'

'Abraham.'

'Yes, Lord.'

'I think that you ought to know that I'm now going to descend on Sodom. The sins of that city cry out to heaven, and injustice reigns. I want to see that city with my own eyes; I'm afraid that there's nothing for it but to destroy it.'

Abraham stood before God as though nailed to the ground. He didn't know what to say. A moment ago he was the happiest person on earth, an expectant father with a son in the offing – and now suddenly these ominous words about Sodom, about Lot and all those others who could only expect disaster. Abraham truly doesn't know what to say. He tries to meet God's gaze, but God is looking down, as if something is written there in the sand. He too seems to be nailed to the ground.

What must Abraham do? Give way? Open up the way to Sodom for God and thus bring devastation upon the city? Abraham saw Lot and his people before him and he knew what he had to do: stand there. Abraham wouldn't budge. He was even bold enough to take a step forward. Gently he put his hand on God's arm: 'Lord, surely you don't want to destroy the righteous with the godless? Just imagine that there are still fifty righteous there. Shouldn't the ruler of the whole earth do right? Far be this from you.'

It's unprecedented, the way in which Israel presents God and a human being to us here: God stands somewhat tentativetly on Abraham's property, wondering whether he should tell Abraham something and, when he's told him, reluctant to go. It's as if he's standing there waiting to see whether Abraham, his friend, will stand up for Lot and the others. As though he wanted to provoke the one who is to receive so much blessing and may expect not to stand aside, now that the destruction of Sodom is imminent.

And in front of him is the patriarch Abraham, who stands between God and Sodom and will not yield, a believer who is already summoning up all his courage and even takes a step forward rather than standing aside. It's only one step, but what a step forwards! Earlier Abraham was portrayed to us in his faint-heartedness, but this is a great move. How bold the step is with which he comes to God, and the gesture with which he puts his hand on God's arm to dissuade him from his disastrous move. 'Don't do it, Lord! Far be it from you! Surely you're a righteous God? Let me recall your promises. You promised that a great people will be born from Sarah and me, a people called from the midst of the peoples to be transparent to you and to preserve your way by doing justice and righteousness. That's the way you showed me. Now I'm showing it to you.'

We can't believe our ears. Here all the proportions are wrong. It seems that Abraham has more sense of justice and righteousness than God. But of course that's precisely how God wants Abraham to be: dedicated with all his heart to keeping the commandments and to revering his holy name, by standing up for all those who are oppressed. That's what God is looking for: a person with a conscience, the father of a conscientious people, to whom he can entrust care of the earth and those who dwell there.

'Lord, perhaps there are still righteous people in Sodom. If there are only fifty good people, then save the wicked for their sake.'

Abraham doesn't ask, 'O God, don't let the good suffer with the evil.' No, he asks for the unrighteous to be saved because of the righteous.

'Abraham, if I find fifty righteous in this city, I shall spare it for their sake.'

'But Lord, with due respect, if there are five short, a handful, will that make any difference to you?'

'Even if I find forty-five, I shall not destroy Sodom, Abraham.'

'Forgive me, Lord, I'm only an ordinary person and I have no pretensions, but if there are only forty, would it still be possible?'

God nodded.

'I hope that you won't be cross, Lord, but if there are no more than thirty…'

'Then I will spare this city for the sake of those thirty.'

'And twenty?'

God nodded again.

'You mustn't be cross, Lord, if I speak to you once more, but if no more than ten are found, please, could you possibly... ten...?'

Abraham is bartering, haggling as if he were in the market. Voltaire, that man of the Enlightenment, had to laugh at this haggler, who can't even refrain from bargaining with God

But Voltaire failed to grasp this story. He didn't see that here we have one of the greatest and boldest stories in the literature of the world. Here we have a breathtaking vision of what faith can be. Much faith is disguised fatalism: 'Everything happens as it must, and what am I to do about it?' Abraham ventures to doubt that. The faith of the father of believers looks different. He comes close and asks for God's mercy on the city. Abraham intercedes for the just and the unjust. He holds God to his word and God is clearly pleased with his passionate plea. 'Abraham, I can tell that you're a true Israelite. You've a great love of humanity. That's what I intended when I created Adam – that's what I envisaged when I called you from Haran.'

Fifty, forty-five, forty, thirty, twenty, ten.

Abraham doesn't dare to haggle any further. A synagogue can't exist with less than ten people. Abraham stops at ten. He doesn't dare to think that the divine mercy can go any lower.

Those ten are Israel in the midst of the people, the *goyim*: God's firstborn, bearer of the blessing. For the sake of this one, salvation may be expected for all. Without this one there is no future for anybody.

21

THE DESTRUCTION OF SODOM AND GOMORRAH

GENESIS 19

Abraham and Lot. They didn't go together Their ways parted. They live in two worlds. It's the difference between night and day.

Abraham has pitched his tents under the oaks of Mamre.

Lot is as firmly established as a house in Sodom.

In Abraham's world, hospitality is honoured; the good earth also gives forth its fragrance for the stranger. Abraham sits down to a meal with no less a person than God himself; they talk together as friends.

In Lot's world, hospitality is violated; they don't heed either God's commandment or one another; all intimacy has gone. That's no way for friends to behave.

No, Abraham and Lot have grown apart.

One lives under the promise: he has a son on the way, and the sun rises upon him.

The other can only expect disaster, for what is happening in Sodom simply can't go on. Of course, anything is possible, but not this. To think that such things happen! One day the sun will no longer rise on Sodom, since God hasn't made the light for such a city. One day Sodom will no longer exist.

To labour the point: these stories aren't about the fates of two individuals, the exciting adventures of an uncle and his nephew. Israel imagines two types of faith: the messianic type and the pagan type. Abraham shows us the way to life; Lot shows us the way to death.

The angels have flown fast, for after leaving Mamre at noon, that same evening they arrive in Sodom. Lot is sitting in the gate and sees two strangers approach. 'May I invite you to my house to have a meal and spend the night there?'

Lot has still remembered one lesson from Abraham: you must be hospitable. Israel knows what it is to be a stranger, a sojourner, far from your fatherland and your mother tongue. So the Bible constantly tells the people of God that they must respect hospitality. 'You who were yourselves strangers in a distant land should continue to remember how that felt. You should sympathize with the strangers within your gate. This is what the Lord says: "If you come to them, you come to me. If you harm them, you harm me."'

Moreover, any violation of hospitality is a serious offence in the eyes of the Eternal One, and that is now precisely the sin which Sodom commits. For when night fell – we have to brace ourselves, since this is a quite different story from the previous one: it's really the difference between day and night – the men of Sodom crowded together before Lot's house and asked for the two guests: 'Give us those men, we want to have intercourse with them.'

That's damnably gross. That's not the way to treat people or for a friend to treat a friend. It's inhuman. This is rape – and rape is just not on. Of course it can happen, anything can; but it's not right.

We aren't talking about homosexuality. Homosexuality is the love and affection of one person for another person of the same sex. In this story there's no question of love and affection. This story isn't about love; it's about a city from which all love has departed. This is a story about humiliation and violation, and especially about the violation of the law of hospitality, and it is clearly meant to illustrate how, in this world which has departed from God, human relations have gone wrong. None of the later passages in the Bible in which there is mention of Sodom and Gomorrah are ever about what comes wrongly to be called sodomy; they're always about the violation of law and the maltreatment of the defenceless. Thus when speaking to his disciples Jesus names the two cities as *the* ghastly model of a lack of hospitality towards the stranger: *'If they do not receive you, then depart from that house, from that town, shake the dust from off your feet, for I tell you that it will be better for the land of Sodom and Gomorrah in the day of judgment than for that town.'*

Back to Sodom, where the people are thronging. *Give us those men!* Lot, at his wits' end, goes outside and offers his own daughters; in his eyes the shame and humiliation that would be done to them would be less serious than what would be done to his guests. But the mob has gone mad and now its fury is directed towards Lot, who after all is a stranger within its gates. 'You're a foreigner and you want to tell us how to behave? Go back to your own country; leave us!' And certainly they would have murdered Lot had not the two angels quickly brought their host into the safety of his house. They bolt the door and strike the gathering mob with blindness, so that none of them can see their hands before their eyes, let alone find Lot's front door.

It's always the same story: hospitality is violated; there is discrimination against strangers; pogroms are imminent. And in the whole city not even ten righteous people can be found to honour justice in God's name and to try to avert the disaster.

Then everything happens very fast. For one thing should be clear: this loveless Sodom cannot exist. It's a city in which the cry for justice is no longer heard. It's a city which turns everything upside down. So this city must itself be turned upside down. It's as though God says to this city, 'Your will be done.'

Abraham has a future. He will be blessed. And he will be a blessing. But this blessing has a limit. Those who curse Abraham, those who do violence to the true humanity that he represents, have no future.

Look, dawn is breaking over there. The day is breaking on which Sodom will no longer see the sun. Now it's crisis time. The angels urge Lot to hurry. 'Escape quickly, you and your wife and your daughters. Take refuge in flight. One stone will not be left standing on another. Get away, flee to the hills.'

But Lot delays. Does he have to leave everything behind? He still doesn't realize the urgency of the matter and he's afraid of the hills. So he asks whether he can flee to nearby Zoar: 'It's only a small town.' He can.

Typical of Lot! Always half-hearted. He wants to go and he doesn't want to go. He knows about the sin of the great city and then wants to go to a small one. He delays. We need to hear the narrator telling the story in Hebrew: *Yit-mah-mah*. 'Go,' scream the angels. And Lot, 'But... but... but.' And the angels scream again, 'Not buts... go!' And because now there really is no time to lose, they take Lot by the hand and his wife by her hand and their daughters by their hands. 'Go, go! Don't look back!'

But Lot's wife does look back. And she becomes a pillar of salt.

All the guides who take modern tourists through the barren, in-hospitable landscape of the Salt Mountains point out their own version of

Lot's wife, fossilized in that awesome setting: the woman who was so attached to this city, and who at the decisive moment stood with her back to her calling and got stuck there, became her own monument. It's as if she has to illustrate the saying of Jesus: *'No one who has put his hand to the plough and looks back to what lies behind him is fit for the kingdom of God.'**

The sun rose. The morning broke.

But not for Sodom. A people that gives in to evil will lose more than body and possessions; their light will be quenched.

Abraham got up from his camp site, went to the place where he had stood before God, and looked in the direction of Sodom and Gomorrah. All he saw was smoke, smoke which rose from the earth like the smoke of a smelting furnace.

Lot escaped. He fled to Zoar. *The sun had risen upon the earth when Lot arrived in Zoar.* He was saved. Abraham had prayed for him.

The avalanche of sulphur and fire rusheds past Zoar. Lot may live there, thanks to God's angels, but he isn't happy. He doesn't trust God and himself, and he flees further with his two daughters, into the hills, to a cave. The three survivors of the disaster.

What happens now?

The inhabitants of the cave seem to have their own ideas of what a fruitful life is. Unlike the two sons of Noah, who covered the shame of their drunken father with the cloak of love, Lot's two daughters give their father more wine to drink than is good for him; they uncover his shame and make themselves pregnant by this drunken donor.

After a few months Lot sits there with two boys on his knee, Moab and Ammon: sons and grandsons at the same time.

Centuries later, a Yiddish legend has it, the Queen of Sheba, on a visit to King Solomon, turned this episode into a riddle. A woman said to her son: 'Your father is my father and your grandfather is my husband; you are my son and I am your sister.' Who was this woman?

The wise Solomon knew the answer: 'Lot's daughter.'

22

THE CHILD BROUGHT BY LAUGHTER

GENESIS 20 AND 21

The caravan moves on. Abraham travels to the south and pitches his tents in the land of Gerar. Will he be safe there? Will Sarah be safe there? For Abimelech is king of Gerar. What if his eye lights on Sarah and he wants to incorporate her into his harem, as the Pharaoh of Egypt did earlier? This ruler, too, probably won't hesitate to do away with Abraham.

'Sarah, tell him that you're my sister.'

The father of believers is just an ordinary man: he can scale the heights and plumb the depths. He prays for Lot and his people, but immediately afterwards he abandons Sarah.

'Sarah, is Abraham your husband?'

'No, your majesty, he's my brother.'

Is she speaking the truth? But what difference can it make to him? 'In that case it's my privilege to welcome you into my harem.'

Abraham didn't get a wink of sleep that night. Sarah probably didn't either. Abraham didn't need much imagination to envisage the scene that was now taking place in the king's bedroom. Poor Sarah, once again abandoned to the passion of a foreign ruler. But now it's all different. For Sarah's womb has been opened since the Eternal One came on a visit in Mamre. Is Sarah's firstborn not to be of the seed of Abraham but prince of Gerar? God forbid! Perhaps there was a disaster in the palace.

No, nothing happened there. The king of Gerar suddenly seemed unable to perform. That night he was a floppy king. Strange! What was going on?

The king had a dream. God appeared and revealed to him what he already probably knew deep down: 'Abimelech, you're sharing your bed with a married woman; you're a child of death.'

'A married woman, Lord? This woman isn't married. She's Abraham's sister. The man told me himself, and she confirmed it. Truly, Lord, I'm an honest man and my hands are innocent.'

'It was I, Abimelech, who made you impotent. I wanted to preserve you. Or rather, I wanted to preserve the helpless Sarah.'

The next day the king summoned Abraham to the palace: 'Have I sinned against you, that you did what may not be done?'

'Sir, I thought that there was no fear of God here. That's why I did what I did.'

What chutzpah of Abraham to talk of fear of God! Again a pagan has taught the father of believers a lesson. And in deep awe of Sarah's God, Israel's *Pater Omnipotens*, Abimelech returned Sarah to Abraham, laden with gifts. 'See, my land is open to you, you may dwell wherever you will.'

Put to shame, Abraham then prayed for the king of Gerar. And God cured Abimelech, so that fortunately he was once again quickly his old self. His wife and his slave girls became pregnant and bore him princes and princesses.

Sarah too gave birth. Through the grace of God she who for a lifetime had been barren gave life to a son, Isaac. *Yitzhak, the child brought by laughter.* Their firstborn. The bearer of the blessing. Listen to that liberating laugh in Abraham's tent!

Abraham was one hundred years old when Isaac was born to him. The boy grew and thrived, and when after three years he was weaned, Abraham held a great feast, because it called for a party.

When the child came in, the whole household rejoiced. Only Ishmael didn't rejoice. Ishmael mocked Isaac to his face. What was this about now? Pride because he was older? Jealousy because although he was the first to be born he wasn't the firstborn? Was paganism here mocking Israel as a ridiculous people, which would have done better not to have existed? Was Ishmael laughing at Isaac's God? Can we hear the age-old dispute between Jews and Arabs here?

Mother Sarah flared up angrily when she saw how Hagar's child was laughing at Isaac. Only her Isaac might laugh. Sarah wanted happiness only for herself: 'Abraham, drive this slave girl away, and that son of hers.'

How will this turn out? Shall we hear again the remark with which the tragedy began years ago, when Sarah had proposed that Hagar, her

Egyptian slave, should be a surrogate mother: *Abraham listened to Sarah's voice?*

No, we hear something else. For Abraham can't bear to think about driving his son, Hagar's son, into the wilderness. He can't bear to think of having to listen to Sarah's voice.

Then the voice of God resounds. And what Abraham has really known all along becomes clear to him: he won't get out of it unscathed. '*Abraham, listen to Sarah's voice.*'

This is shocking. Because Abraham listened to Sarah's voice once before, the child was born who doesn't have the promise and the blessing. By listening to Sarah's voice now, Abraham must break with him. Ishmael will be taken care of, but he will not be the firstborn. There must be a break. Next morning Abraham will have to say good-bye to the boy and his mother.

There are people who think that there's a solution to every problem in life. But sometimes there isn't, at least not without pain. We suffer from the consequences of our deeds; others suffer from them, and that's unavoidable. Abraham has to tear out of the book of his life the page on which he was wrong to write. The one who prematurely began to answer his own prayers must break with Ishmael, his impatience incarnate. He must bear the consequences of his own unbelief.

And how will things go with Ishmael? Surely the poor boy can't be made to pay the price? If he isn't the promised one, the one with the blessing, surely he isn't excluded from every promise, every blessing? Surely God will also look after him? Don't all people count with you, O God of Israel? How are things to go now with Ishmael? And with his mother Hagar?

Early in the morning Abraham sends them away, with pain in his heart. But he can't do otherwise. Abraham must cut into his own flesh. Farewell, Ishmael. Farewell, Hagar. À Dieu!

À Dieu?

Abraham gives them bread and a skin of water, the last thing that he can do for them. But a few days later everything is gone, and now what? 'There's water, mother. There's water!' But little Ishmael is mistaken. Hagar lays him down in the shadow of a bush. She goes to sit a little way off, a bowshot away; she can't bear to see the death of her child. The boy cries. Hagar puts her fingers in her ears; she can't listen to this. Ishmael will surely die. His name means *God hears*. Has God got his fingers in his ears too?

And God heard the voice of the boy. An angel of God called from heaven to Hagar and said to her: 'Hagar, fear not, for God has heard the voice of the boy. Stand up, pick up the boy, and hold him fast. A great people shall be born from him.'

God opened Hagar's eyes and she saw a well close by. She filled the skin with water and gave the boy some of it to drink.

God was with the boy and he grew up and lived in the wilderness. He became an archer. His mother took a wife for him from Egypt.

The Book doesn't leave any room for misunderstanding: God also looks after Ishmael. Ishmael also shares in the promise. He shares in the blessing. The water of life is also for him. Isaac and Ishmael, the two of them belong together. They are and remain children of one Father.

23

ABRAHAM'S SACRIFICE

GENESIS 22

Now it happened that God put Abraham to the test.

'Abraham!'

'Here I am, Lord.'

'Now take your only son, the one you love, Isaac, and go to the land of Moriah and offer him there as a burnt offering on one of the mountains that I shall tell you of.'

Early in the morning Abraham rose, cut wood for the burnt offering, saddled his ass, took two servants with him and Isaac his son, and went to the place of which God had told him.

He went!

Abraham, in God's name, why did you go? You're like a religious fanatic. Recently you pleaded with God so fervently for sinful Sodom; why do you now abandon your own innocent child?

Or do we have to put the blame on God? What kind of a macabre game is he playing with this father and his son? Of course God may put a person's faith to the test. But does that have to be done so fiercely, so cruelly and inexorably, with a vulnerable and defenceless child as the victim?

Or must we make the narrator responsible? For of course God and Abraham can only say and do what the author *makes* them say and do. What is this man really trying to tell us? Beyond question he is a gifted author, and his story is full of mysteries and a wondrous beauty. But why at the same time does he provoke so much aversion? Couldn't he have put the same thought differently, in more accessible and less cruel images? Think of the disaster he caused with this story! For centuries he's saddled people with the thought of a sadistic God. In so doing he's cultivated masochistic believers, pious people who began to think that in religion you have to switch off your thoughts and feelings; theologians who devised a heavenly Father who allowed his own son to be nailed to the cross. These believers also became hard and inexorable in their turn.

For a brief moment we thought, hoped, that with this story Israel is opposing the pagan practice of child sacrifice. But the narrator makes God bless Abraham only when it proves that he is indeed willing to offer what is most precious to him on earth, so sadly that cannot be the case.

So what does the narrator want to say?

'Abraham!'

'Here I am, Lord.'

'Take your only son, the one whom you love, Isaac, and go to the land of Moriah and sacrifice him there as a burnt offering on one of the mountains that I shall tell you of.'

And he went.

This patriarchal history also began in the same way: 'Abraham, go from your land, your family, your father's house, to the land that I shall show you.' And he went.

At the end of this history we hear those opening words once again: 'Abraham, go.' And he went.

The one story matches the other.

It began with Abraham having to break with his father, with his natural past.

It ends with his having to break with his son, his natural future.

Abraham must begin by sacrificing what he takes for granted: his land, his father's house. He must take a risk with the promise. And he's done that, the father of believers. However, his pilgrimage hasn't been unblemished: Ishmael has been born, the son whom he shouldn't have had. And when God once again half confirmed that he would certainly grant his promise, Abraham more or less laughed at God.

It's as if now, at the end of his pilgrimage, this past plays a role once again. It's as if before the curtain falls, God is once again perplexing Abraham in order to put right that bitter laugh, and to end at the level on which he began. If Abraham is now in true faith to be able to receive his son Isaac, whom he had not been able to receive in true faith, then Isaac must first be given back to God.

'Abraham!'

'Here I am, Lord.'

'Take your only son, the one you love, Isaac, and go to the land of Moriah and sacrifice him there as a burnt offering on one of the mountains that I shall tell you of.'

The story isn't about a God who requires blind obedience. It's about whether Abraham's faith will hold.
    'Abraham!'
    'Here I am, Lord.'
    'Go.'
    And he went.

It must have been a difficult journey. Think what was at stake here! Everything! This son, his only son, his long-awaited son, whom he loves, Isaac, will soon no longer be in the land of the living. That means that his long-awaited birth will have been in vain. Moreover, Abraham's exodus from his father's house will have been in vain. The Voice which he heard will have proved an illusion, as will the whole of his faith. In that case, there is no truth in this business about the one in our midst, the firstborn, the one with the blessing, through whom the Eternal One wants the whole human family to know that history is a history of salvation and not a history of disaster. In that case we indeed live on this planet in a terrifying void, surrounded only by silence. In that case there is little else here to tell than what can be told of Lot's life: we live from disaster to disaster, until after the last disaster there will be nothing.
    Wasn't all that at stake when Abraham climbed the mountain with Isaac? Everything was at stake. How in heaven's name did he make the climb up the mountain? How did he manage to continue to believe so confidently that he and the boy weren't heading for a dead end? Where did he get the resources from to tell the two servants so trustingly, half-way along the journey, to wait there until he and the boy *returned* together?

On the third day Abraham lifted up his eyes and saw the place from afar.
    In Israel's story, *'on the third day'* means that a decisive moment has arrived. *'On the third day* things take a turn.' And then heaven is always involved.
    On the third day Abraham lifted up his eyes and saw the place from afar. He took the wood for the sacrifice, put it on the shoulders of Isaac,

his son, and himself carried the fire and the knife in his hand. And so the two went on together.

Then Isaac said to Abraham, his father, 'My father!'

'Here I am, my son.'

'Look, here's the fire and the wood, but where is the lamb for the burnt offering?'

'God will provide the lamb for the burnt offering, my son.'

And so the two went on together.

Abraham knows that Isaac is from God. And God will not abandon what he has begun. 'God will see, my son.'

Abraham says what he cannot say, yet must say. This is the language of faith, just as it was also the language of faith when he talked earlier to the servants about their return. Isaac heard it clearly and thought: if my father trusts God like that, then I shall trust my father.

'God will see, my son.'

Abraham trusts in what the Eternal One has in view. He relies on what God sees. 'God will see, my son.'

So the two went on together.

They came to the place which God had told him of. There Abraham built the altar, put the wood on it, bound Isaac his son, and put him on the altar, on top of the wood. Abraham stretched out his hand, and took the knife to kill his son.

'Abraham! Abraham!'

'Here I am.'

'Do not stretch out your hand to the boy, do nothing to him. Truly, now I know that you fear God and have not withheld your son, your only son, from me.'

Abraham has surrendered his son to the future which his God has in view. *Abraham believed that God was able to raise Isaac even from the dead; hence in a way of speaking he did receive him back.* *

Once again Abraham has heard the Voice. He hasn't gone out from his land and his father's house in vain. Isaac hasn't been born in vain, the one in our midst, the one with the blessing, God's incarnate sign that history isn't a history of disaster that keeps moving from catastrophe to catastrophe, but will prove to be a history of salvation.

Abraham lifted up his eyes and looked, and see, a ram, caught in a thicket by his horns; and Abraham went and took the ram and offered it as a burnt offering instead of his son.

And Abraham called that place 'God will see.'

24

THE DEATH OF SARAH

GENESIS 23

Through the night of doubt and sorrow
onward goes the pilgrim band.*

And right at the head of this band we see the figure of the patriarch Abraham, the nomad of faith who has begun the pilgrimage through time and through foreign lands. As the firstborn on earth he had an inkling that life isn't a cycle but a way, and as a firstborn he took this way. That's how it began.

Israel, God's firstborn, told a story about this. In Abraham, Abraham's children told of their faith. In so doing at the same time they told of the adventure of all faith, for the calling of the firstborn holds for the whole human family. Moreover people from all times and all lands have also listened to Israel's stories. Suppose it's true! Many have recognized themselves in that distant figure, at the head of the band, with his victories and his defeats, his courage and his cowardice, his anxieties and his dreams. In him they have come to see the father of all believers.

We too have followed him on his wanderings, this stranger of no fixed abode, this displaced person. We've hoped with him and despaired with him on his long journey. He's had to break with Hagar and with Ishmael, and he's also lost sight of Lot.

But Sarah remained with him all those years. They were inseparable. They were promised a land. And their descendants were to be as numerous as the stars of the sky, as the sand on the seashore. This promise made them laugh. But they didn't wait in vain: Isaac saw the light of day, the child brought by laughter. Almost not born, and later almost not preserved. And how will things go on now, since Isaac still has no wife? As for the promised land, Abraham still can't call a single acre his own. For he's remained an alien. How will it all end, now that it's ending?

For Sarah is going to die.

Abraham has sat with her all night; it can't last much longer. He holds her hand, and from time to time dabs her face with a cloth. Sometimes she just looks at him, but usually she keeps her eyes shut. Sarah has come to the end. She too is a displaced person. She will die far from home and be buried in strange ground. Or in a place of her own?

Then suddenly there was the moment when Abraham was alone with his thoughts and with everything, for Sarah had died. He wanted to pray, but he couldn't. He was so weary and so alone. And always those questions. Such a breath, such a last breath, where does it go?

Abraham went out of the tent in search of space, fresh air. He involuntarily lifted up his eyes to heaven: the stars twinkled as if nothing had happened. Suppose that it's all just imagination and suppose that the promise and therefore also the promised land are nonsense! God is silent. Just as now Sarah is also silent. Where in God's name must he bury her?

Abraham went in again, to Sarah's death bed, to weep and lament over her.

Then he rose up from before the face of his dead.

For there is a time to weep and lament, and there is a time to rise up from before the face of the dead. Abraham is sorrowful, but the sorrow doesn't have him in its grip. It's his faith, shaky though it is, that makes him get up. He still has something to do.

In the opening of the tent Abraham turned round and looked once again at Sarah's white and still face, the face that had accompanied him all those years, from the beginning of the journey until now, first radiant with youthful splendour and later adorned with the beauty of old age. How many miles had she gone with him? In good days and in bad, in sickness in health, for richer for poorer, she had gone with him – now he looks at her one more time, though she can no longer look at him. Once again he looks at her dear face: Sarah, his wife, his lover, his companion, the mother of his son. Their life has been a life face to face.

Abraham rose up from before the face of his dead. He has to go on, on with the pilgrim band. Not that many people are making this pilgrimage: to tell the truth there are just the two of them, him and Isaac. But when courage is lost, all is lost. Abraham gets up. In a day or two he will order his servant Eliezer to look for a wife for his son. And already he can't believe it any more than Sarah: Isaac will become the father of a people, as numerous as the stars of heaven and the sand of the seashore. A promise is a promise. And as for the land...

'Where are you going, father?'

'Not far, I still have something to do.'

Abraham goes to the gate where the city fathers are accustomed to gather, the sons of Heth, the people of the land of Canaan.

'I know that I am only a stranger and sojourner among you. Nevertheless will you give me a burial place of my own, so that I may bury my dead from before my face?'

'You may surely bury your dead in one of our graves. None of us will refuse you his burial place to bury your dead.'

That sounds very kind of the sons of Heth, but in saying this they are refusing what Abraham asked for. He had asked for a grave *of his own*. His heart longs to possess a little bit of the promised land, a little bit of Canaan where the old pilgrim can bury his beloved from before his face, a small patch of the land as a sign that God's promise of the whole of the land will be fulfilled. But the sons of Canaan have no desire to let this stranger and sojourner acquire his own grave, a perpetual domain.

Abraham knelt down: *'If you are willing that I should bury my dead from before my face, hear me and entreat for me Ephron, the son of Zohar, that he may give me the cave of Machpelah, which lies in the corner of his field. I will gladly give him the full price, to acquire for myself my own burial place among you.'*

'I give it to you,' said Ephron, the son of Zohar. 'The field and the cave I give to you. Before the eyes of the sons of my people I give it to you. Bury your dead.'

Notice Ephron's words, *I give it to you,* three times. Here the lord Ephron is negotiating courteously and shrewdly, but unconsciously he is doing so with the great words of the promise: *'Abraham, this is the land that I shall give you.'* Abraham must now dig deep into his pocket, for business is business, and the lord Ephron will only sell the cave along with the field. A Canaanite package deal. *'Land for four hundred shekels of silver, what is that between you and me?'*

It's an extortionate price. The villain is certainly asking half as much again more than its worth. But the words of Ephron, Zohar's son, must have been music to Abraham's ears. The purchase is concluded in the fine legal language of the land registry.

Why didn't Abraham bargain with the lord Ephron, who proved not to be much of a lord? Perhaps because of this music in his ears. For Ephron it's business, but for Abraham it's holy ground, and you don't haggle over that. '*Land for four hundred shekels of silver,*' said Ephron. *Land! Erets!* That's the word! Ephron himself didn't hear what he was saying, but Abraham heard it all too well. *Promised land!* At four hundred pieces of silver the *erets* is almost a gift.

Then Abraham buried his wife Sarah in the cave of the field of Machpelah, over against Mamre in the land of Canaan.

That has to be added: *in the land of Canaan*. This one piece of land means everything to Abraham. In it he can see the fulfilment of God's promise. Just as he can see it in this one son.

25

THE SERVANT IN SEARCH OF
A WIFE

GENESIS 24

Abraham's journey is almost at an end. He's old and weary of life. And lonely, now that Sarah has died. Fortunately he's almost finished his task, and it won't be long before he finds his last resting place next to her, in the cave in the field of Machpelah. Then Isaac will be alone. An orphan. Will he manage? It isn't easy to live on your own and it isn't easy to believe on your own, and you certainly can't become a father on your own.

Isaac needs a wife urgently – until he has one, Abraham won't be able to die in peace. But where is he going to get a wife for his son? From the daughters of the Canaanites in whose midst he lives? God forbid! If he does, what has begun with him will come to a dead end before it's really got going. No, a bride from here would be a disaster!

'Eliezer!'

'Here I am, master.'

'Put your hand under my loins and swear by the Lord, the God of heaven and the God of earth, that you will not take a wife for my son from the daughters of the Canaanites in whose midst I live. You must go to my land and to my family, and there take a wife for my son, for Isaac.'

Eliezer has to put his hand under Abraham's loins, the place of his seed, and swear to him for the sake of that seed, for the sake of his son Isaac, that he will go to Haran, his land, his family. Long ago the journey had begun there. 'Go from your land, your family,' said the Voice. Now that his journey is almost at an end, we hear Abraham again speaking of his land and family. He fervently hopes that Eliezer will find a wife there who is ready to make the same journey.

Eliezer is frightened. Abraham knows that he is called. Trusting in the

Voice, he left Haran to go to Canaan. But who says that now a woman will also feel called to take this way in obedience? '*My lord, if the woman is not prepared to follow me to this land, must I then send your son back to Haran, back to the land from which you departed?*'

How lonely a man can suddenly be! Has this faithful servant, who's been with him for I don't know how long, and who has shared joys and sorrows with him, never understood what inspired his master all those years? The Voice from on high, the distant vision, has that all passed Eliezer by? Does the man from Damascus regard this journey only as a trip to no man's land? Does he think deep in his heart that Isaac can just as well retrace Abraham's footsteps, to settle back into the old ways in Haran?

Abraham feels his heart go cold. Is that simply because of Eliezer's failure to understand, or is it also because his own doubts have been revived again? Who is crazy now? Perhaps Eliezer is right. Perhaps this is a foolish adventure. Is there really a God who calls? Is there such a thing as 'history', a way to take in obedience, a pilgrimage with a starting-point and a destination? Who says that it leads up somewhere?

'In that case shall I send your son back again?'

'No, not back, Eliezer. We mustn't go that way!'

What a fine hero we have! He's no hero. One word from his servant and the father of believers almost abandons his faith. At the same time he feels that this mustn't be, so he gives himself a good telling-off: '*Why are you so heavy, O my soul, and why are you so disquieted within me? Hope in God, and forget not one of his blessings.*'*

Then he counts these blessings, one by one. There are three of them, and that's a sacred number. '*Listen carefully, Eliezer. The God who has taken me from my father's house and the land of my family, the God who has called me and has sworn to me, 'To your seed shall I give this land,' this God, Eliezer, will send his angels before you so that you take a wife from there for my son.*'

So Eliezer doesn't need to worry so much. Nor does Abraham. Now once again he knows where he is with this God. He's already experienced so many benefits from this God in the past, and therefore the future is certain. Just believe that, Eliezer!

God *has* done. God *will* do.

But meanwhile a human being, in this case a woman, has to do something: she has to be willing to go. What if she isn't? *'If the woman is not prepared to go, Eliezer, then you are free from this oath. But you may not make my son* (Abraham repeats this one more time to be sure) *return there. And now, farewell. May the Lord bless you and keep you.'*

Then Eliezer put his hand under Abraham's loins, the place of his blessed seed. 'I swear it to you.'

With ten camels, packed with many precious gifts, he set out on the journey.

Arriving one evening in Haran, Eliezer made the camels kneel down by a spring. No animal kneels as impressively as a camel does. Eliezer also knelt: 'O Lord, you are the God of Abraham my master. Show your faithfulness. Here I am standing by the well. Soon the young women will come to draw water. May it be that the young woman to whom I say, "Please let down your jar, that I may drink," and who says, "Drink, sir, and I will also water your camels", is the one whom you have destined for your servant Isaac. By her I shall know that you have shown your faithfulness to my master.'

No sooner had Eliezer said 'Amen' than a young woman came up: Rebecca, the granddaughter of Abraham's brother Nahor. Gracefully she went down to the well, the jar on her shoulder, filled it, and came up again. Eliezer approached her: 'Please let down your jar, that I may drink.'

'Drink, sir, and I will also water your camels.'

You should have seen how skilfully this Rebecca did it all! She adroitly let the jar slide into her hand and gave Eliezer a drink; she hastened to give the camels a drink too, and was back down at the well again to draw more water.

When the camels had drunk enough, Abraham's servant took a gold ring from his saddlebag along with two heavy gold bracelets.

'Whose daughter are you? Please tell me. And is there room in your father's house for me to spend the night?'

'I'm Rebecca, daughter of Bethuel. We've plenty of straw and fodder, and also a place where you can spend the night.'

Eliezer knelt down again: 'O Lord, God of Abraham, blessed are you for not having ceased your faithfulness to my master and for having guided my way to the house of my master's brother.' Eliezer was convinced that in Rebecca he had found the wife for Isaac. It would be up to Isaac and Rebecca to hand on the faith of Abraham and Sarah, the inspired pioneers, to coming generations.

Meanwhile Rebecca had run back home and related what had happened to her. With great delight she showed the precious ring and the gold bracelets which Eliezer had given her. 'Such a nice man, by the well.'

Laban, her brother, impressed by the gold and her account, hastened down to the well: *'Come, you blessed one of God, why are you standing outside when I have already prepared the house for you and for the camels?'*

Servants brought Eliezer water to wash with; the animals were un-saddled and given fodder and straw. Brother Laban invited Eliezer to the evening meal. But he refused. *'I shall not eat until I have spoken my words.'*

'Speak.'

Eliezer spoke. First he spoke of Abraham's journey. God had promised him a land and a son. He told how long and hard the journey had been, but he also told of the piece of land that Abraham had finally acquired and of the birth of the child brought by laughter: Isaac. A lonely young man, of course, especially after the death of Sarah, his mother.

Then Eliezer told of *his* journey. He told how his master had bidden him seek a wife for Isaac. He told of his journey from Canaan to Haran and of his encounter by the well. He told of his prayer to Abraham's God and how even before he had said 'Amen' his prayer had already been heard, because Rebecca had come to him and said and done precisely what he had prayed that she should say and do. *'Now, if you will show faithful-ness to Abraham, my master, tell me – and if not, also tell me.'*

In Laban's eyes none of this could be chance; God was behind it. *'This is from the Lord. Who am I to speak good or evil of it? I give you Rebecca. Let her be the wife of your master's son.'*

Doesn't Rebecca have a say in this, too? Not really. Rebecca is being given in marriage; the tradition is that this is arranged without consulting the woman.

Indeed, but wasn't it quite contrary to tradition too that (and this is what matters) after Abraham it was a *woman* who declared herself willing to move out of Haran? The narrator wants not only a *patriarch* to leave his *father's house* in faith, but also a *matriarch* to leave her *mother's house* in faith.

How will the narrator resolve this? How can the woman say yes when she isn't being asked anything?

The marriage contract is concluded, Eliezer unpacks yet more jewellery and attractive garments for the bride and her family, and there is eating and drinking. It's already late when everyone goes to bed.

The next day Eliezer indicates that he wants to leave. But Rebecca's mother can't believe that she must now say good-bye to her daughter so soon. 'Please let her stay with us a while. Wait ten days.'

'God has so blessed my mission. I pray you, let me go to my master today.'

'Let's ask Rebecca.'

They call Rebecca.

'Rebecca, will you go?'

'I will go.'

She went. All her dear ones saw her off. What a pity that they couldn't accompany her to the bridegroom's house! Before they said good-bye, at a turn in the road, they called out a blessing to Rebecca: *'Our sister, may you become the mother of thousands of ten thousands, and may your descendants inherit the gate of those that hate them!'*

So she went.

Isaac is waiting over there in his tent, by the well Lachai-Roi. He's missing his mother and he's missing a wife. When will Eliezer come? Perhaps he will return without having achieved anything. Evening falls. He goes outside to meditate in the field. A lonely young man. Must he live on his own and believe on his own? How can he be the son with the blessing if he doesn't have a people?

In the distance he sees camels approaching.

And Rebecca, high up on her mount, sees in the distance a young man alone in the field. Is he coming to meet her? Is he...?

'That's Isaac, my master.' Rebecca slips down from her camel, puts on her veil and covers herself.

That evening, sitting by the well Lachai-roi, Eliezer told his story about the well in Haran. 'Please let down your jar, that I may drink.' 'Drink, sir, and I shall also water your camels.'

Isaac looked at Rebecca: a lovely figure, a source of life. 'Thank God that you went, Rebecca. Come.'

Isaac brought her into his mother Sarah's tent, and he took Rebecca, and she became his wife and he came to love her. So Isaac found comfort after his mother's death.

26

THE DEATH OF ABRAHAM

GENESIS 25.7-11

Then Abraham also died. Isaac and his brother Ishmael, who had become an archer in the wilderness, came to bury their father. Sometimes death brings together those whom life had parted. United, the two sons bore their dead father to the cave in the field of Machpelah. They laid him next to Sarah, his wife, Isaac's mother. This is holy ground on which they are standing, worth more than all the silver shekels in the world: the pledge of the new earth.

After that their ways parted again. Each had to be a blessing in his place. Ishmael returned to the wilderness.

Isaac went to live by the well Lachai-Roi, *the Living One who sees me.* It's the place which once and for all speaks of God's faithfulness to Abraham's two sons. It's the place where Hagar saw an angel when she had fled from Sarah. It's the place where Isaac saw Rebecca for the first time. The well Lachai-Roi is above all a place where human beings can meet God and one another. It's a well of stories.

This is where this history comes to an end.

Israel is reticent about a life after death. The lands around teemed with belief in immortality, and there was vigorous speculation about what was to be expected. In reaction, Israel preferred to keep silent. Keep, quiet, just wait, yes, of course all will be new, we needn't worry about that any further. The dead shouldn't be our concern. They're God's concern. Let's just pay attention to the here and now, to life and living together face to face.

So this is where the story of Abraham comes to an end.

But there is also this. Once the Sadducees came to Jesus.* They were religious people who, unlike the Pharisees and also unlike Jesus himself, didn't believe in the resurrection of the dead. They wanted to argue with Jesus.

Of course the resurrection isn't a good subject for an argument. No one knows anything about it. No one can assert for sure that the other has got it wrong. One can only ask cautiously how the other has come to believe or not to believe in the resurrection.

'Don't you know the Torah?' retorted Jesus.

To think that there was one Sadducee who didn't know the Torah! They swore by the Torah, and because the Torah doesn't say a word about the resurrection of the dead, for them there *was* no resurrection of the dead.

'In that case, may I remind you of the story of Moses and the burning bush?' said Jesus. 'Do you know what God said to him then? "I am the God of Abraham, Isaac and Jacob." Now doesn't that suggest that our God is a God of the living and not of the dead? My God is the God of Abraham, Isaac and Jacob. He was their God all the days of their life, and he's remained their God, beyond the bounds of death, to the day of Moses and to the present day. He hasn't suddenly stopped being God. He has held them fast. And he also holds me fast in life and in death.'

> *Through the night of doubt and sorrow*
> *onward goes the pilgrim band.*

And right at the front of this band we see the figures of the patriarchs and the matriarchs, the pilgrims who began this journey. There too go their sons and their daughters, so many of them, countless, an endless line, the saints of all times, as numerous as the stars in the sky, as the sand on the seashore. And at the end of their journey they all died as strangers.

So the pilgrim band goes on. At least for as long as the story goes.

A rabbi wrote in a letter* to his grandson: 'From this distant father Abraham to my own father, our fathers have handed down a truth which lived in their body and which now lives on in me. Shall I not then hand on this truth to those that are born of me? Will you accept it from me, my child? Will you hand it on again? Perhaps you will want to give it up. If so, then let it be for a greater truth. If there is one.'

27

THE FIRSTBORN

GENESIS 25.19-34

These are the generations of Isaac, the son of Abraham: Isaac was forty years old when he took Rebecca, the daughter of Bethuel, as his wife.

With her he found consolation after the death of his mother. But a new sorrow was waiting for Isaac. Rebecca was barren. So you could argue that it's a bit premature to have the heading to this story say that it will be about the generations of Isaac. There aren't any! Rebecca is the second matriarch in a row who can't give birth. What's up? It's a miracle that Israel saw the light of day.

It's precisely this notion that is developed in these stories. It isn't someone's own fertility, someone's own potency, that caused Israel to be born. This is no human work. God is involved. Israel isn't made in Israel. Israel is made in heaven.

Isaac prayed. 'Father in heaven, Rebecca, my beloved, who for your sake and mine left her mother's house in Haran, will not give birth unless from on high you...'

Isaac's prayer is heard. Rebecca becomes pregnant. And with twins into the bargain. It's as if God had to make amends.

'Can you feel that there are two of them, Rebecca?'

'Yes, they're already playing together. And sometimes they quarrel. It's just as if they're fighting over who will get out first.'

Rebecca was worried. What was going on here? She asked God.

'Two peoples are in your womb, Rebecca. Two nations will separate from your body. The one will be stronger than the other; the older shall serve the younger.'

One will be stronger than the other, of course. That's how things are. But the older serving the younger? By nature that's *not* how things are.

No, *by nature* that's not how things are. But that's how they are in *Israel*. In the stories of Israel, that strange latecomer to the world of great peoples, nature is constantly stood on its head. There the roles are reversed. Just as fertility and potency don't bring the blessing.

Two peoples are in your womb.

We're not just talking about two brothers. We're talking about the history of humankind, focussed on the people of God and the brother peoples, the *goyim*. We're talking about two types of life and faith. There is messianic life and there is pagan life, and these two lifestyles don't go together. The ways part. You can live like Cain or like Abel, like Abraham or like Lot, like Isaac or like Ishmael, like Jacob or like Esau. One figure constantly depicts the messianic life and a contrasting figure depicts pagan life. However, the narrator doesn't paint everything in black and white, and so it can happen that sometimes a pagan messianic figure can be thoroughly put to shame by a messianic pagan.

'It's just as if they're fighting over who will get out first,' said Rebecca,

Not only were the twin brothers at loggerheads with each other before they were born; during the birth itself they went on fighting vigorously to see who would be first. Esau won. *The Rough One.* As rough as the mountains where he was going to live when their ways parted. Immediately after him Jacob was born. He came out on the heels of his brother; indeed he was grasping Esau's heel in his hand in a final attempt to get past his brother at the last moment. *The Leg-puller.*

Twins, but they weren't like each other at all. While the smooth Jacob sits at home with his mother in the tent, the rough Esau wanders in storm and wind through forest and field. He loves hunting and game, just like his father.

'Why is it, Esau, that you come home only to eat and sleep? Why don't you ever sit quietly at home, like Jacob? You ought to understand that this isn't a hotel.'

'Let him be, wife, he's still young.'

One day Jacob ('our Jacob's such a good cook') made lentil soup. He was just about to take a bowl to his mother when Esau returned from the hunt, hungry and worn out, exhausted. *'O do let me have some of that red stuff, that red stuff there!'*

Esau smells soup and Jacob smells his chance: 'All right, if you give me your birthright now, at once.'

'My birthright? What use is that to me? I'm starving to death and we die anyway; we must die, and we always die earlier than we think. You can have that birthright.'

'Swear it to me now, immediately.'

Esau swore it to him. So he despised his birthright.

Clever Jacob. A smooth young man. Nevertheless he's on the track of the mystery of the birthright. Esau isn't. The Rough One simply sees what's there. His hunger is limited to a bowl of soup. He knows the ways through wood and forest, but he isn't bothered with what lies over the horizon. He lives in hills and in valleys, but he doesn't see God anywhere. He doesn't ask about the reason for his birth or the goal of his life. Birthright? I'm going to die. But as long as the ladle's in the pot, who cares?

Jacob, although he's a creep, wants to know the whys and wherefores. He's in search of the blessing. He isn't completely frank with his brother; he's the cunning one as opposed to the rough one. But he's the man who has an inkling of the secret of history. He sees it as his calling to be the firstborn. As the one who is blessed he will have to father the firstborn and the one with the blessing before he dies, so that the story of God and humankind can go on, from generation to generation.

Esau has no idea of Jacob's deepest motives. He doesn't see himself as a creature and doesn't enquire about a Creator. Let's eat, drink and be merry, for tomorrow we die!

Jacob gave him what he asked for: eating and drinking, bread and lentil soup.

Esau ate, drank, got up and went.

Where to?

To a life without mysteries, and also without any breaks in it. Without thinking, without looking, without questioning, remaining outside the tradition. Soon their ways will part.

Esau got up and went.

And Jacob, what's the world coming to with Jacob?

28

THE WELLS

GENESIS 26

'Isaac,' said God one night, 'look at the stars of the sky. That's how numerous your descendants will be. All the peoples of the earth will be blessed by your seed. What I promised your father, I also promise you. Take my blessing with you and hand it on to your son.'

And Isaac did that. He did so in faith which was moving and complied with what was simple. No great adventures are told of him. He didn't argue like his father Abraham, far less wrestle like Jacob, his son. He's the only one of Israel's patriarchs who doesn't change his name. In other words, there are no great crises in this life, no essential changes. Really we hear only how he was the son of his father and the father of his son. He was a guardian of the tradition, a man called to hand on what he had received. Isaac knows that this 'God with us' didn't begin with him and wouldn't end with him either. The promise was already there before he opened his eyes, and it would still be there when he closed them. What was given to his father would live on in his son. He had received the blessing. He preserved the blessing. And he handed on the blessing to the next generation.

Isaac plays the main role only in three stories, but remarkably we already know these stories from what happened to Abraham. So three times we have evidence that Isaac is the true heir. Like father, like son.

A famine also broke out during Isaac's lifetime. He went to Gerar, to the land of the Philistines. He even thought about going down to Egypt and seeking his salvation there, but God told him not to do it.

Then, like Abraham before him, he was very afraid that his attractive wife would arouse the desire of the king. That would cost him his head.

'She's my sister,' he lied.

But when the king of the Philistines looked out of the window one fine day and saw Isaac and Rebecca in the house opposite making love, he understood that he had been deceived.

'Didn't you tell me that she was your sister? Why didn't you tell the truth?'

'I was afraid, your majesty; I feared for my life if I told the truth.'

'And meanwhile I was running the risk of sharing my bed with a married woman, Mr Isaac.'

Like his father Abraham, Isaac too had moments of weakness.

The third story also has a well-known theme: the eternal dispute over the wells.

Isaac sowed in that land and harvested that year a hundredfold, for the Lord blessed him. Isaac became great; he steadily became greater until he had become very great. Sheep and goats, cows, camels, servants, maids: Isaac becomes a rich and prosperous man. God is good to him. The sun rises upon him. How blessed this man is!

The blessing of Israel is a sun which rises above you, great, steadily greater, until it has become very great.

> *The Lord bless you and keep you.*
> *The Lord make his countenance shine upon you and be gracious to you.*
> *The Lord lift up his countenance upon you and give you peace.*

That's a wish for salvation at the beginning of every new day that God gives you. *Shalom.* Peace. May the light come to be in you and around you, so that you know what you're living for, what you're sowing for and what you're reaping for. May God give you peace, again and again, morning after morning. May you become great, steadily greater, until you've become very great. A blessed one of God!

But the one who is blessed is also the one who is envied.* And envy can rapidly turn to hatred. A conflict develops over the wells. Again, just as with father Abraham, King Abimelech turns up to deny Isaac the right to use these wells. Now don't be clever and ask whether this uncircumcised Philistine has eternal life, that he can turn up again here, or cunningly suppose that this king from Abraham's time probably had a son who took after his father and also had precisely the same name. No, history repeats itself; it's always the same old story: the one who is blessed is the one who is envied and the one who is envied is the one who is hated. So it goes on from generation to generation. For ever and ever there is war over wells. Wells of water, oil wells, Philistines, Palestinians, there's nothing new under the sun.

Besides, in the days in which the narrator sets these stories, the Philistines hadn't even settled in Israel. So he isn't telling the history of a particular time. He's telling a truth of all times. Well, well.

Isaac has become great, steadily greater, until he's become very great. So we don't have long to wait: the pagans come marching in, choking with jealousy. They want to make Isaac small again. 'Get out of here,' says Abimelech, 'you've grown too big for me.'

How must Isaac, the messianic man, the hated man with the blessing, resolve this?

Isaac yields. He goes a long way with his cattle. Then he digs the wells which father Abraham had once dug, but which the Philistines had stopped up after his death. Isaac restored to the wells the name that Abraham had given them. So he brings his father's heritage to new life. He also strikes a spring himself, and thus adds to his father's heritage.

This arouses the hatred of the Philistines. The hostile shepherds turn up again. 'That's our water. Get out of here.'

What must Isaac do now?

He's wise enough to keep quiet and strong enough not to strike back. He calls this well *Esek, quarrel.* The source of a quarrel. Again he moves on, clearly ready to go the necessary miles. This strange Hebrew seems to have quite a different source on which he can draw. Again he puts up his tents elsewhere and there too he digs the wells which his father had dug and which the Philistines have stopped up.

When, after a great deal of labour, living water again wells up, and Isaac has given the spring the name with which his father had once baptized it, his tormentors again take up arms to dispute his grassy pasture: 'That water's also ours.' Then Isaac also retreated from there. He called this well *Sitnah. Opposition. Satan's water.*

Isaac moves on. The foxes have holes and the birds of the air have nests, but Isaac moves on, in hope of blessing. What does this bring him except for thirst and scorn and loss of face?

The story goes that it gave him peace. He had become great, steadily greater, until he was so great that he could be small and non-violent. To put it in present-day language, he argued for peaceful co-existence between Israel and the neighbouring peoples. Not to be a hawk and not to strike back can be actions of great wisdom and of great power. Isaac reaches his goal by constantly yielding. The miles that he went eventually led to peace. Isaac had not made his sacrifices in vain; from now on the Philistines gave him space. Isaac is thus free to see the hand of God here. Again he digs a well. *Rehoboth. The Lord has made space.*

From there he goes to Beersheba. Here he pitches his tents and builds an altar to God. Again the Philistines turn up. Fear strikes Isaac's heart when for the umpteenth time he sees king Abimelech approaching, accompanied by two cronies, his mate Ahuzzath, and Philcol, the chief of the army. *Wealth and Big Mouth.* One could think of a more pleasant visit.

'What brings you here? Do you hate me? You've chased me away, time and again, until I've finally ended up here. Why are you pursuing me?'

'We've come because we've seen with our own eyes that you have God's blessing. Let's make a covenant. Let's live together in peace.'

Are these people afraid of the one with the blessing and his God? Or do they want to share in his prosperity? Or are they in search of the secret of this messianic man and are they asking whether there's also room for them with his God?

And they had a meal.

The solemn sealing of a non-aggression treaty. One could also say that there is messianic life on earth. In the midst of the wilderness God's firstborn has dug for water and Beersheba is a little oasis for Hebrews and pagans. Isn't the blessing for the whole human family?

29

THE BLESSING

GENESIS 27

There were just two pupils at the Beersheba Bible School, Jacob and Esau.*
Why weren't they at ordinary school? Because Isaac preferred private
schooling. In our isolation lies our strength, he used to say.

Granted, this was still only a little Bible; it contained only the first few
chapters of Genesis. But it was also only a little school and, more important, the few stories that they did have really contained everything.
Jacob in particular couldn't get enough of them. 'Sir, tell us again about
the creation of the heavens and the earth and what happened next.'

Then the teacher began again from Adam: 'In the beginning God
created the heavens and the earth.' After that he told of Cain, who had no
eye for his brother Abel. He could even murder him! And the teacher
told about the peoples, the *goyim*, who could no longer understand one
another's language and were dispersed over the earth.

The teacher stopped. He looked at his watch.

'Go on, sir,' said Jacob, 'Go on. More.'

'Our teacher wants to go home,' said Esau, who certainly wanted to go
home.

But home was more Jacob's cup of tea. Esau preferred to be outside. He
had just made a new bow and arrow and needed to try it out. He wanted
to go hunting with the boys from the local school, and he was beginning
to get tired of these stories. Moreover, he was hungry.

Jacob was different. He was hungry for these stories. He kept thinking
about them, young though he was. There was a mystery in them, and so
he wanted the teacher to go on telling them, because now it got really
exciting: the story of grandfather Abraham who was called by God to leave
the world of the *goyim*. From him a people was to be born which would be
a blessing for all peoples, a people that knew what God was after with the
heavens and the earth.

'How is it, sir, that God chose Abraham and his seed of all people to be bearers of the blessing? I mean, surely there were others, older and stronger than he was?'

'To be honest, I don't know,' said the teacher. 'But I do know that God isn't like human beings. He even turns things round. Then the last become the first. Just like Cain and Abel, you know. But I agree with you, it's amazing.'

'Yes,' said Jacob, 'quite amazing. I must think hard about it.'

'You do that,' said the teacher.

Esau's friends were already standing outside waiting for him.

'Tell mother that I'll be home before dark,' said Esau. 'And tell father that I'll bring a good piece of meat for him.'

Jacob walked home by himself. A loner. Not like the others. Always occupied with, shall we say, the things that can't be seen, with the secret of history. A pity that his teacher didn't go on with the story. Of course he could also ask father Isaac at home, but last time he didn't seem to have much to say in answer to the questions that Jacob shot at him; he would have preferred Esau to shoot something for him. Then Jacob resorted to Rebecca. Mother could also tell good stories. For example, about how Abraham and Isaac had handed on the blessing.

'Yes, naturally,' said Jacob. 'He was the firstborn.'

'No, not naturally,' said Rebecca, who understood that Jacob hadn't yet learnt this at school. 'For really Ishmael was grandfather's firstborn: uncle Ishmael, who has *goy*'s blood. Abraham couldn't wait for God to grant his promise in his own time and he took a wife from the *goyim*. God later forgave him, of course, but he shouldn't have done it. What he did was quite natural, but you know that our God is different. With him the oldest serves the youngest. The last become the first.'

'Yes,' said Jacob, 'that's what our teacher, too, is always saying.'

Then silence fell in the tent.

What were they thinking about, those two?

'What are you thinking about, mother?'

'Me, nothing. Go outside and play. Where's Esau?'

'Hunting,' said Jacob. 'Hunting with the boys. He should be home before dark.'

Rebecca sighed. She said nothing.

Father Isaac had grown old. He'd gone blind. How long would he still have to live?

'Esau.'

'Here I am, father.'

'I'm an old man, my son, my days are numbered. So take your bow and arrow, go into the field, shoot some game and prepare it the way I like best. Then bring it to me. You and I will have a meal. Then I shall give you the blessing before I die.'

Mother Rebecca hears Isaac's words. At the same time she hears the Voice from her dream of long ago: *'Two peoples are in your womb; the older shall serve the younger.'* Isn't this the moment to give God a helping hand? The end is a good one, and don't the means justify the end?

'Jacob, quickly bring two he-goats. I'll prepare them the way that your father likes best. Take them to him, so that he eats of them and gives you the blessing before he dies.'

'But what when he lays his hand on me? I'm smooth, and Esau is hairy. What if father touches me? He'll notice that I'm a deceiver. He'll curse me instead of blessing me.'

Rebecca knows what to do. She dresses Jacob in Esau's clothes, and uses the skin of a he-goat to cover his smooth neck and hands. Thus equipped, a little while later Jacob goes into Isaac's tent.

'Father.'

'Here I am, my son. Who are you?'

'I am Esau, your firstborn. Here's the game. Eat some of it, father, and then give me the blessing.'

'Are you back already?'

'Yes, it was very quick. The Lord your God gave me a speedy hunt.'

To be honest, it's a credit to Jacob that he talks about the Lord *your* God. At this moment the Lord is not *his* God. Jacob himself is playing God.

'Come closer, that I may touch you and know for certain that you're my son Esau.'

Jacob came closer, with a thumping heart. Isaac touched him.

'I don't understand it. The voice is Jacob's voice, but the hands are the hands of Esau. Are you really Esau?'

'Yes, father.'

'Bring me the game, my son. Then I shall eat and give you the blessing.'

Jacob brought it to him and Isaac ate. He also brought him wine, and Isaac drank. 'Come closer, my son, and kiss me.'

Jacob came closer and kissed him. Isaac smelt the smell of the field in his clothes and gave him the blessing: *'See, the smell of my son is as the smell of a field which the Lord has blessed. May God give you of the dew of heaven, and of the oil of the earth. Peoples shall serve you, and nations bow down to you. Be ruler over your brothers, and your mother's sons shall bow down before you. Cursed be everyone who curses you, and blessed be every one who blesses you.'*

No sooner had Isaac spoken, hardly had Jacob left the tent, than Esau appeared, back from the hunt.

'Father, here's the game you asked for.'

'Who are you?'

'I'm Esau, your son, your firstborn.'

Isaac shook with fear. 'Then who was it who has just brought me game, so that I ate? Who was it to whom I gave the blessing and is now the one with the blessing?'

Esau uttered a loud, bitter, cry. 'Bless me, me too, my father!'

'Your brother Jacob has come with lies and deceit and has taken away your blessing.'

'Isn't he rightly called Jacob? *Deceiver!* Twice already he's deceived me. First of all he took away my birthright, and now he's also stolen the blessing. Father, do you still have a blessing? Surely you've more than that one blessing?'

No, there's only one. Jacob is the blessed one and blessed he will be. A word of such power cannot be turned back. The blessing for all is contained in the blessing of this one. But what consolation is that to Esau?

'Bless me, me too, my father!'

However, the blessing which Isaac allows himself to be persuaded to give can only be a confirmation of Jacob's victory. *'Far from the oil of the earth shall you live, far from the dew of heaven.'*

So can these two no longer live together as brothers? Is no reconciliation possible?

Behold how good and pleasant it is
when brothers dwell in unity!

It is like precious oil,
which falls like dew on the mountains.
*For there the Lord commands his blessing.**

But that's still in the future.

30

JACOB'S LADDER

GENESIS 28

Jacob and Esau, each plays his role in the sacred theatre of Israel.

Esau, the strong, hairy Esau, portrays the *goyim*, the natural way of living. He knows no mysteries; he squanders his birthright on a bowl of soup. Tradition, what is that? What should he hand down? He knows no other origin than his birth and no other destiny than his death.

Jacob portrays the true Israelite. Granted, everything's wrong with this scoundrel: he lies and cheats and a whole lot of water will have to flow down the Jabbok before he can bear the name of Israel with honour. But he has heard the same Voice which called Abraham from his land; he knows the mystery of the firstborn; he knows about the blessing. It's Jacob who will hand on the blessing to the next generation.

That is, if Esau in his anger hasn't killed him before then, as once Cain killed Abel. For again a fratricide threatens. *Esau said in his heart: the days of mourning for my father are approaching, then I shall kill Jacob my brother.*

As soon as father Isaac has laid down his weary head, Jacob's head will roll.

'Flee, my son, flee to Haran, flee to my brother Laban, and remain there some days until Esau's wrath is assuaged!' That's how mother Rebecca arranges things. She also hastens to Isaac, but with a rather different story: 'Isaac, what if our Jacob marries a wife from here, just like Esau? That would be the end of me.'

Is that what she left Haran for, like Abraham before her? What if the people of God dissolves into the world of the great peoples? Will little Israel, before it is properly established, disregard the Voice and disappear again like a tiny drop of water into the sea of the *goyim*, from where God called it to appear?

Esau, the hunter, has taken Canaanite wives for himself. He had no sooner left Bible School than he lay with *goyse* women. 'God forbid, Isaac, that the same thing should happen with Jacob. Don't let Jacob take a wife from the daughters of Canaan.'

Isaac summoned Jacob. 'Don't marry a daughter of Canaan, my son. Arise, go to Haran, to your mother's father, and there choose a wife from the daughters of Laban, your mother's brother. God bless you. May he make you fruitful and numerous, a great people, living in the land that he promised to Abraham.'

Jacob goes away from the land. He has gone beyond bounds in a way that he shouldn't have done, and now there are boundaries that he has to cross. Esau's bitter cry is still ringing in his ears. Jacob flees like a thief in the night. He has said farewell to his blind father. How pale and weary the old man was when they said good-bye! Will he ever see him again? And mother Rebecca? She had been so worried, busy with clothes and food for his journey. Up above on the hill he had turned round towards her one more time, waving cheerfully and bravely. The deceiver. For he isn't cheerful and he isn't brave. He's afraid. Miles of loneliness ahead and no way back. Good-bye, Canaan. It's just as if there is no place for him there before God's face as long as he's at odds with his brother. Will he ever return here?

The sun has set. One last time Jacob lays himself to rest on the ground of the land that the Eternal One promised to father Abraham. Tomorrow he will travel in the direction of Haran.

Jacob is going the way of Abraham, but the other way round. Can he just go on like that? Can he just slip out of the land, over the border, and quietly disappear? It's a critical moment. God is almost back to the beginning with Israel. If the Eternal One doesn't want his people to go round in a circle, then Jacob has to return to Canaan.

One last time he lies down to sleep in the land. A stone is his pillow. Tomorrow he will be in a foreign land. Alone.

Alone?

And look, a ladder, set down on the earth, the top of the ladder touched heaven.

This is a great surprise, since it's a long time since we've heard anything about heaven. We heard about Jacob's deceit on his mother's prompting, about his father's bitterness and Esau's wrath, but not a word about heaven.

Look, a ladder, set down on the earth from heaven.

It's difficult the other way round. You can't set a ladder against heaven. In the land of Babel, where Joseph is now going, they tried that once. They were going to build a gigantic stepped tower to heaven. It was a crazy status symbol of people who knew no bounds and wanted to be like God. Arrogance in stone. It didn't work. You can't set a ladder against heaven.

But heaven can set down a ladder on earth. *Look, a ladder, set down on the earth, the top of the ladder touched the heaven. And look, angels were ascending and descending on it.*

As they ascend, they carry up Jacob's distress, his shame, his guilt, his sorrow for what was and his anxiety about what is to come.

As they descend, they carry God's consolation with them. *Look, God has put himself there: 'Jacob, I am God, the God of Abraham and the God of Isaac. The land on which you lie, to you I shall give it, and to your seed, which shall be numerous. Look, I am with you. I shall preserve you wherever you go, and I shall bring you back to this land.'*

This puts Jacob's journey to Haran, where Abraham's journey began, in the perspective of his return. The future which began with Abraham will go on with Jacob, here, in this place, in this land. Just as one day the people Israel will return from exile, so the sun of God's grace will rise again here over Jacob.

That's the secret of the place where Jacob dreamed: salvation can be expected there. This place stands for the *erets Yisrael,* which in turn stands for the whole *erets.* 'Jacob, this is the place where I show myself. And from here that shall be known throughout the land and to the ends of the earth. Salvation is to be expected, Jacob, for you and for all who are born of you.'

Jacob awoke from his sleep: *Truly, God is here and I did not know it. How fearful is this place! This is none other than a house of God. This is the gate of heaven.*

Gate of heaven. Or *Babel* in Babylonian. So whoever seeks this gate, the place where heaven and earth touch, mustn't be in Babel but here, in this place, in this land.

Jacob set on end the stone which had served him as a pillow, as a monument. He poured oil on the stone and he called the name of the place Bethel, *House of God.* 'If God will be my God, preserve me on this way that I have to go, give me food and clothing, and let me return in peace to my father's house, then this monument has rightly proved a house of God. Then in my joy I can only share with others what God gave me in such abundance.'

Jacob lifted up his feet and went to the land of the sons of the East.
    An exile, but not an exile without hope. On the way to much loneliness, but not alone. Jacob has a dream, and far from home he will be able to live by it. And one day he will return here.

31

THE MEETING WITH RACHEL

GENESIS 29.1-14

Jacob lifted up his feet and went to the land of the sons of the East.

That's a rather cumbrous and unusual way of saying that Jacob got up and set off. But the story-teller clearly wants to emphasize this, and he's right to do so, for this isn't just any journey that Jacob is undertaking. He's leaving his home in some confusion; he has to go alone through the wilderness, and how will things be in the land of the sons of the East?

He looked, and see, a well in the field.

Strange! One moment Jacob is packing his bags in Bethel, lifting up his feet and setting out on the journey of a lifetime, and the next moment he's sitting a couple of hundred miles further on and is already where he needs to be. That was fast! It seems as if the angels of Bethel have given our dreamer wings! Not a word about the dangers on the way, the pain, the hunger and the loneliness. Why are we told nothing about Jacob's deprivations? Is it because all the suffering ultimately doesn't count in the face of the glory that is revealed to him?

He looked, and see, a well in the field. And see, three flocks of sheep and goats were lying beside it, for out of that well the flocks were watered.

Another well story. Everything takes place by wells. The well is a place of tender encounters and of murder and death. The possession of villages and nomadic tribes, wells are as precious as they're the objects of dispute. In the cool of the evening women tell one another the stories of the day there, and in the cool of the morning the stories of the night. Shepherds gather their flocks there to water them. Abraham's servant found a wife for Isaac there, and on his flight from Egypt Moses met Jethro's daughter there.

Jacob looked, and see, a well in the field. And see, three flocks of sheep and goats. But there was a big stone on the mouth of the well.

Yes, for water is precious, so a good heavy stone can really do no harm. You can't remove such a thing all by yourself; you have to be with others. Now the shepherds there had arranged things so that they waited until everyone was present. Then they rolled the stone from the well – one, two, three, up! – and watered their sheep, and after that they rolled the stone back over the mouth of the well – boom! – to its place. That was carefully organized: everyone knew where they had to hold it, otherwise there would only have been quarrels.

'Brothers,' Jacob said to the shepherds, 'What's this place called?'

'Haran.'

The brothers aren't very talkative. But our Jacob's in the right place. He's in Haran! For the time being, at any rate, he's at his destination.

'Do you know Laban, the son of Nahor?'

'Yes, we do.'

Another long speech. The shepherds aren't very friendly. Tired of the chatter, they clearly want to be left in peace. What's this strange fellow doing here?

'Is there peace with Laban? *Shalom*?'

'Yes, peace. Look, there comes his daughter Rachel with the sheep.'

Look! And don't talk too much, stranger, that's not good.

Jacob looks, and see, over there Rachel, Laban's daughter, is approaching with her sheep. It's a splendid sight: the undulating flock and behind it the beautiful figure of Rachel, lithe of step, coming down the hill with her animals. Peace indeed. Such an attractive girl and so many plump sheep: if that isn't *shalom*, what is? Jacob gets an irresistible longing to be alone with her. A moment ago there was the suspicion that these shepherds wanted Jacob out of the way, but now it's clear that Jacob would very much like to see the shepherds clearing out.

'I don't know whether it's struck you,' says Jacob, 'but it's now mid-day. As far as I can see this isn't exactly the best moment to bring the flocks together. So my suggestion, brothers, would be to water the animals and go, then you'll still be able to pasture the animals for a good while.'

The shepherds of Haran won't budge: 'That heavy stone isn't taken from the well until we're all here. And we aren't all here. Don't you understand?'

Rachel was now close. How glorious she looked, this shepherd girl with her flock! A picture. At the beginning of his journey Jacob had seen angels in the dark night. Now at the end of his journey he sees an angel again, but in the clear light of day: a being of flesh and blood. Or is he dreaming again?

Now when Jacob saw Rachel the daughter of Laban, his mother's brother, and the sheep of Laban, his mother's brother, Jacob went up and rolled the stone from the well and gave water to the sheep of Laban, his mother's brother.

As if he were Esau. So strong! The beautiful Rachel and the shepherds of Haran unleashed unsuspected powers in him. While the men were watching with undisguised contempt to see how his pride would come before a fall, Jacob strained every muscle of his body and all by himself rolled the heavy stone from the mouth of the well. Like someone taking the cork out of a bottle, according to an old rabbi.

Jacob kissed Rachel and wept. 'I am Jacob, a blood relative of your father, for I am a son of Rebecca.'

Calvin writes in his Bible commentary that probably Jacob first said who he was and only after that kissed Rebecca.

Calvin was a great divine, but unfortunately somewhat deficient in romantic feelings. For at first Rachel knows no more than that a complete stranger has toiled away for her. So gallant! And strong! Only after he kissed her did he tell her of their family connection. The first kiss would never have been such an overwhelming experience for the unsuspecting girl had Jacob observed etiquette.

Another divine, the thirteenth-century Spanish rabbi Maimonides, could tell from reliable sources that Jacob didn't kiss Rachel on the mouth but on her forehead. He too was no expert in romance.

Don't let's quarrel over it. Be it as it may, Jacob has finally found the peace for which he so longed, the *shalom* promised him by the angels who were descending the ladder from heaven. Don't let's argue when he kissed Rachel and where. Let's simply rejoice at this couple's happiness.

The sheep don't understand why their shepherdess is suddenly so anxious to get home. 'Father, listen to what's happened to me.' And no sooner had Laban heard the report about Jacob than he rushed to meet him, embraced him, and brought him to his house. Jacob told Laban everything that had happened. And Laban said, *'Surely you are my bone and my flesh.'*

Those are words from paradise: *bone of my bone and flesh of my flesh.*
What is more like paradise than people belonging together? Jacob has
found a brother.

Talking about brothers, how are things at home, Jacob? How are things
with your brother Esau?

32

THE TWO SISTERS

GENESIS 29.15-30.24

And Jacob stayed with Laban the days of a month.

Was that about the amount of time that mother Rebecca had at the back of her mind when she told Jacob that he had to flee, because Esau was seeking to kill him? 'Flee, my boy, flee to my brother Laban *for some days*, until Esau's wrath has cooled.'

For some days... But the journey itself lasted I don't know how long! Did Rebecca say that simply to comfort her child? Or because she thought that Jacob would find a beloved and because she knew from experience how quickly time goes for lovers?

Jacob fell in love with Rachel. You couldn't find such a pretty and joyful shepherd girl in all Haran. Her older sister, Leah, for example, was no match for her, Leah with the dull eyes.

Jacob fell in love with Rachel, and Rachel fell in love with Jacob. And Laban saw it. Laban, who had given Jacob such a brotherly welcome into his home: *'Surely you are my bone and my flesh.'*

'Jacob, you've now been with us for more than a few days. You're my brother. But is that a reason why you should be serving me for nothing? Tell me what your wages must be.'

'I would very much like to marry Rachel, uncle.'

'Rachel? But surely you know that Leah is the oldest?'

'Yes, I know that. But I love Rachel so much.'

'I've seen that. And you're right. She's an angel. I would rather give her to you than to anyone else. Work seven years for me, and Rachel is yours.'

Jacob served Laban seven years with delight, because he knew who he was doing it for. Time flew by.

'Uncle, I've now worked seven years for you, give me Rachel as my wife.'

'Did it seem a long time to you, my boy?'

'No, uncle, the years have gone by quickly; in my eyes they were *a few days.*'

A marriage is celebrated. A great country marriage. There's singing and dancing, eating and drinking. Yes, above all there's a great deal of drinking: brother Laban, otherwise economy personified, was generous in pouring the wine. So the hours of the wedding flew by.

Night fell. The first night of the marriage. Jacob led the veiled Rachel to the bridal chamber and entered her.

Day broke. Jacob awoke with the woman of his dreams in his arms. But... it was Leah! Leah with the dull eyes! Jacob screamed with anger and sorrow. Laban had deceived him. To be treated like that by one's family. He calls himself my brother! *'My bone and my flesh...'*

Indeed, of the same bone and the same flesh. For what is this, if not a copy of Jacob's own quick-change trick of years ago? Laban is giving our hero a taste of his own medicine. Once he deceived his father, veiled in darkness through blindness. 'I'm Esau, father.' But look, it was Jacob. Now the deceiver is deceived in the darkness of the night. And look, it was Leah.

Jacob is unhappy. And furious. 'A scandal,' he screams, 'a scandal before God and men.'

But Laban shrugs his shoulders. 'Oh well,' he says, 'people don't do that sort of thing here, my boy. It's not our custom for the youngest to go before the oldest. Besides, it doesn't mean that I don't want to give you Rachel as your wife. Let me make it up to you, Jacob. I'll give her to you as your wife now, and in exchange you must serve me for another seven years from today.'

This is the first case in world history of a bride on hire purchase. So Jacob got what was coming to him. The deceived bridegroom still has another *few days* to go. So perhaps it's best to leave him alone with his thoughts. For how have things been in the meanwhile with Leah and Rachel, the two sisters who've been manoeuvred into such an impossible situation by their father?

Alas, the relations between these two sisters are as sorry as those between the brothers Jacob and Esau. The women are caught up in a murderous rivalry, and that's not at all uplifting. The paternal and maternal ancestors of Israel knew something about this. It's strange that such a people didn't prefer to keep quiet about its past. Why is all that human, all too human, plotting and scheming set down in black and white?

Probably this is a way of depicting the wonder of election in black and white. Jacob engages in lying and deceiving, but through the lying and deceiving the Lord carries through his plans. Laban is a villain, but he's also a brother. Rachel and Leah are out for each other's lives, but in the meantime they do build the house of Israel. A few poor actors and actresses are on the stage; they bungle things, act by act, but they're nevertheless children of God. There is more than their muddle. God is also still there.

And God is as he prefers to be: opting for the least, the weak, the scorned.

Like all the matriarchs of Israel, Leah and Rachel are barren. In other words, like the origin of heaven and earth in the beginning, the origin of Israel in the midst of the peoples is a miracle of God. Powerful he-men and voluptuous mother figures may set the tone in paganism, but in Israel they don't get anywhere. There it's God who gives life.

Leah and Rachel are barren. But Leah is also unloved. And God saw her misery. He had pity on Leah and opened her womb. We hear in the names of the sons to whom she gave life how great was her loneliness and how deep her sorrow:

Reuben. *Because the Lord has looked upon my affliction, surely now my husband will love me.*

Simeon. *Truly the Lord has heard that I am not loved, and he has given me this son also.*

Levi. *Now my husband will cling to me, because I have borne him three sons.*

Judah. *Now I shall praise God.*

A brave person! She continues to hope. But Jacob continues to love Rachel none the less, although she gives him no children.

Rachel is near to desperation. Has she somehow been born behind God's back, and will she die there childless? 'Jacob, give me children, or I shall die! Must my way lead into a dead end?'

'What can I do about it, Rachel? I'm not God.'

Clearly Jacob regarded Rachel's cry of distress as an attack on him. At the same time there's something attractive about his answer. Indeed he isn't God. At first he had secretly thought that he was. But on the journey of his life he has clearly begun to doubt that. So there's now room for faith. Faith always begins when a person confesses that he or she isn't God. 'I'm not God, Rachel. What can I do about it?'

'What you can do is to father a child by my slave-girl Bilhah. Let her give birth for me.'

A surrogate mother will give Rachel her rights. So a son is also born to Rachel, to whom she gives the name Dan: *God has finally secured my rights*. And yet another son sees the light of life, thanks to Rachel's slave girl: Naphtali, *Fought for with my sister*. What's in a name?

Leah, whose womb now seems to be closed again, doesn't want to get left behind and also chooses a surrogate to give birth in her place. Our Jacob has a lot to do: Gad is born, *Good fortune*. And his brother Asher, *Happiness*. Why these names, Leah? Are you really so happy-go-lucky?

And then we hear nothing of these sons, who against their will are involved in this dispute and whose names bear witness that their mothers are more concerned with their own lives than with those of their sons. Laban has played a sordid game with Leah, Rachel and Jacob, and now these three in turn play a sordid game with one another and with their children.

One day, at the time of the wheat harvest, Reuben, Leah's oldest son, found love apples in the field, fruit which stimulates the senses and which when put under the bed promotes fertility. 'Just look, mother, what I found in the field.'

Rachel comes to hear the news. It would be a child of Leah's who found the love apples! What need does Leah have of them? It's a long time since Jacob slept with her, so there are no senses to stimulate, and as for Leah's fertility, that's the last thing that must be encouraged.

Once the brothers Jacob and Esau negotiated over a bowl of lentil soup.

Now the sisters Rachel and Leah negotiate over a bowl of love potion. It's humiliating to Rachel to have to ask Leah for it. But she must. She needs the stuff. Those who are desperate will grab at anything.

'Leah, may I have those love apples?'

'You? But you've already got Jacob, my husband. Do you now want my son's fruits too?'

'If you give them to me, Jacob is yours for the night.'

In the evening twilight Jacob returns from the field. Full of desire Leah runs to meet him. 'Come, Jacob. I've hired you for the night in exchange for the love fruit that Reuben found.'

Hired! She actually says that. Jacob has become the gigolo of his own wives. Moreover, whether Leah secretly kept back some of this 'passion fruit' we don't know, but we do know that it was a fruitful night, since nine months later Issachar is born: *Man of hire.* Fathered by a hireling.

How does that feel, Jacob?

And Rachel, how were things going with her? Did the apples under the bed bring her happiness?

No, they didn't. For poor Rachel of course it was the umpteenth disappointment, but for Israel's faith it was better like that. For faith isn't like magic. Magic turns faith upside down. With magic people try to use God instead of allowing themselves to be used by God. Magic is a method of using the Almighty for one's own purposes. Those who believe, let the power come as it were from outside themselves. Grafefully or gracelessly, they entrust themselves to the Eternal One.

This is a trust that has to grow. That's why our story goes the way it does. Jacob and Rachel have to learn it in a long process.

But fortunately the God who opts for the most insignificant, who raises up the humiliated, now also looks on the low estate of his handmaiden Rachel. At long last God opens her womb. Joseph is born. *May God add!* May God give me another son! The more the merrier.

A bizarre story. But all the same, through all this sorry, petty business the promise which was once given begins to be fulfilled. A people has been promised to Abraham, Isaac and Jacob, and it really beings to look as if it's coming. Don't ask how, but the human family is taking shape.

God has promised a people. And a land.

Yes, that's also true, the land.

Jacob, what are you thinking of? Oughtn't you to be going back to your land?

33

THE RETURN

GENESIS 30.25-31.55

When at long last the Eternal One had also opened Rachel's womb, Jacob thought that the moment had come to return to his land. Were his father and mother still alive? And how would things be with his brother Esau?

'Let me depart, Laban, along with my wives and my children.'

Better not, Laban thinks. For this Jacob is worth his weight in gold. He's a man with a blessing, someone who spreads blessing everywhere. There are people like that. Wherever they set foot, everything flourishes and comes to maturity. You see *shalom* blossoming in the footsteps of the one with the blessing. So Laban very much wants to keep Jacob at home. The boss even becomes humble. *'If I have found favour in your eyes, name your wages, and I will give it to you.'*

It's not every day that an immigrant worker is spoken to in that way.

Jacob, just as cunning as before, decides to postpone his departure a bit and opens the negotiations:

'Since my arrival, the little that you had has increased abundantly. God has blessed you in my footsteps. But now the time has come for me to think of my own house and home.'

'What shall I give you, Jacob?'

'Nothing, uncle, you needn't give me anything. But I would like to be able to have a few sheep and goats. Let's make an agreement: I shall continue to pasture your sheep and goats. But first today I shall go through the flock and take out all the brown sheep and spotted goats. My sons shall pasture them, three days' journey from here. I shall pasture the rest of the flock, the white sheep and the brown goats, for you. The brown sheep and the spotted goats that are born shall belong to me.'

Laban can't believe his ears: Jacob will have to breed brown sheep from white sheep and spotted goats from brown goats! He's a clever young man who can manage that.

'I gladly agree,' he says, and hides a laugh.

But Jacob will have the last laugh.

He picks branches of poplar, almond and plane, cuts white strips in the bark and puts the twigs in the animals' troughs at mating time. This is a trick to which even Mendel's laws must yield, since promptly brown lambs and spotted goats are born. Whenever the strongest sheep are mating, Jacob puts the branches in the troughs, but if the sheep or goats are weak, he doesn't. The weak animals are for Laban, the strong ones for Jacob.

His revenge is sweet. There's no greater pleasure than malicious pleasure. For centuries shepherds round their campfires told the story in great detail: Laban was fooled, a servant who was treated badly got the better of his master, a vagrant became the shepherd prince, a newspaper boy became a millionaire.

But Jacob sees the hand of God in it: 'Rachel, Leah, the God of my father has been with me. Now I know that he is calling me to return to my land. Come with me.'

It's indeed time to leave Haran. Relations have been seriously disrupted, and Jacob has acquired enough possessions to stand on his own feet. At the same time you can hear from his voice and see from his attitude that this is a different Jacob from the insecure exile who came here years ago, full of himself. Here too speaks a man who has begun to understand something of his calling and who wants to go back to the place where his life went off the rails.

'Rachel, Leah, will you go with me?'

They go with him.

And they feel so little affection for their father that they depart from Haran secretly. When Laban is away from home for a few days to shear the sheep, they see their chance and go.

Jacob knows the way. From his outward journey, of course. But perhaps even more because it's the way which father Abraham once took in great faith, when a Voice called him. And because this is the way which mother Rebecca took when she had heard the Voice in Eliezer's words. It's the way of the one with the blessing.

Now Jacob also takes that way. The God of Abraham and Sarah, the God of Isaac and Rebecca, is calling. And Esau, his brother, is calling. Jacob retraces his steps. Homewards.

But Rachel feels that this journey is a break with her past. She knows of the God who motivates Jacob, but she can't yet trust this God completely, That's why she was so quiet on the day of departure. Once again she walked through the stalls and the sheds and past the places in the garden where she had buried her dead animals, climbed trees and loved Jacob. Once again she walked through the house, the room where she was born, the quarters where she was a girl and became a woman. Once again she stood quietly by the household altar, where she learned to pray and knew that she was close to the gods. It seems a long time ago now. The gods of olden days. Suddenly, in a wave of emotion and without anyone seeing her, she took the images from the altar and hid them under her garments. Better not go on a journey without them. To go in blind faith to an unknown land is asking too much of Rachel. On the frontier of two worlds she seeks support in the gods of her youth. There she will still have something from home. And perhaps these images will bring good fortune.

Laban is furious when three days later he returns from shearing the sheep to discover that his children and grandchildren have gone. He doesn't waste a moment and chases after them with his sons. He'll get them!

No he won't. For by night the Eternal One appears to him in a dream and urges him to do no harm to Jacob.

After journeying for seven days Laban and his followers catch up with the caravan. 'Jacob, what have you done to me? You've misled me, and carried away my daughters as prisoners. Why this secret flight? Why didn't you bid us an open and honest farewell? I would have seen you off with rejoicing, with songs and drum and lyre. Why did you grudge me kissing my daughters farewell? I could have done you evil, but your God has appeared to me and urged me to let you depart in peace.'

'I was afraid. I thought that you would never let your daughters go, that you would rob me of them.'

'Why have you stolen my gods?'

'Your gods? By God, I swear to you that I don't have your gods. The person in whose possession you find your gods here shall not live.'

Unsuspecting, Jacob has brought his beloved wife to the brink of death. Rachel has hidden the gods in her tent, under her saddle.

The search begins. Laban searches Jacob's tent from top to bottom. Leah's tent and that of the two slave girls are turned upside down. No gods.

Then Laban enters Rachel's tent. She's sitting there in a corner on her saddle, the picture of innocence.

'Are you looking for something?'

'Yes, I am.'

'What are you looking for, may I ask?'

'I'm looking for our gods.'

'I'm afraid I can't help you. Excuse me if I don't get up, but the way of women is upon me...'

Israel has great fun telling the story. Those gods? You can sit on them. An unclean woman puts them under her skirts and they disappear. No more humiliating place could be imagined. You shall be the god of Laban and the Labanese.

But whether Rachel was so happy with this way of telling the story is another matter. She was still attached to those gods.

Jacob and Laban each go their own way. They part in peace. They've spent many years together. But it ends happily: 'Jacob, let's make a covenant, you and I. Let this stone bear witness to it. Mizpah shall be the name of this stone. *Watcher between you and me.* In a short time we won't be seeing each other again. I won't know if you neglect my daughters. So let God be witness to this covenant between you and me. I shall never go with hostile intentions past the stone that we set up here. Nor must you.'

The treaty is concluded. They offered a sacrifice and had a meal.

The next day – it was still early – Laban blessed his children and kissed them good-bye.

Thus all at once a dove flutters through this history. The two deceivers, the former serf and the man who enslaved him, finally rise above themselves. God has prevented them from parting in discord.

34

THE WRESTLING AT THE RIVER

GENESIS 32

Jacob returns to Canaan. He has made a non-aggression pact with Laban. He need no longer fear danger from the brother *behind* him. But what about Esau, the brother *before* him? Is he out for a fight? Jacob senses that there can be no homecoming to the land and no future without a reconciliation. As long as they don't dwell together as brothers there will be no peace.

Jacob returns from exile in hope of blessing. Will God, the Lord of this land, let him enter it immediately? Over there lies Bethel, the place where he left the land long ago. At that time angels had escorted him out of it. In his last night in God's land they had unveiled to him the mystery of that land, in a dream in which he saw heaven opening. The dream had comforted him all those years.

And look, in a new vision the same angels are actually standing waiting for him. *An army of God!* Why is that army standing there? Is it a guard of honour for a lost son who is returning? Does heaven still have a bone to pick with him? Is this Esau's army, ready to advance in attack?

All kinds of things haunt Jacob's soul now that he is approaching the frontier of Canaan. Years ago he left the country at this point with no more than a staff in his hand. Now he's returning with wives and children and menservants and maidservants and cattle. He's richly blessed. And yet, what does it benefit a person to win the whole world if he suffers damage to his soul? Jacob has won the whole world. But who is he? Is his name still *Deceiver*?

A man on the frontier.

Jacob decides to send messengers to Esau, with a message in which he calls his brother master and himself servant. It's a peaceful greeting. How the greeting is received over there we aren't told. On their return, the messengers report only that Esau is on his way with four hundred men.

Jacob is afraid. Cunning as ever, he divides his caravan in two. If one group is attacked, the other will still be able to escape. He can't do more. Except to pray: 'O God, God of my father Abraham, God of my father Isaac, grant that I may return to my land and to my kinsfolk; save me from the hand of my brother Esau! You've said that you will do good to me and will make my seed as numerous as the sand of the seashore. May I remind you of this promise?'

Jacob prepares a princely gift for Esau: two hundred she-goats and twenty he-goats, two hundred ewes and twenty rams, thirty milch camels and their colts, forty cows, ten bulls, twenty she-asses and ten he-asses. Jacob gives them into the hands of his servants: 'Go ahead of me and leave space between the different flocks and herds.'

A cunning fox! It's already a great gift, but this makes it seem even more. Now he's turning this one gift into a stream of gifts. No sooner has Esau received the one gift than he will be surprised by the next.

First he finds two hundred bleating she-goats in his way. *'Whose are these? Where are they going to?'*

'They are for you, sir, from Jacob your servant. Look, he is coming behind us.'

Then twenty bleating he-goats bar his way, and again after an interval the two hundred ewes, followed in turn by the rams and the thirty milch camels with their colts. And time and again Esau asks, with increasing amazement, *'Whose are these? Where are they going to?'* And time and again the drivers with the same refrain: *'They are for you, sir, from Jacob your servant. Look, he is coming behind us.'* No sooner has this carnival of animals passed than after them come the forty cows, with the bulls, she-asses and he-asses in their wake. One flock after another, so many waves to break the force of Esau's anger. *'And Jacob is coming behind us.'*

The firstborn comes last.

In this way Jacob's present went before him. *'I want to appease Esau's angry face with the gift that goes before me. Perhaps he will lift up my face.'*

That night in the camp Jacob arose, took his wives and children, and crossed the ford of the river Jabbok. He took everyone over to the other side. But he himself remained behind alone. Just as Moses withdrew in solitude to seek God and come to himself, just as Elijah took refuge on

Mount Horeb, just as Jesus sought the silence of the wilderness to pray and to fast and to fight with the devil, so Jacob laid himself to rest in solitude on the river bank.

Suddenly a figure appears in the dark. Someone grabs Jacob and they begin to wrestle.

Who is this someone? Who is this dark frontier guard who watches over this area? What kind of river demon is this which shuns the light? Is it the creditor of his soul who comes to him this night to make the reckoning? Is it Esau who is pressing hard upon him? Is Jacob at odds with himself, and is this a fight with his own shadow? Or is this mysterious form an angel? Is Jacob wrestling with God? Must he pay a toll before he can be ferried over?

The dark night of the soul. Everyone is on the other side of the ford; he's alone. It's eerie, and he can no longer avoid all the questions. Who am I? Where am I going? I've gained the whole world, but at the cost of whom and what? Is there more than the blessing of the possessions that I've gathered?

'Let me go, for day is dawning,' says the figure in the dark. Is he afraid of being recognized? Who is he?

'I shall not let you go unless you bless me.'

'What is your name?'

'My name is... Jacob.'

The story of his life hinges on this. Jacob is his name. *Deceiver, Leg-puller.* And as soon as he gives his name, it's as if the whole of his existence is examined, including his inner turmoil. The name always expresses someone's being. You are what you're called. You are what you say. 'What is your name? Who are you really?'

The angels on high prick up their ears. What will Jacob say? Who are you?... Hadn't his blind father once asked him that?

'I am Jacob.'

A confession. A brave confession in one word. Jacob will no longer seek his salvation in deception and cheating. He no longer shields himself with what he has, since all that is over on the other side. He no longer wants desperately to deny his shadow side. 'What is my name? My name is Jacob.'

'Your name shall no longer be Jacob but Israel, for you have fought with God and with men, and you have overcome.'

Jacob is not blessed as Jacob. He is blessed as *Israel.* Jacob is a thing of the past. 'I'm wiping out this name,' says the figure by the water. 'I baptize you Israel. *The one who fought with God.* For you've fought courageously, Jacob. Your sins are forgiven. Now you may cross over. You may dwell in the land. Your place is there, Israel.'

Who is this figure? In heaven's name, who is speaking?

'If I may ask, do tell me, what is *your* name?'

And that's something that Israel may not ask. It's asking too much. How can a mortal know the being of the God of heaven and earth and name him by name? It's beyond our understanding and power of expression. 'Why do you ask me my name?'

Israel doesn't hear God's name. But he does receive the blessing. Isn't the name hidden in the blessing?

Israel called this place Peniel. *I have seen God face to face.*

Then the sun rose upon him. 'Shine today especially for Israel,' said the angels to the sun. For they still remembered very clearly, years ago in Bethel, when the sun had set on him. It had long been night for Jacob. Now, with a new name, he may once again enter the land reborn, in radiant sunlight.

He walks with a slight limp, drags his leg a bit. Trouble with his hip.

It's a souvenir of the angel. Before the sun rose he touched Israel's hip. The place of his potency, his power, his future. Israel has difficulty walking. He limps a bit.

Someone who fights with God doesn't emerge from the fight untouched. With every step he takes into the country he will be painfully aware that he can't hand on the blessing in his own strength.

Israel may bask in the sun of God's grace.

But he also has to take care, with that hip.

35

THE RECONCILIATION

GENESIS 33 AND 35

Jacob called the name of that place Peniel. *I have seen God face to face.* Then he goes on. The sun has risen on him.

Over there Esau, his brother, is waiting. Will that also be a meeting *face to face?*

Jacob enters the land, a man who has sorted things out with God and himself, and now wants to sort things out with his brother. Messengers have brought him the news that Esau is coming to meet the caravan with four hundred men. Is this to prevent him going further into the land? Or is Esau coming to welcome him?

Jacob divides his children between the two surrogate mothers and between Leah and Rachel. He puts the surrogate mothers with their children first, Leah and her children next, and Rachel and Joseph after that. He himself goes at the head of the group.

From afar he sees Esau approaching. He prostrates himself before him seven times. Esau rushes up, falls on his neck and kisses him.

They weep.

Esau saw first the two surrogate mothers and their children approaching, then Leah and her children, followed by Rachel and Joseph. 'Who are they, Jacob?'

'They're my wives, Esau, and the children who have been given me by God's grace.'

'And what were those flocks and herds that I kept meeting on the way?'

'That's a gift to find grace in the eyes of my lord.'

'O brother, I've so much, you keep them.'

Jacob calls Esau lord and Esau calls Jacob brother. Brother! It's Esau who first uses this loaded word. From now on Jacob may also use it again. No brother can give his brother a greater sign of reconciliation. In Haran, Laban hastened to meet Jacob, to make him a slave instead of a brother.

Now that Jacob is returning from his slavery, Esau hastens to meet him and makes him a brother instead of a slave.

However, it's very important to Jacob that Esau should accept his present. He's so rich in blessing, and there's nothing he wants more than for his brother to share in this blessing.

'*Esau, I pray you, accept this gift from my hand, accept my blessing.*'

As if Jacob were restoring to Esau the blessing that he had stolen from him.

And Esau accepted Jacob's gift of blessing.

Do the two brothers now continue to live together in a brotherly way?

Sadly, not. That might perhaps be possible in another story, but not in this one. In this story the two of them must continue to play the role assigned to them from the beginning. That's how the biblical narrative wants it to be. This isn't a description of two lives but a picture of two ways: the messianic way of living and the non-messianic way, the way of Israel and the way of the peoples. So in the story the distance between the two must remain. To make things quite clear, the ways must part again, just as Abraham and Lot went separate ways, and Isaac and Ishmael.

'Well,' says Esau, 'let's journey on from here, Jacob.'

Jacob knows where Esau wants to go. To the hill-country of Seir. It's *hairy* there, a rough stretch, real Esau country. Not a land for Jacob. He'll be out of place there.

How can he say that without hurting Esau? Jacob wants to go his own way, but they must part as brothers.

'You go before us to Seir, Esau. The children are frail and I've so many young animals to look after – if I overdrive the animals they'll collapse on the way. Please go ahead and don't be annoyed. Let me go on gently, at the pace of the cattle and the children, until I too reach Seir.'

Not that Jacob really plans to go to Seir. He's courteously telling his brother that his destination lies elsewhere. And Esau understands that.

'Shall I leave servants behind to go with you?'

'That's not necessary. Just let me go.'

The brothers embrace.

'Farewell, Jacob.'

'Farewell, Esau. See you soon.'

'See you soon.'

Esau returns to the shaggy hill-country of Seir, which lies just outside Canaan. Hunting grounds for a hunter.

Jacob has to live a different life, more as a shepherd who tends his flocks, as a father who goes at the pace of the children. Jacob can't live in Seir; he builds himself a house elsewhere, and he makes booths for the sheep and cattle. He calls this place Succoth: *The Place of Booths.*

These are booths like Israel built in the wilderness after the exodus from Egypt, booths like Israel still builds to the present day at Succoth, the Feast of Booths. A true Israelite must be careful about building a house on earth; before you know it, you're going to *settle* somewhere. But our house isn't in this time; here we're on a journey. Beware of houses and castles, not to mention palaces and pyramids. If you aren't careful, you'll be captive in Egypt once again, and we've just been liberated from there; we mustn't go back. A person must keep moving, travelling. Here we're guests, pilgrims on the way.

The ways part: Esau goes to Seir and Jacob to Succoth.

And from Succoth the journey continues further, for later we find Jacob in Shechem and later still in Bethel. Then the caravan approaches Bethlehem.

There, in Bethlehem, Rachel dies, in the field of Ephrathah. She dies in childbirth. 'Give me a child or I shall die,' she once cried to Jacob. Now she dies through a child. Years ago she gave birth to Joseph. *May God give me another son.* Now, after years of painful waiting, she dies at the birth of her second child. 'It's a son!' cries the midwife, hoping to give the exhausted Rachel new courage to live. 'A son!' But Rachel is finished, 'He shall be called Ben-oni,' she says weeping. *Son of my misfortune.*

'No,' says Jacob, 'he shall be called Ben-jamin. *Son of good fortune* shall be his name, *Son of my right hand.*'

Then Rachel died.

Jacob buried his beloved, beside the road, in the field of Ephrathah. Before he went on, he put a stone on her grave, the most beautiful he could find.

Did David still see this stone when he was looking after his sheep in Bethlehem?

And did the shepherds who were watching their flocks in Ephrathah's fields when David's Son was born still realize what it was?

Jacob's journey continues. The foxes have holes and the birds of the air make nests, but those who are called to live a messianic life have nowhere to lay their head.

Father Isaac still lives in Mamre, old and weary of life. How long ago was it that we were told that the old blind man felt his own end approaching? Now that end will come. Mother Rebecca has already died. Now Isaac too will be gathered to his fathers. It's reported to his sons.

Look, there's Esau. Esau from Seir.

And there's Jacob. From I don't know where.

The brothers stand together by Isaac's bed. Side by side. Not one after the other, as they once did. Children of one father.

36

THE MASTER DREAMER

GENESIS 37

These are the generations of Jacob: Joseph...

Joseph? But Joseph wasn't the firstborn! Wasn't Joseph a latecomer? Reuben was Jacob's firstborn son, wasn't he?

That's right, Reuben was born first. But Reuben ruined things for himself by going to bed with his father's concubine - '*Reuben... you shall not have pre-eminence, because you went up to your father's bed.*'*

So why isn't Simeon the firstborn, then, or Levi, since these two come immediately after Reuben?

Another sad story: Simeon and Levi ruled themselves out when they used cowardly deceit and cruel violence to avenge the rape of their sister Dinah.*

Then isn't Judah Jacob's firstborn?

Yes, Judah *is* the firstborn, but the storyteller first directs all his attention to Joseph, Judah's lost brother.

Once again, this isn't simply a story about two men. This story was told after the first exile, and in Joseph the storyteller is thinking of the northern kingdom of Israel. Judah stands for the southern kingdom. The northern kingdom never returned from exile. Joseph is gone. Only Judah remains. From now on the southern kingdom will give its name to all Israel; now all the sons of Jacob, all the children of Israel, will be called *Judaeans, Jews.*

Joseph is gone. Where is Joseph? Judah, where is your lost brother? What kind of future can you and your brothers hope for after the exile, without Joseph?

Joseph will be the chief character in our story, but the story is really about Judah and his brothers. For isn't it the case that there will only be a future for Jacob/Israel when Judah and his brothers rediscover Joseph, and when the twelve of them live together again as brothers?

Joseph, seventeen years old, was shepherding the flock with his brothers. His father loved him more than all his other sons. He made him a coat of many colours.

If only Jacob hadn't done that! And if only Joseph hadn't paraded around in it. He was the son of Jacob's old age, the son of his favourite wife, the son both of them had longed for so deeply. It's as though Jacob has transferred all his affection, his fiery, many-coloured love for Rachel, who died so early, to Joseph, his long-awaited son. Does he perhaps expect Joseph to complete the life Rachel left unfinished? But that's no life for a child. No good will come of it; it will cause a lot of suffering. *When his brothers saw that their father loved him more than them, they began to hate him. They could not speak peaceably to him.*

'Well, if it isn't Joseph.'

The brothers see him coming from a long way off, the heir apparent in his multi-coloured garment. He strides along in his regalia as if he's immortal. He isn't wearing working gear for binding sheaves in the noonday sun, nor anything you'd put on at night to watch over the flocks. 'Look, here he comes.'

'Brothers, I had a dream last night. A wonderful dream. We were binding the sheaves in the field and lo and behold, my sheaf stood upright. And your sheaves stood round it, and bowed down to my sheaf.'

Joseph, did you have to say that? It's bad enough to have such dreams, but do keep them to yourself!

'What? Do you want to become king over us? King? You? Do you want to rule over us? You?' The brothers are furious.

A shepherd boy dreaming a dream fit for a king. That's what makes his brothers hate him. He's the apple of his father's eye, but not of his brothers'. 'Do you want to become king over us? King? You?'

Joseph, despised by his brothers by day, turns the tables at night and dreams a second dream. Keep your mouth shut this time, Joseph! Don't go telling them this one, too!

But Joseph, jaunty and oblivious to all danger, describes his dream, which far outstrips the one he had before. It's a fantasy more grandiose than any mortal could have: 'I had such a fine dream: the sun and the moon and the eleven stars bowed down to me.'

Now the rage of Judah and his brothers truly knows no bounds, and even father Jacob is horrified by such overweening pride. What kind of revolting self-glorification is this? 'What are you thinking of, Joseph? Do you really imagine that I and your mother and your brothers...?'

Thus well before Freud Jacob knew that we live out our hidden desires in our dreams. And father Jacob knew more than that. At least, he suspected more than that. *He kept this saying in mind.* Just as later, when it's said of Mary that she kept in her heart the words she couldn't understand. Father Jacob listened to the presumptuous dream of a conceited adolescent with delusions of grandeur. Yet this fantasy seemed to Jacob to be worth remembering, as though he felt that a deep sense was also hidden somewhere in this nonsense. Could it be that he heard something in it of a messianic kingdom stretching out over the fields of the world, indeed rising above it and even touching heaven?

Judah and his brothers couldn't care less. They've begun to hate Joseph. It would have been better if this long-awaited one had never been born. It would be better for him simply to disappear, this conceited dreamer standing between them and their father's love.

The brothers have left home to graze their flocks near Shechem.

'Joseph.'

'Yes, father?'

'How do you think your brothers are? Do you think they're living in *shalom* out there, in peace? Go and see whether they're at peace.'

But that's asking for trouble, Jacob. You know the friction between Joseph and his brothers. *They could not speak peaceably to him.* So why send Joseph out all alone to see his brothers?

Joseph heads for Shechem, but he doesn't find his brothers. Lost on the plains, he wanders around out there. Not a soul in sight.

And a man found Joseph wandering in the fields.

What a strange report. It doesn't say that Joseph found a man. Joseph couldn't find a living soul anywhere. A man found him.

'What are you looking for?'

'I'm looking for my brothers. Do you perhaps know where they're feeding their flocks?'

'They set off from here and I heard them say, 'Let's go to Dothan.'

Who is this man who found Joseph? Is it an angel? If so, it's rather a strange angel! His words lead Joseph to his brothers, but also into deep trouble and captivity, a captivity which is to prove a blessing to his brothers. A strange angel, if angel it is: pointing the way to humiliation and exaltation.

'Thank you very much,' Joseph said.

'At your service.'

Later on, Joseph must have thought back on the man who found him and asked what he was looking for.

'Look, boys, there's Joseph, our master dreamer.'

And they know: this is their chance, now's the time. 'We'll kill him, throw him in that well over there and say that a wild animal got him.'

Before Joseph can even ask whether peace is with them, it becomes clear to him that there is no peace here. Judah and his brothers tear the coat of many colours off his back. Joseph is undressed.

That undressing, there's always something mysterious about it. Those of us who are no longer little children do it ourselves. If someone else undresses you, it's always either the most holy or the most unholy of deeds. It's an act either of love or of contempt. It's the difference between night and day, between confirmation or denial of a person. Joseph is undressed, stripped of his life. A fraternal conflict seems about to turn into fratricide.

But can't anyone stop this?

Yes, there's one person who can stop it: Reuben, Jacob's firstborn. He may once have gone up to his father's bed, and so he may no longer be regarded as the firstborn, but here he's his brother's keeper: 'Let's not shed any blood. We mustn't kill him. Why don't we just throw Joseph into this well?'

In this way he hopes to keep Joseph out of the hands of his brothers, and to return him to his father safe and sound. Fortunately, his brothers listen; they don't kill Joseph, but content themselves with throwing him into the dry well. A stone's throw from the well they sit down for a meal and eat their bread. Joseph can hear their voices and calls from the depths, but they pay him no heed.

Reuben gets up.

'What are you doing, Reuben, don't you want any more?'

'I'm not hungry. I'm going to gather some wood for the fire.'

And look, a caravan of Ishmaelites comes by, camels laden with gum and balsam and resin, headed for Egypt.

'Reuben's right,' says Judah. 'What good would it do us to kill Joseph? Let's not get his blood on our hands; he's our brother, our own flesh. Why don't we sell him to the Ishmaelites?'

Not a bad idea of Judah's! They can even make some money out of their victim. Besides, a slave in Egypt won't live long. This is murder by instalments, without bloodshed.

'Joseph, grab hold of the rope.'

Is this terrifying dream finally over? Are his brothers going to let him go peacefully back to his father's house?

No, the terrifying dream is just beginning! Joseph is sold for twenty pieces of silver. Not much money for a man. Joseph is going for a rock-bottom price. A clearance sale!

It was late by the time that Reuben returned with the firewood. He walked straight over to the well. 'Joseph.' No reply. 'Are you there, Joseph?' No sign of life. Oh my God, they've murdered him, they've gone and done it. 'The boy isn't there. You murdered him!'

'We sold him.'

'Sold him? And what about me, what am I supposed to do now?'

Reuben isn't worried about what will happen to Joseph; he's only thinking of himself. Does this mean that his plea to the brothers to spare Joseph was prompted by something other than noble sentiment? Was he actually less concerned with a brother in need than with winning back his position as firstborn in his father's eyes?

The brothers have torn Joseph's coat to shreds and drenched them with the blood of a kid. That's how they go back to Hebron. Have they really fooled themselves into believing that they will bask in the warmth of their father's love, now that Joseph is no longer around?

'Father, look what we found, isn't this Joseph's coat, the one that you gave him? Doesn't it look as if...?'

Jacob once deceived his own father with Esau's clothes. Now his own sons are using Joseph's clothes to deceive him.

Jacob sees Joseph's royal robe, torn and drenched in blood, takes it in his arms, presses it to his chest and weeps. 'Joseph, my son, my son. O God, why, why? You spared Abraham's son. There was an animal in the thicket that gave its blood... Isaac was allowed to live. Why must Joseph die, the son of my dearest, Rachel's child?'

Weeping bitterly in sackcloth and ashes, Jacob is inconsolable. 'From this day on I mourn, and in mourning l will remain until the day that I descend to meet my son in the realm of the dead.'

Thank God, it's not as Jacob thinks. The blood is the blood of an animal. Joseph isn't dead. And everyone knows it. Joseph knows it, his brothers know it, and God knows it. The only one who doesn't know it, and whose ignorance is breaking him up, is Jacob. Jacob, who deceived *his* father in his youth: a deception that also had something to do with a kid...

But there's a grain of truth in his assumption that his son has descended to the realm of the dead: chained to one of the merchants' camels, Joseph is going down to Egypt. It's a descent into hell. A royal child has been cast from his throne; a star has fallen, a dream has flown. All that's left of Joseph is a frightened captive.

37

TAMAR

GENESIS 38

'*What do we gain from it if we kill Joseph? Why do we not sell him?*'

That was Judah's proposal. The firstborn. The bearer of the blessing. The brother who has to be a blessing to his brothers.

Joseph is indeed blessed with such a brother! He's been sold as a slave and, chained to a camel, he's had to go down to Egypt. In all probability, end of story.

And Judah: is there anything else to tell about Judah?

Yes, Judah also goes down. To a precarious level. *It happened at that time that Judah went down, away from his brothers.*

So Judah does precisely what the one with the blessing mustn't do: he parts company with his brothers. How? By going his own way and marrying a Canaanite woman. Here he's on a downhill slope, for what if Israel dissolves into the world of the peoples? Then God will lose his people. Then it will be all up with the testing ground of God and humankind. Where in God's name will the brother peoples get the blessing from if Israel, God's firstborn and bearer of the blessing, fails?

Judah isn't available to talk to. He's busy getting three sons by his Canaanite wife: Er, Onan and Shelah.

Er, his firstborn, marries Tamar. *Date Palm.* A beautiful, noble name for a beautiful, noble figure. She appears only once on the scene in the Bible, but she nevertheless plays a significant role, since all by herself she's understood more of Israel's secret than many sons of Israel put together.

Tamar becomes a widow because *her husband was wicked in the eyes of the Lord, and the Lord killed him.*

Clearly Er died prematurely, and the narrator sees this as a punishment from God. Or is he telling us in religious language that by his manner of living, Er brought down disaster upon himself?

Be this as it may, the man is dead and Tamar is left behind childless. That's always a bitter fate, and it certainly was in those days, since children, especially sons, were a support in old age. And in *Israel* the fate of the childless woman is a particularly bitter disaster: one day the messiah will see the light of day, but it will never be as the fruit of her womb. She won't be there, in her descendants, when the messiah is born. It's as if God is saying, 'I don't need you for salvation to go on.'

It's against this background that we must see levirate marriage in Israel: if a man dies and his wife is left behind childless, then it's the task of her brother-in-law to produce descendants by the widow, in the name of his dead brother, *so that his name is not wiped out from Israel.*

Perhaps you need to get used to the notion. I don't know whether you think it an unattractive one. But the idea which underlies it should be clear: it's a measure which is dictated by both social and religious motives, and it's a scandal before God and humankind if someone evades this duty.

That brings us to Onan, Er's brother, who literally withdraws from his obligation towards Tamar, *for as soon as he entered his brother's wife, he let his seed fall on the earth, so as not to give his brother any offspring.*

As laconically as before, the narrator reports that God was so angry about this that he also killed Onan. Would the narrator later have regretted this when from above he impotently watched how here below generations of children were threatened with sin and damnation if they practised the sin of Onan? They were told that onanism was an abomination before the Lord God.

However, Onan's sin was not onanism. The technical term for what he did is *coitus interruptus*. It wasn't 'self-satisfaction'.

Onan is in fact busy satisfying himself in another way. He's only thinking of his own interests. If Tamar has offspring, there will immediately be less to inherit. But to enter her all the same... The pleasure without the burden.

Here's another brother who doesn't want to do his brotherly duty. Onan refuses to do right by his sister-in-law. Through his lack of love Tamar will not become a mother, and a mother in Israel, the bearer of salvation. Will God allow that to happen?

It was evil in the eyes of God, and he also killed Onan.

Someone who grudges another their future isn't worthy of a future himself. The narrator wants us to be clear about that.

Father Judah had three sons, and now he has only one, Shelah. Must he now also lose his third son to this *femme fatale*? Fortunately the boy is still too young. 'Be patient, Tamar. Go home and live with your father, and wait there until Shelah has grown up.'

Of course she can wait till the cows come home. Judah has made himself a sacred promise to keep his youngest son out of Tamar's arms and thus out of the arms of death. Tamar doesn't matter.

Is *Date Palm* going to bow to her fate?

One day Judah goes into the hills to shear his sheep. It's a ritual which recurs every year. The great sheep-shearing feast concludes it; a celebration is called for when the wool has been sold and purses are full. Judah lives it up.

He sees a woman sitting by the wayside, a veiled woman. The message conveyed by her manner and her clothing leaves nothing to the imagination: she's a prostitute. Of course there are such fallen women.

'For a kid,' says Judah, who doesn't have a kid with him.

'What pledge will you give me?'

'Whatever you like.'

'Give me your signet ring, your cord and the staff that is in your hand.'

Judah is already putty in her hands, and begins his striptease. He divests himself of his signet ring, his cord and the staff in his hand. He puts aside all the signs of his dignity.

And then this prostitute. She too takes off her clothes, but with a shyness that you wouldn't expect of a woman of her profession. She keeps her veil on. This didn't disturb Judah. After all, he wasn't concerned to meet her face to face...

When he got home, Judah asked a friend to take the kid to the woman in exchange for the pledge.

Strange, she wasn't sitting in her place. '*Can you perhaps tell me where I can find the temple prostitute who...*'

The temple prostitute! It's nice of Judah's friend to embellish Judah's not very respectable actions with such a respectable word. But the people in the area know nothing about her: 'We don't have that sort of woman here, sir, fortunately, if I may say so.'

Three months later Judah hears that Tamar is pregnant. 'The filthy whore! Not married and pregnant! To the stake with her!'

For of course you can't have such a thing in a respectable family. The whoring Judah is blinded by the fire of his passion, but Tamar the whore will be consumed by fire. Here's a classic example of a victim who gets the blame and of the different criteria by which men and women are measured.

What does Tamar carry in her hands on the way to the stake? A signet ring, a cord and a staff. *'These come from the man who made me pregnant. Perhaps you will be so kind as to take them to my father-in-law. Doesn't it look as if...'*

The same words which Judah and his brothers used when they came to father Jacob with Joseph's bloodstained coat, torn and drenched with blood. *'Doesn't it look as if...'* Tamar stands straight as a palm in front of the men who are to judge her.

'Judah, could it be that...?'

The colour drains from Judah's face. He has to own up, with his double morality. What must he do? What must he say?

'She is more righteous than I am. She is a tsaddiq.*'*

And that in turn is royal of Judah. Tamar is in the right. He himself unknowingly performed with this woman the action that his sons had owed her. It's to his credit that he chivalrously recognizes that she's righteous.

In this story men lose their way and are unfaithful to their calling. In this male world a woman gets her rights by herself. She wants to be a mother, moreover a mother in Israel. Tamar has understood Israel's secret.

Judah is put to shame. He's a man with a past. But thanks to Tamar, he's also a man with a future: a new leaf is being written in the book of generations. And there's something that he doesn't yet know: King David will be born into Judah's family. And David's son, long awaited. It was Tamar who through her courageous deed paved the way for their coming. Through the true passion of this matriarch in Israel, sitting by the side of the road, Judah has been put on the right track. What does the psalmist say? *The righteous shall flourish as a palm tree.**

Judah confesses his guilt. 'She's a righteous woman.'

Judah also has to make amends to his brother Joseph. Will these two ever be reconciled? May we hope that Tamar has made another man of Judah?

And it happened that when Tamar gave birth there were twins in her womb.

Earlier Judah had lost two sons. Now two sons are born to him. One of them stuck his hand out and the midwife quickly tied a scarlet thread round it: 'This one came out first.' But the baby withdrew his hand again, and immediately afterwards his brother came out. The midwife gave him the name Peres. *How powerfully you have broken through!* Only after that did his brother appear. Overtaken at the last moment.

He was called Zerah, *Scarlet.* He was the first to announce himself, the baby with the scarlet thread, but he wasn't the firstborn. This is a new version of an old fact: the last become first and the first last.

Centuries later, this secret of Israel was to become the great theme in the preaching of another son of Judah: 'Many last shall be first and whoever exalts himself shall be humbled.'

And when after his death, one of his friends, Matthew, sat at his desk to relate the story of this messianic man, and he mentioned the names of the men from whom he was born, from Abraham on, the evangelist couldn't omit the name of Tamar from the names of the women from whom he was born.

Hail, Tamar, you are blessed among women and blessed is the fruit of your womb.

38

AT POTIPHAR'S

GENESIS 39

But how are things with Joseph, the master dreamer, who has been banished so harshly from the land of his dreams?

Joseph is for sale. He stands half-naked in the market in Egypt, while prospective purchasers come along to inspect the goods from the Ishmaelite caravan which has just arrived. But he's a different Joseph from the Joseph who set out from Dothan. The vain Joseph of before, who had delusions about being God, has died on the way. Another Joseph has arisen. The caravan drivers already noticed on the way that there was something about this young man. He was more than his sufferings. There was the very way in which he asked, 'Where are you taking me?', as if he believed in some other purpose. As if he thought that he had a special destiny. A remarkable boy. In the evening, in long conversations by the fire, suddenly moved, he could utter with a wonderful reverence the name of a strange God whom they didn't know.

One day there was suddenly shouting at the head of the caravan. The first pyramids were looming up in the distance. Egypt was in sight. Now Joseph would finally see with his own eyes the royal tombs of which he had never heard more than talk, with deep awe.

'Isn't it tremendous?' said the merchants.

Joseph had kept quiet. What was he, the son of Abraham, Isaac and Jacob, to do here in Egypt? 'O God of my fathers, stand by me.'

Joseph is standing in the market. He's for sale.

What do you look at when you're buying a slave? At his legs, his arms and his shoulders if you're looking for a labourer. Potiphar, the captain of Pharaoh's palace guard, is looking for a household slave. He looks at the hands, the eyes and the neck.

'Where did you get this one from?'

'From Canaan, sir. He's no ordinary slave, I swear.'

'How much? All right. I'll buy him.'

No, he's no ordinary slave, this Hebrew. He's one with a blessing.

It began with Adam. *God blessed him. God called him a human being.* 'I shall be with you so that you can be a human being, so that you can develop, so that you can manage. You shall be human. Not inferior, nor someone who gets above himself. A human being.'

God doesn't want to belittle human beings; he wants to make them great. *'Abraham, I shall make your name great and you shall be a blessing and with you all peoples will be blessed.'*

What had begun with Adam and Abraham went on with Isaac: *he became great, steadily greater, until he had become very great.*

With Jacob it went yet further: where Jacob lived, the Lord gave his blessing.

Now it's up to Joseph to be a blessing as the one with the blessing. Indeed he is no ordinary slave. As soon as he was deep down there in the well, he began to grow. The grain of wheat which fell into the earth and died began to bear fruit. Joseph copes. Wherever he puts his feet, peace blossoms. Joseph too is becoming great, steadily greater, until he becomes very great.

'Joseph, come here. Mend the oil lamp, will you?'

The thing can't be repaired. Potiphar has known that all along, but he's curious to see how his new slave will perform.

'It's burning again, sir.'

'What did you say?'

'This lamp's burning again.'

Amazing, no matter what business this young man takes on, he copes. A pair of golden hands. And a good mind. In due course Potiphar no longer undertakes anything without first asking Joseph what he thinks of it. And he ends up entrusting all his affairs to Joseph: *all that he had he gave into Joseph's hand.* At home and in the country, everything goes smoothly; there's singing and laughter, and everyone enjoys their work. Formerly peace was hard to find in the house, but now that's over. Things are going well with Joseph: he's a man with a blessing: great, steadily greater, until he becomes very great. *Everything in his hand.*

Can Joseph become even greater?

Yes, he can.

'Joseph, come and lie with me.'

Mrs Potiphar. The young foreigner in the house, his eyes, his hands, his neck... Mrs Potiphar is in love with him. And lonely. The captain of the palace guard is often away on journeys.

'Come and lie with me, Joseph.'

And what does Joseph say?

Joseph says: *'My master has given everything in the house into my hands. In this house he himself is not greater than I am. He has withheld nothing from me except for you, his wife.'*

Joseph has become great. Very great. But how great can a person become and still remain human? What are the limits of greatness?

'Not greater than Potiphar,' says Joseph. He can even appropriate the last thing that has been withheld from him. Everything is possible. But it cannot be. For this is the limit to the growth of the one with the blessing. One more step and Joseph would have gone too far.

Here we have more than 'the chaste Joseph'. This is no pique at a failed advance; this is a temptation story which goes far beyond the relationships of the boudoir. Here, more than the virtue of chastity, the courage of the messianic man is being celebrated. For that's the anxious question: will the one with the blessing, far from home, remain faithful to his calling? Will Israel in a foreign land, in exile, remain God's blessed among the peoples, or will it get the worst of it in the arms of paganism?

The question here is one of preserving creation. There are limits for human beings. There are limits to growth. When human beings don't respect these limits, they meet their downfall.

'Come and lie with me, Joseph.'

But Joseph did not listen to her. She calls and she calls, and of course Joseph hears her, but he doesn't give in. This isn't repression on Joseph's part. It's a choice.

Potiphar's wife, filled with desire and unaccustomed to a disobedient slave, seizes him by his garment, pulls him to her and wants to embrace him, but Joseph tears himself loose and flees, leaving his garment behind in her hand. How will she get out of this?

'Help, help! I'm being raped.'

Mrs Potiphar begins to scream, for those who haven't screamed aren't thought to have been raped.* 'Help,' she cries with the garment in her hand, 'Help!'

Slaves and slave girls come running.

'That man, that Hebrew man, he wanted to lie with me... and I... and I screamed as hard as I could. Then he ran away and left his garment here, next to me.' *Next to me*, says Mrs Potiphar sharp-wittedly. She doesn't make a mistake; she doesn't say *in my hand*!

'Oh madam, how terrible!'

Madam upset, the staff upset, everyone upset. That's how things are at court. But don't think that her servants believe a word of it; all along they suspected that she had her eye on Joseph. But they play along with her. That's how everyone keeps fooling everyone else. 'How terrible, madam. And that Hebrew man!'

When Mrs Potiphar wanted to seduce Joseph, she knew his name perfectly well. But now that her plan has failed, she calls him *that Hebrew man*. Foreigners can't keep their hands to themselves. Everyone knows that.

Potiphar comes home and smells trouble.

'What's up?' he says to the slave girl who is washing his feet.

'Your wife says that Joseph...' The girl tells her story in a tone which makes him suspect that she doesn't believe her mistress, and Potiphar is afraid that she has the right end of the stick.

'Potiphar, that slave whom you brought into the house to make a mock of me, that Hebrew slave, you won't believe it but...' and his wife accuses Joseph of the act that she herself desired.

It's not Joseph who is making a mock of her; she's doing that herself.

This is quite a different story from the one we've just heard, about Judah and Tamar. Judah fell far from home, Joseph remains upright far from home. Tamar got Judah's signet ring, cord and staff legitimately; Potiphar's wife has stolen Joseph's garment. Tamar's name is mentioned with honour; the narrator prefers to withhold the name of Potiphar's wife.

'Potiphar, that Hebrew slave...'

And does Potiphar opt for his wife or for his slave?

Potiphar's a politician. Potiphar doesn't take sides. He doesn't want to abandon his wife, but he doesn't want to abandon his favourite slave either. 'It's a scandal,' he says to his wife, but he contents himself with putting the Hebrew man in prison; he doesn't have Joseph killed, and everyone in the house knows why.

Joseph is put in prison.

Once he lost his royal robe and had to go down to Egypt.

Now he's lost even his slave's garment and has to descend still deeper. Joseph disappears from sight again into an underground prison.

But fortunately he copes, again. In the prison of the prison which is Egypt, this messianic man again makes something of heaven visible. He gains the trust of the guards and of his fellow prisoners. The peace which has been lost in Potiphar's house blossoms in gaol. Under the ground, the one with the blessing again begins to flourish and grow. *And the keeper of the prison gave all the prisoners into his hand; and whatever was to be done there, he left it in Joseph's hands.*

Joseph becomes great.

Steadily greater.

Until finally the walls of the prison can no longer hold back his greatness.

39

THE CUPBEARER AND THE BAKER

GENESIS 40

'Good morning, did you sleep well?'

A new day has has dawned, although this is hardly noticeable in the Pharaoh's underground prison. Nevertheless, it's a new day, and if you lose heart you lose everything.

'Did you sleep well?'

Joseph is taking round the food, although you can hardly call it food: some water and some bread. Nevertheless, it's food, and if you lose heart you lose everything.

However, the Pharaoh's cupbearer and his baker, fellow-prisoners with Joseph, seem to have lost heart completely, and Joseph tries to cheer them up a bit. 'You in particular should find this refined food and drink worth sampling.'

The cupbearer and the baker aren't in the mood for the gallows humour of this slave from the land of the Hebrews. 'Slept well?' No, they haven't slept well. They've dreamed and they're a prey to confusion. 'If only we had someone who could interpret our dreams.'

'Interpret dreams?' says Joseph, the master dreamer. 'Isn't interpreting dreams God's business? Tell me your dreams.'

Remarkable! If interpreting dreams is God's business, then it isn't Joseph's business, is it? After all, Joseph isn't God. He had certainly dreamed that at home, in his arrogance, but surely he'd been cured of it?

Yes, he'd been cured of it. We won't see Joseph playing God again. But we shall see him playing along with God. A person mustn't think too highly of himself, but not too lowly either. You aren't God, but that doesn't mean that you're nothing.

Joseph's brothers had thrown him into a well and sold him for a handful of silver pieces. Ishmaelites had sold him on for two handfuls of silver pieces, and after he had risen high, an Egyptian woman had brought him low. But he has remained faithful to his calling, this man with the blessing. Aggrieved, Joseph could have succumbed to self-pity, but he took up his cross and coped. The little Hebrew exile never forgot the dream which God gave his people to dream, and so he wasn't lost for the messiahship. Either you're the one with God's blessing or you aren't. The one who is, who wants to be, knows that he's called to be a blessing on earth and if need be under the earth. In prison, Joseph won the trust of both the guards and his fellow prisoners. He was a grain of wheat which germinated again underground, a blessing for all.

'Good morning, did you sleep well?'

No, the cupbearer and the baker didn't sleep well. At least they didn't wake up well. Each dreamed a dream and their hearts were disturbed. What could this dream mean? They looked bewildered. What was hanging over their head? 'Who will interpret our dreams?'

'Tell me your dreams.'

But why are the cupbearer and the baker in prison anyway? What crime have they committed?

We don't know. A rabbi conjectured that there had been a speck of dirt in the Pharaoh's wine and a stone in his bread. You don't need to tell a rabbi anything about the arbitrariness of angry rulers. Or did he take his suggestion from the dreams of the cupbearer and the baker?

'I dreamed,' said the chief cupbearer, 'and look, there was a vine in front of me and on the vine were three branches. Thereupon the branches began to shoot; they blossomed and bore bunches of ripe grapes. The Pharaoh's cup was in my hand and I took the grapes, pressed them and put the cup into Pharaoh's hand.'

'This is the meaning of your dream,' said Joseph. 'The three branches are three days...'

Joseph's interpretation is obvious: in three days the Pharaoh will celebrate his birthday. According to ancient custom some prisoners will then receive a free pardon and others will go to the scaffold. No wonder that the cupbearer and the baker are having such disturbed sleep!

'The three branches are three days. After three days the Pharaoh will raise up your head and restore you to your post. You will put the cup into the Pharaoh's hand as you were accustomed to do when you were still the king's cupbearer.'

The baker takes heart. 'And now me! I dreamed, and look, on my head there were three baskets of bread. In the top basket were all kinds of food for the Pharaoh, of the sort that a baker prepares. But birds devoured it, from the basket on top of my head.'

'This is the meaning of your dream. The three baskets are three days. After three days the Pharaoh will raise up your head, above you. He will hang you on a stake and the birds will eat your flesh.'

Why may the cupbearer remain alive and why must the baker die? No one knows. The rabbi with his fantasy about the dirt in Pharaoh's wine sees in the cupbearer's dream how carefully the man tries to make good his mistake: he takes no risk; he personally supervises the growth of the grapes, presses them with his own hands and himself offers the cup to the Pharaoh. By contrast, the baker brings the Pharaoh bread which hasn't been baked under his supervision. Surely that means that he hasn't learnt a lesson from what has happened?

'In three days,' said Joseph to the cupbearer, 'the Pharaoh will raise up your head and you will again be the king's cupbearer.'

'In three days,' said Joseph to the baker, 'the Pharaoh will raise up your head and you will hang.'

Both men are to be raised up. *On the third day*. It's a well-known motif in the Bible. The great decisions are always taken on the third day, and they're usually on matters of life and death.

And it happened on the third day that the Pharaoh arranged a feast for his birthday. He raised up the head of the cupbearer and he raised up the head of the baker. The cupbearer gave drink to the Pharaoh. The baker gave food to the birds. Long live the Pharaoh! Happy birthday to you!

The chief cupbearer poured wine as before. *But he did not remember Joseph. He forgot him.*

Painful. Joseph had just asked the cupbearer so urgently not to forget him when he was a free man again. *'Remember me, when it is well with you, and do me the kindness, I pray you, to make mention of me to Pharaoh, and so get me out of this house. For I was indeed stolen out of the land of the Hebrews; and here also I have done nothing that they should put me into the dungeon. Remember me!'*

Unkempt men in the prison, fighting against degeneration, the wretched of the earth, comrades in pain. Far in the distance they hear the noises of the street, life, free life. How long still? Are they forgotten? Is there anyone up there who is thinking about them?

Then the door opens, a strip of light comes in, and someone is let out. What a hubbub that creates among those who have to remain! 'Take this letter for me...' 'Give greetings to...' 'Go for me to...', and Joseph says, 'Remember me, don't forget me, keep me in mind.'

But the cupbearer forgot him.

Why? Is he a heartless man? Does he want to forget that grim time in prison as quickly as possible? Or doesn't he want to remind the Pharaoh of his imprisonment, afraid that he will be in disgrace a second time? For it only needs something to happen at such a court and you're out of favour and then you'll hang. So keep your mouth shut and remain polite: 'Yes, your majesty; no, your majesty. Shall I pour you another cup, your majesty?'

But lose heart, lose everything. And fortunately we shall hear more of how Joseph, the Hebrew man with a past, who was sold for a handful of silver pieces, who died and was buried, descended into prison, rose again from the dead, and went up to the palace and sits at the right hand of the king.

The story matches the story of another Hebrew man, centuries later. Sold for a handful of silver pieces, he underwent his punishment an innocent man. 'Remember me,' said a man hanging next to him, 'remember me when you come into your kingdom. Don't forget me, keep me in mind when you are raised up.'

'Today you shall be with me in paradise,' said the Hebrew man, and yielded up the spirit.

The story goes that he was raised on the third day.

40

THE PHARAOH HAS A DREAM

GENESIS 41

'Good morning, Pharaoh, did you sleep well?'

The cupbearer and the baker bring the king of Egypt his royal breakfast in bed. The new baker, of course; the old one was hanged two years ago.

'Did you sleep well, Pharaoh?'

'No I didn't. I had a dream. A bad dream. Two dreams, in fact. I'm worried. Call all the sages and wise men of the land together for them to interpret my dreams.'

A story full of dreams.

The master dreamer Joseph began it. 'I'm the greatest,' he dreamed. His brothers thought differently. They would knock him into shape.

The cupbearer and the baker also dreamed. When the cupbearer comes to think of it... But he wants to forget that dark page in his history as quickly as possible, so he forgot Joseph too. That's two years ago now, and all that time Joseph is stuck in prison. *Two years of days*, says the narrator. Two years, day after day after day.

Now the king has also had a dream. In the third year. Now the story will take a decisive turn. It has to.

The Pharaoh has had two dreams and his heart is disturbed, 'Call together all the wise men and soothsayers of the land.'

A story full of dreams. God is at work. What happens on the earth and what happens under the earth doesn't leave heaven unmoved. God is still there, though hidden. The Pharaoh dreams and gropes in the dark. Soon Joseph's star will rise again and shine.

'I dreamed that I was standing by the river and look, seven cows came up out of the river, sleek and fat, and they fed in the reeds. And look, seven other cows came up out of the river, gaunt and thin, and they went to stand next to

those other cows on the river bank. And the gaunt and thin cows swallowed up the sleek and fat cows. Then I woke up.

After I had gone to sleep again I dreamed a second time. And look, seven ears of corn sprouted on one stem, fat and good. But look, another seven ears sprouted, thin and blighted by the east wind. And the seven thin and blighted ears swallowed up the seven fat and full ears. Then I woke up. Tell me what my dreams mean.'

The king looks at his servants in desperation. Isn't there anyone who can see some light in these dark dreams?

Alas, the wise and learned men of Egypt can't give an answer: the sages and priests, soothsayers, clairvoyants, augurs, astrologers, sorcerers and magicians are at a loss. Why? Are these dreams really so difficult to interpret? Or is the interpretation so dangerous that no one dares to stick his neck out? Before you know it you're getting the chop. Or you land up in prison and are forgotten.

The Pharaoh is at the end of his tether. The king of Egypt, son of the Sun God, dreams dreams which turn his whole world order upside down and puts the whole court in turmoil. The scholars of the kingdom, though surrounded with an aura of sanctity, cannot say the word of deliverance. Isn't there anyone..? In God's name, couldn't one person get up and...?

'Joseph, get up!'

'What did you say?'

'Get up, Joseph, you must appear before the Pharaoh. The king had disturbing dreams last night and no one can interpret them. Then the cupbearer thought...'

The cupbearer! For *two years of days* he had forgotten him, but now at last he's broken his silence. 'Your majesty, may I say a word to you?' For the cupbearer saw the anxiety of his king and he remembered his own imprisonment and the words of liberation spoken by that Hebrew with his Hebrew God. Wasn't that what the king needed, now that no one in Egypt could say the word of deliverance? 'O king, may I be allowed... I know of a man in the prison...'

Joseph is brought up. In a wing of the palace a slave girl runs the bath, and the king's barber hastens to an adjacent room, while the king's tailor also arrives with a choice of colourful garments. This will be another complete change for Joseph. All his experience has been of clothes being taken off his back, by his own brothers or by his master's wife. Is he dreaming?

Soon Joseph is standing before the throne, pale, with his mother Rachel's big eyes, still barely used to the daylight. The most powerful man in the world encounters the least of men, a slave, moreover a slave from abroad and a prisoner. The king must be at the end of his tether to resort to this puny being.

'My cupbearer has told me about you. Is it true that you only need to hear a dream and you already know the interpretation?'

'Not I, your majesty – my God will speak and give you peace.'

Joseph no longer has any desire to be a star. He will let God's light shine. He's a string on God's harp.*

'Tell me what my dreams mean.'

'Your two dreams are one, your majesty. Seven fat cows, seven full ears: those are seven years of plenty. Seven thin cows, seven empty ears, blighted by the east wind: they will be seven years of hunger. After seven years of plenty you are to expect seven years of famine, and the famine will be so severe that you forget all the plenty of the previous years. God has shown you what he will do. You've dreamed it twice. So God's word is sure. He's hastening to fulfil it.'

The Pharaoh is terrified. This Hebrew is putting into words what he already knows deep down inside, but didn't want to know. It's as if Joseph is opening a curtain, and what was hidden in the dark is suddenly coming to light. The Pharaoh is terrified.

'All is not yet lost, your majesty. I would advise you to gather and store food in the seven years of plenty for the seven lean years which follow. To do that you need to build granaries.'

The most powerful man in the world meets the least of men. He listens and he revives. He is terrified by Joseph's words, but this man before his throne not only makes him aware of his fear, but also makes it bearable: 'Build granaries.' His dreams don't mean an unavoidable catastrophe; perhaps disaster can be avoided and the spell can be broken. 'May Pharaoh find a wise and intelligent man...' and then Joseph sets out so clearly and eloquently what this wise and intelligent man must do to save the land from disaster that the king immediately knows that he doesn't need to look far for this wise and intelligent man. This man is already standing in front of him: Joseph!

The king listens to Joseph's words and revives: 'Could we find someone like this, a man in whom is the spirit of God? Henceforth you shall be my regent. You shall be called Zaphenath-paneach. *He speaks and one revives.'*

And again Joseph becomes great, again he becomes steadily greater, again he becomes very great. Again everything is given into his hands except the throne. *'Only by the throne shall I be greater than you.'* There's always a limit that must be respected. There's always someone above you. You must never think too highly of yourself. You must be a string, on God's harp.

'Look, I give you the land of Egypt,' said the king, and he took his signet ring off his hand and gave it to Joseph, along with a gold chain, linen garments and a chariot. He also gave him as wife Asenath, daughter of Potiphera, priest of On. From the sound of her name we can hear that in this way that sorry business in the past has been reconciled. And the fact that the priest of On is Egypt's highest priest means no more and no less than the recognition of Joseph's God, the Eternal One of Israel, who interprets dreams. *He speaks and one revives.*

Joseph goes through Egypt and divides the land into five provinces. In this way he makes it so to speak a promised land, for five is the number of Israel: four plus One. Four for the points of the compass; one for God. Israel is entrusted with binding the wide world to the One. Isn't that written in the five books of the holy Torah?

Joseph goes through the land, gathers up the surplus, builds granaries, and piles up the grain like the sand on the seashore. 'Think of later. Think of our children who will live after us and who won't live if we've heedlessly consumed everything.'

Joseph himself also has children: two sons are born to him. He gives them Hebrew names. His firstborn is called Manasseh, *For God made me forget all my troubles and the house of my father.* He called his second son Ephraim, *For God has made me fruitful in the land of my misery.*

Yes, Joseph has become so fruitful in the land of his misery, so great, greater, greatest that his fame extends far beyond the frontiers of the land. When the lean years begin, you see the peoples coming. 'We've heard that you have bread.'

'You must go to the Hebrew man,' says the Pharaoh. 'He has bread.'

'I've heard that there is bread in Egypt,' says a father to his sons, far away in a hungry Canaan.

Then his sons set out.

41

BALSAM, GUM AND RESIN

GENESIS 42

He is regent of Egypt and his name is Zaphenath-paneach. Formerly he used to be called Joseph, but that was a long time ago, and he's more concerned with the future: in seven years of prosperity enough food must be gathered and stored in granaries for the seven lean years which are to follow. Formerly? You'd better forget formerly, formerly is a thing of the past. Joseph is caught up in his work, his wife, his sons. He calls the oldest Manasseh, *For God made me forget all my troubles and the house of my father.*

Or does this name just indicate that Joseph hasn't completely forgotten his former difficulties and his father's house? He's a free man now, he loves and is loved, and he has respect and a reputation. But he seems to fix the sorrow of his life in the name of his firstborn. It sounds like a prayer, 'O God, make me forget.'

He calls his second son Ephraim. *For God has made me fruitful in the land of my misery.* That too sounds ambiguous. Joseph may indeed be fruitful, but he is and remains an exile; there's a pain which doesn't go away. How are things with father Jacob and with Benjamin, who was also born from Rachel's womb, and with the others? He once dreamed that they prostrated themselves before him on the ground. In anger they tore his clothes from his body and wanted to kill him. 'Don't do it,' cried Reuben, the oldest, and they threw him into a well and went a little way off to sit and eat bread. Don't think that they tossed him a chunk. Perhaps they would have murdered him had not a caravan happened to come by, laden with balsam, gum and resin. So they received some silver pieces... Now and then he still dreamed of it, and then he screamed in the middle of the night and woke up in a state. Then his wife would put her hand on his hot brow. 'What is it, Zaphenath?'

'It's nothing, darling. It's nothing.'

No, he hadn't forgotten them. And when the lean years arrived and even people from Canaan came to Egypt for food, driven by hunger, Joseph already half expected that one day his brothers would also be standing at the gate. Better not think about it. But he just had to. He may be regent of Egypt, bear an Egyptian name and speak Egyptian, have an Egyptian wife and wear Egyptian clothes, but inside there's still a homeless Hebrew shepherd boy called Joseph who is homesick.

Then, one fine day, he sees his brothers appear. They stand at the back of the line, but he immediately recognizes them in the garments of his people, which are so familiar to him. They come closer, gradually closer. What must he say? What shall he do? There are ten of them. Has he counted right? Yes, ten. So who isn't there? Isn't Benjamin there? Surely nothing's happened to Benjamin?

The brothers fall to the earth and prostrate themselves. A dream from a time long past becomes reality, but Joseph doesn't feel a sense of triumph and the brothers know nothing of it.

Joseph summons an interpreter. 'Where have you come from?'

'From Canaan, sir, to buy food.'

'You're spies, enemy agents, come to spy out the weak places in this land.'

'No, sir, no! We're here to buy food, honest people, not spies. We're brothers, sons of one man from Canaan, twelve in number – the youngest has remained at home with father and one is no more.'

Fortunately what they say isn't true: the one who is no more is sitting before them on his throne. And is it true that they're brothers?

'You're spies in my eyes until you've proved that you're speaking the truth. Listen to what I command you: I want nine men to remain here and the tenth to go back to your land and bring me the youngest. What is his name?'

'Benjamin, sir.'

'Let him bring me Benjamin. If not, I shall regard you as spies.'

Barely has the interpreter translated these words than the king's servants take the men from Canaan away prisoner and throw them into Egypt's underground prison. Joseph's brothers in the well. They're innocent, but of course these things happen sometimes.

On the third day Joseph has them brought before him again. His voice sounds as hard as before, but his request is milder. It's now enough for him that one hostage should remain; the other nine may go with grain to their father's house, provided that they promise to return with Benjamin.

Why Joseph has had second thoughts the story doesn't tell, but what both orders have in common is that Joseph always separates one brother from the rest. The brothers can discover how that feels. At least if they have any brotherly feelings!

Fear strikes their hearts. What's happening here? Is this a punishment for sin? 'Is this happening to us because we are guilty of the death of Joseph our brother? We saw the fear in his soul when he begged us for mercy, but we didn't listen to him. Must we now atone for his blood?'

The translator leaves this out, but Joseph understands his brothers word for word and hastily turns away, because he has to weep. Indeed, that is what happened. Deaf to his cry for mercy, they had sat a little way off and eaten, not sharing their bread with him. Blind to the fear in his soul, they had sold him. Isn't it time for them to talk about guilt?

Before the eyes of his brothers, Simeon is bound and taken away. Then there were only nine. Dejected, they began the return journey to Canaan, to father Jacob. Laden with grain and with provisions for the journey, certainly, but also with an unquiet heart. This drama isn't yet at an end.

That evening one of them opens his pack to give some fodder to his ass. He's horrified: on the top he finds the silver pieces which he had given to the regent of Egypt in exchange for the grain. What's going on here? When they get home, to their amazement the other brothers also find that their silver has been returned.

Father Jacob is beside himself when he hears that he has to let little Benjamin go down to Egypt. He won't think of it: 'Joseph is dead, Simeon a hostage; I don't want to lose Benjamin as well, the only child of Rachel that is left to me. It would be the death of me.'

But what does Jacob want? Is hunger then to be the death of him? For the grain runs out, and what then? Joseph again asks his sons to go down to Egypt to buy grain.

'Not without Benjamin, father. The journey would be in vain; the man in Egypt won't give us his grain unless the youngest is in our midst.'

'Why did you tell that Egyptian about Benjamin?'

'That man wanted to know everything! He asked, 'Is your father still alive? And do you have another brother?' How could we suspect that he would say, 'Bring the young man here?''

Judah, Jacob's firstborn, speaks: 'Father, I pray you, let the boy go with us. Otherwise we shall perish of hunger, we and you and our children. I myself will stand surety for Benjamin. If I do not bring him safely back home, I shall be guilty before you for all time. Now let us go, father. Had we not delayed we could already have been there and back twice.'

Judah ties his life to that of little Benjamin. Now as firstborn he is as it were his brother's keeper. Do you hear that, Joseph, far in the distance, how Judah wants to bear responsibility and take up the cause of the least?

Jacob gives in. 'Go then. Take precious gifts with you, honey, almonds, balsam, gum and resin. And twice as much silver, and also the silver that you found in your sacks. And take Benjamin with you. May the almighty God have mercy on you before the face of the Egyptian man, so that he lets Simeon go along with Benjamin. As for me, if I must become childless, I shall become childless...'

Again the caravan of brothers sets off. With Rachel's son in their midst, with twice as much silver, with balsam, gum and resin. It smacks somewhat of the scene of long ago. A picture of former times, which has not yet come to rest.

42

BREAD AND CUP

GENESIS 43 AND 44

Joseph already saw his brothers approaching from afar, ten in number. 'Bring those men from Canaan to my house,' he said, 'I want to have a meal with them.'

'The king is expecting you at his table,' the king's servant tells them. 'May I go before you to the palace?'

To the palace? What will happen there? What does this Egyptian ruler want? Will he make them slaves? Just before the palace gate they accost the king's servant: 'With your permission, sir, this is the second time we've come here – when we got home we found in our bags the silver that we brought you earlier in exchange for our grain. There must have been a mistake somewhere. Look, we've brought it back with us.'

'Don't be afraid. It must have been your God, the God of your fathers, who gave you this treasure in your bags – after all, didn't I receive your silver?'

The brothers are brought into the dining hall, where they are reunited with Simeon. He looks a bit pale, this hostage, but he's clearly relieved to see his brothers back safe and sound.

After a wait, Zaphenath-paneach appears. The brothers can't prostrate themselves quickly and deeply enough. 'Accept our gifts, your majesty.'

'How is it with you father, is he still alive?'

'It is well with our father, he is still alive.'

'And is that the Benjamin of the family?'

'And is that the Benjamin of the family?', repeats the translator in Hebrew.

Joseph can barely wait for the answer. He wants to embrace him, his dearest brother, born of the same womb. Tears spring into his eyes and he has to turn away. He leaves the hall, escapes into a side room and weeps.

Then he washes his face, pulls himself together and again enters the dining hall. 'Please be seated. My servants will show you to your places.'

The oldest of the brothers has to sit at the head of the table, the next oldest beside him, and so on. Does the king then know who is who? What kind of an eerie palace is this? What kind of a play is being performed here? And whereas before they were just onlookers, now they themselves are taking part in it.

'Serve the bread.'

Servants bring in the bread. Some for Joseph's table, some for the table of the Hebrews and some for the table of the Egyptians, all separate. *For Egyptians cannot eat bread with Hebrews.* Egyptians clearly don't like that.

And the Hebrew brothers, can they eat bread together while one of them is sitting separately?

Of course not, but these things happen... The brothers eat their bread, Joseph is close by but he doesn't sit with them. Who is the director of this bizarre performance?

The director sits apart. Alone. He's recalling a scene of long past. A picture of former times which has not yet been laid to rest.

This is about the question of bread and the question of guilt. The two questions seem to belong together. Give us today our daily bread and forgive us our trespasses. Does the question of guilt crop up where daily bread isn't eaten together? Eating together is a sign of fellowship and brotherhood. It's still too early for that. The guilt isn't yet confessed and therefore isn't yet forgiven.

They all eat their bread separately, the Egyptians, Joseph, his brothers. Benjamin gets five times as much as the rest. Why? 'You're still a growing lad,' they joke. The wine flows abundantly and they no longer understand why recently they were still so afraid. Nonsense! The suffering is past, the hunger, the anxiety, the uncertainty, happily it is all past. All's well that ends well. 'Yes, pour me another, your majesty, *lehayim.*'

'May you have a long life,' says the translator.

There's drinking, and at the request of Zaphenath-paneach a Hebrew song is sung. The king seems to like it. Then he nods to his butler: 'Fill their bags with grain, as much as they can carry. Put everyone's silver back into them. And put my cup, my silver drinking cup, in the top of the youngest one's bag.'

It gets light. The day dawns. 'Now you must go.'

'Thank you, your majesty .'

'Farewell, and a good journey.'

Barely have the brothers left the city than at the king's request his servant chases after them. 'Why do you recompense good with evil? Why have you stolen our king's cup, the silver drinking cup with which he does soothsaying?'

'Truly, sir, we are innocent. We brought back to the king the silver that we found in our bags when we got home. Why should we steal his cup now? Search our bags, by all means. And if you find your king's cup in the pack of one of us here, let him die, and we shall all be the king's slaves.'

'No, only the one with whom the cup is found shall be the king's slave. The rest can return home.'

Why does this servant say that? Why separate one of them from the rest?

The bags are unloaded and searched thoroughly, beginning with the oldest brother's bag. Not a cup to be found. Finally Benjamin's pack is opened. Then their world collapses: Joseph's silver cup shines brightly in the sunlight. O God!

'Come with me to the palace,' the butler commands Benjamin.

That's how this story began, years ago, with a brother who was his father's favourite and who was made to go all alone as a slave to Egypt. Is history repeating itself? Or have the brothers meanwhile learned what true brotherhood is?

They don't leave Benjamin in the lurch. Defeated and confused, they go back with him to the palace, their garments rent. They mourn for Benjamin, who will be a slave in Egypt. They mourn for their old father, who is spared nothing in this life. They mourn for themselves, for they will miss their brother. Will they ever see their father's house again? That's how Joseph must have felt when he was carried off, long ago, into slavery.

A prey to despair, the brothers enter the palace for the third time. For the third time they prostrate themselves before the king's face.

'What deed is this that you have done? Didn't you know that a man like me can prophesy? And then you steal my cup?'

From olden times a cup has symbolized the life of its owner. The cup is the person. Therefore a silver cup at one's birth, with one's name engraved on it, is a profound present. This cup is a prayer: 'May your life be as unique and precious and lasting as this cup. May your life have a rich content. May your cup overflow.'

On the night before Jesus died, when he passed the cup round among his friends, he did it for them all to drink out of. He did it so that they should share in the content of his life.

'Why did you steal my cup?'
    'We didn't steal that cup, sir.'
    No, they didn't steal that cup.
    But they stole a life.
    The cup is the cup of the man whose life they stole.

43

THE BOOKS ARE OPENED

GENESIS 44 AND 45

'Why did you steal my cup?'

Jacob is engaged in a cat and mouse game with his brothers. Why? He's playing with them. Because once upon a time they played with him like that? Let's be honest, you and I, we're sitting chuckling: chickens are coming home to roost because a brother is playing a dirty trick. But is that such a good theme for the Book of God and humankind...?

'Why did you steal my cup?'

Is this the same man who the night before broke bread with them so hospitably and so generously poured out his good wine? His eyes are hard now, and there's a bitter line to his mouth. What kind of unpredictable person is this? He has two faces. One is cold and inexorable: 'You're spies! Thieves, who recompensed good with evil!' The other is friendly and concerned: 'Did you have a good journey? How's your father? Sit down at the table, let's have a meal.'

'Why did you steal my cup? Didn't you know that I can prophesy?'

They heard about that on the way, in the caravanserais, about Egyptian soothsayers who can predict the future by gazing into the liquid in a cup. It made them think of their dead brother Joseph, who also had this gift of prophesying. At least, that's what he claimed. However, he didn't see the future in a cup but in his dreams. Then he saw, for example, that they would all bow down before him... But this Egyptian prince with his piercing eyes will certainly have gifts of prophecy. He's a clairvoyant, who sees more than they do. It's as though he's looking straight through them.

'Why have you done this?'

Now something has to happen. Now one of them must say something. Benjamin is in danger. And what do you do if you're your brother's keeper? What do you do if your brother is in need?

Judah steps forward. The firstborn. 'Sir, what must we say to you, what shall we speak, how shall we justify ourselves? *God has found out the guilt of your servants.*'

Judah before the throne.

This is how it will be at the end of time, if we may believe an age-old fantasy: one day we shall stand before the throne of the Eternal One. Then the books will be opened.

It's as if the scene were already being depicted here and now: the dénouement, after so many years: the disclosure before the king's throne of all that has been said and kept quiet about, all that has been done and hasn't been done. All that has been evaded in life now returns: nothing remains hidden; everything comes to light. '*God has found out the guilt of your servants.*'

What guilt? They're innocent of the theft of the cup. Does Judah mean the crime committed against Joseph? That was more than twenty years ago! Indeed at first their consciences played up a bit, when they saw the sorrowful face of their grieving father or heard in their dreams Joseph's cry of misery, begging for mercy. But they'd agreed to be as silent as the grave, and silent they were. Over the years they smoothed out the rough edges in their souls; you can't keep looking back, you have to go on. Guilt? Who's talking about guilt? What guilt?

There they stand, the eleven before the one. They bow and bow, like the sheaves and the stars once did in Joseph's dream. A handful of Hebrew shepherds, and in front of them the man who also owes his brilliant career to their treachery and the faith that the Keeper of Israel neither slumbers nor sleeps. The question of bread had brought them together again, and then the question of guilt immediately cropped up, from God knows where. And now there's repentance: 'God has found out the guilt of your servants. Not only shall Benjamin be your slave, sir, we shall all be your slaves.'

'Far be it from me! Only the one who has stolen my cup shall be my slave. Let the rest of you return to your father, in peace.'

Why again is one separated from the others? Does this man really think that the brothers can go in peace while one of them disappears into slavery?

Indeed, that is precisely what this man thinks. And this man has his reasons for doing so. This man wants to know whether an atrocity of years ago could be repeated, or whether in the meantime it has dawned on the others that true brotherhood is impossible without concern for the weakest, the smallest brother.

Judah before the throne, the firstborn.

'My lord, do not be angry if your servant speaks yet another word to you. You asked your servants, "Do you still have a father, a brother?" "Yes, we said, we have an old father and a child of his old age, the youngest, who means everything to him." That child's brother, born of the same mother, is dead. You said to your servants, "Bring the youngest to me, that I may see him with my own eyes." We said to my lord that our father certainly wouldn't let his dearest child go. You answered that we wouldn't be able to come here again without the boy. We conveyed your words faithfully to our father. Driven by hunger, he asked us to return to you again to buy grain. We said, "Father, not without our brother, the little one; we cannot come into the presence of the Egyptian ruler unless our brother, the smallest one, is with us." Your servant, our father, answered: "Rachel, my wife, bore me two sons. One of them has departed from me and I shall never see him again. I must accept that a wild beast has torn him in pieces. Will you now also take away my second son? If misfortune strikes him, my grey hair will descend into the realm of the dead in pain." Therefore, Lord, if we should return to our father's house and the boy is not with us – my father is so attached to him – then he will die of sorrow. Therefore I pray you, my Lord, take *me*. I have stood surety with my father for the little one. Take *me* in his place, and let him go with his brothers. How could I go up to my father if the boy is not with me? Take me, O king, take me.'

Is this what were you waiting for, Joseph? Is this what you wanted to hear from the mouth of your brothers?

It is what he was waiting for. This is why Joseph has played his game. It looked like the cruel game of a vindictive man, delighting in sweet vengeance. It looked as if he was again playing God, there on his throne. But Joseph wanted to know how much brotherly love they had, and he made them take a course that would end up in their conversion.

Suppose that Joseph had immediately exclaimed, 'I am Joseph.' Then he would have spared them the remorse and the pain about their old father and their anxiety about the defenceless Benjamin. Judah wouldn't have made his offering and God wouldn't have appeared in the story. 'Well I never,' they would have said. 'It's Joseph! Who would have thought it?'

There would have been a cheap happy ending. No conversion. No new beginning.

Now, by Joseph's staging the past has returned, and the guilt which was lost has been found. The books have been opened, and there isn't much more to hide. But at the same time it's possible to breathe again. There's redemption. It's come out; finally it's come out.

For Joseph to frighten his brothers to death like this is almost beyond the pale. But he doesn't want to lose them, he wants to gain them. With Joseph this is the wrestling of love. So no triumphant smile plays on his lips when he sees them so bewildered, one in their anxiety over the smallest of them, Benjamin. He is moved to the depths of his soul. He and they are brothers again. Now the way is open for Joseph to return to their circle. 'Let all my servants leave the room!'

'All, sir?'

'Yes, all.'

The brothers have given up their secret and let the masks fall, showing their true faces – now Joseph must do the same.

'I am Joseph, your brother.'

Joseph weeps.

Tears because something is too good to be true. They had been one another's prisoners all those years. Miles apart, they had haunted one another's lives, day by day. Now they're free from that. The shame is over, the guilt is over, the tragedy is over, the masks have fallen, the lost has been found. Peace, peace at last.

'I am Joseph your brother. Is my father still alive?'

The brothers are amazed. This can't be true. Zaphenath-paneach is speaking to them in perfect Hebrew. The man with the cup who can reveal hidden things, is he Joseph, their lost brother?

Joseph sees their confusion, their anxiety, their unbelief, their hope. 'Come closer!'

Hesitantly the brothers come closer.

'I am Joseph, your brother, whom you sold into Egypt.'

Again there is silence.

Joseph thinks with horror that these last words could have given the wrong impression, as though he needed to torment his brothers just once more. But that isn't his intention. He is moved by the words with which Judah the firstborn has stood up for Benjamin. That was true brotherliness, and Joseph now so wants to share in it. He wants nothing more than for the circle of brothers from which he was cast out, not least for his own fault, to be closed again. 'Come closer. I am Joseph whom you sold, but let that no longer be between us, that is past, for, how shall I put it...'

Joseph is looking for the right words. How can he best put what he feels inside? Everything has found a place. The ghosts are ghosts no longer. He is more than the fate that befell him. He has come through the struggle with both a smaller and with a greater self. He has found peace, the peace that passes all understanding. He has experienced that the Keeper of Israel neither slumbers nor sleeps.

Then the words come to Joseph from within. What he wants to say he can say only in the language of faith. 'Don't be distressed, or torment yourselves, because you sold me here. *For God sent me here ahead of you to keep you alive.*'

'God is behind it,' says Joseph. He says it again, a second time: *'For God sent me here ahead of you.'* He even says it a third time, more strongly than before: *'You did not send me here, but God.'*

How does Joseph come to say this? Is this faith or is it foolishness? Surely God didn't sell Joseph; his brothers did!

Yes, that's the first thing that has to be said: his brothers did it. But, Joseph thinks, that's not the last thing to be said about it. For without obscuring the guilt and without denying the pain, in the curse there was also a blessing. The blessing and the curse aren't either-or. They're both-and. But the last word, brothers, is the blessing. For what shall we say about the curse now that the evil has turned to good like this, if not that it's a blessing from heaven, for you and for me? I did some things to you and you did some things to me, but doesn't the goodness of God shine over all this now?

So Joseph sees the depths and the heights of his life combined in one meaningful bond: 'God has sent me. I am one who has been sent. And it isn't fate that is decisive in this life, but how you encounter it, what you make of it. No, I'm not putting that very well, because what I've made of it is also something that is given me. Of course it's the work of my hands. But even more it's a present that I've received gratefully from God's hand. People do what they do. And from what they do, God weaves his plan. It's both-and. Human work and grace. Without God's grace we would be nowhere, brothers.'

44

FATHER JACOB

GENESIS 45, 46 AND 47

'I am Joseph your brother. Is father still alive?'

Joseph and his brothers fell on one another's necks; they wept with happiness. And this would be the moving conclusion to this story, were it not that there is still one person who knows nothing of all this happiness. For father is still alive.

In fact we haven't heard of him for a long time. Jacob's role seemed to be played out, and he probably also thought that himself, since he's old and full of sorrow. Jacob's world has shrunk. He sits quietly in Hebron in front of his tent, under the old oak. He himself is an old oak. Passers-by think that he's asleep, but he doesn't sleep. He dwells on the past. The older he gets, the more often he has to think of his father. How did he do it, grow old and die? He should have asked him. But at that time he didn't think of growing old and dying. He doesn't really want to think about it even now, for his life doesn't yet seem over. It's as though there is still something unborn lying in wait. Rachel would have understood him. Rachel! The weight of the loss seems only to increase with the years. And he can't get over the loss of Joseph. He can still see him going out that morning, cheerful and well. ''Bye father!' He will never see him again. He should never have let him go.

And why did he now also let Benjamin, Rachel's youngest, go? Why did he give in to pressure from his sons? That damned hunger! And now he's also tormented by the hunger of his heart. ''Bye, father.' ''Bye, son.' He had wanted to say so much more. 'Be careful, Benjamin. May God preserve you.' But he hadn't been able to utter a word.

He sits quietly under that old tree. He tries to pray a bit, but it doesn't really work, just scraps, no more. Benjamin has gone, and where is God now? How did Abraham and Isaac do it? How did they believe?

Then one day he's suddenly startled out of his musings. Noises, over there in the distance. Wagons. Shouts. Benjamin? Benjamin and the others?

Yes, Benjamin. Benjamin and the others. 'Hello, father.'

'Hello, son! Thank God you're back. How was the journey?'

'Good, father, good. Look at all the grain we've got. We got it for nothing.'

'For nothing?'

'Yes, father, for nothing. And also the wagons and these expensive clothes.'

Expensive clothes; that rings a bell with Jacob.

'Who did you get them from, my son? Who gave them to you?'

'The regent of Egypt, father, at the command of the Pharaoh himself.'

'Tell me why. Do you know what moved this man?'

'Yes, father, I do. Don't be frightened when I tell you. You won't believe it. The regent of Egypt isn't an Egyptian. You know him.'

'Someone from here on the throne there? Who is it, my son? Who is it?'

'Don't be frightened, father, when I tell you his name. It's Joseph, father! Joseph's alive!'

Jacob is frightened. He winces, because he doesn't believe it. It can't be true.

When his sons told him untruths that time, long ago, he believed them. Now that they're telling the truth, he can't believe them. Benjamin must have made a mistake. Joseph still alive? There's a voice inside him which resists the thought. As if he's too old for something new. As if he wants to arm himself in advance for a possible second loss.

'Joseph's alive, father! Joseph's alive!'

But Jacob can't just return to a story that he had thought to be long closed.

Then the others also tell their story, each one tumbling over the other with their words. Some speak of the former times, the treachery with which it all began. Others about what happened to them at the Egyptian court. Yet others speak of the Pharaoh's royal offer that all of them, with father Jacob and their families, may live in Egypt until the famine is over. And when Jacob sees the gifts which Joseph has sent for him, it begins to dawn on him that they aren't playing a game with him. This is reality. Unsuspected, glorious reality.

'Look, father, here's the carriage which Joseph chose specially for you to make the journey in. Did you ever see such a carriage?' Jacob walks over to it and touches the wood and the fine fittings, as if he wants to reassure himself that he isn't dreaming. 'Joseph,' he says gently, 'Joseph.' As if in mentioning that name he wants his lips no longer to speak of a dead person but of a living person.

And Israel said: 'My son Joseph still lives. I will go and see him before I die.'

Strange, we don't read that *Jacob* said that. We read that *Israel* said it.

No, it isn't strange at all. The lost brother is found, and soon the twelve will be reunited. There's a future for all Israel.

The preparations for the journey are made. Is Jacob's mind completely on it?

'Are you looking forward to the reunion, father?'

'Of course, my son.'

But when towards nightfall he goes through the stables and over the land and along the vats hewn out of the rock, the work of his hands, he shivers. Must he leave all this behind? You shouldn't transplant an old tree. Will he ever return to this land again? The land promised by God?

'Is there something, father?'

'No, my son, it's nothing. I'm a bit tired, that's all. Sleep well.'

'Sleep well, father.'

While Jacob is still lying brooding a bit, listening to the noises of the night, it's as if he suddenly hears the voice of *his* father. Amazing that he has to think of him increasingly often. And again now. 'We're strangers on earth, my son. We must always be ready to travel. I learned that from father Abraham and I'm teaching it to you. One day God will bring you home.'

Israel set out, with all that he had, and he came to Beersheba.

When as a young man he had had to flee and had reached the frontier of the land, he had seen the heavens open in a dream. Now he's an old man and again he's standing on the frontier of the land that had been promised to Abraham and Isaac. Will the Eternal One now help him again in a dream?

And God said to him in a night vision, 'Jacob, Jacob.'

'Here I am, Lord.'

'I am God, the God of your father. Do not be afraid to go down to

Egypt. I shall make you a great people. I myself will go down with you to Egypt and I will bring you up again from there. But not before Joseph's hand has closed your eyes there.'

The next day they travelled on.

As soon as Joseph receives a report that the caravan is approaching the Egyptian frontier, he has his carriage hitched and rides to meet his father.

'Father!'

They embrace each other. They don't want to let go of each other and so they just stand there, the father and his lost son. 'Now I can die, my son, now I have seen your face.'

Then, before the curtain falls, we are witnesses to another encounter: Jacob is given a special audience by the Pharaoh. It's a loaded moment: Israel and Egypt meet each other. What is that, if not the fulfilment of God's heartfelt wish for this world that Israel and the *goyim* shall meet? It's Joseph, the one with the blessing, who brings them together.

A splendid scene. In the heart of the Egyptian capital, in the state room of the royal palace, the Pharaoh sits on his high throne. Here is the ruler whose enthronement is called the rising of the sun and whose name may never be spoken... This is a style and brilliance of which those under the oak trees in Hebron know nothing. The doors swing open, music sounds, and then in comes this very old Hebrew, the shepherd leader from little Canaan, father Jacob, limping because of his hip. His father went before him in the faith of *his* father that here below we have no abiding city but are only strangers and sojourners. Jacob enters. What in heaven's name is the Pharaoh to say to this man, who is so old and has come so far, whose language he doesn't speak and whose history he doesn't know?

'*How many are the days of the years of your life?*'

The Pharaoh is visibly impressed by the Hebrew before him, Zaphenath-paneach's father, radiating a majesty before which he himself feels small.

'*How many are the days of the years of your life?*'

'*The days of the years of my sojourning are one hundred and thirty years.*'

Where Egypt speaks of *life*, Israel speaks of *sojourning*. For here we are simply guests. Foxes have holes and birds of the air have nests; Pharaohs have palaces. But where is Israel to lay his head?

The Pharaoh has much that Israel doesn't have.

But Israel has something that the Pharaoh doesn't have. For what do we see suddenly happening? Silently father Jacob comes forward. He raises his hands. He has something to give. Something eternal, something holy, something from the Lord who is the shepherd of us all: the blessing. *'The Lord bless you and keep you...'*

'Amen,' says the Pharaoh. He didn't understand a word of it, but he clearly understood that this old Hebrew had wanted to share his most valuable possession with him.

When father Jacob had disappeared through the doors of the state room without saying another word, the Pharaoh understood that the audience was at an end.

The Pharaoh smiled. Joseph saw it clearly when he left the room. The Pharaoh smiled.

45

JACOB'S END APPROACHES

GENESIS 47 AND 48

'I am Joseph, your brother. Is father still alive?'

Yes, father is still alive. But that was years ago now. Now the moment has come when the end of Jacob's life is near. He is one hundred and forty seven years old. In Hebrew, seven and a hundred and forty. If that isn't a good and holy age to yield up the spirit! And of those seven and one hundred and forty years Jacob has been able to spend seventeen in Joseph's presence, an unhoped-for grace. Just as he was also able to share the first seventeen years of Joseph's life at close quarters.

How long had Jacob already been living with death? First there was the loss of Rachel in the field of Ephrathah. Then he thought that he had also lost Joseph, Rachel's firstborn. Jacob was broken: 'In mourning I shall go down to my son in the realm of the dead.' But he didn't go down to the realm of the dead; he went down to Egypt, for the young man was still alive. 'I will see Joseph before I die.' When on the way to Egypt he arrived in Beersheba, on the frontier of the land, he heard God's voice in a dream: 'Do not be afraid. I myself will go down with you to Egypt and I will bring you up again from there. But Joseph's hand will close your eyes there.'

That moment now seems to have come. The end is near. It will be an end which bears its future in it. Jacob has Joseph called.

'Joseph.'

'Yes, father.'

'It is my fervent wish not to be buried here in Egypt but with my fathers in Canaan. I want to go up to the land that God has promised us. Therefore put your hand under my loins, my son, and swear that you will not bury me in Egypt but lay me to rest with my fathers.'

Joseph puts his hand under Jacob's loins, the centre of his vital power. How did God's promise to father Abraham go? 'To you and to your seed I give the land where you dwell as a stranger, and in your seed shall all generations of the earth be blessed.'

'Swear it to me, Joseph.'

Joseph swore it to him.

'When you come back to me, bring your two sons, Ephraim and Manasseh, with you, so that I may give them my blessing.'

'I'll do that, father. See you soon.'

'Your son Joseph has arrived, sir. Manasseh and Ephraim are accompanying him.'

Jacob, old and almost blind, laboriously props himself up in bed, white against the white cushions. One can't imagine that he was once young, vital and full of tricks. He's loved life so passionately. He's tasted its sweetness and its bitterness; he has deceived and he's been deceived. He has learned much, and also unlearned much. Jacob hasn't emerged from the struggle unscathed: his face is marked, he limps because of his hip. But he's emerged from it, and he's received a new name: Israel, *God's fighter*.

'Are you there, Joseph?'

'Yes, father, I'm here.'

'Listen, my son. Before I give Ephraim and Manasseh my blessing, I want to tell you my story once again.'

Jacob tells his story. He tells of his life and of the vicissitudes of his faith.

'It began in Bethel, in the land of Canaan. There the Eternal One appeared to me. I saw him in a dream. At the top of a ladder I saw heaven open and God gave me his blessing: "I shall make you fruitful, and to your seed I shall give this land, to dwell there for ever." That's where it all began, in Bethel.'

Bethel. After the deception. After stealing the blessing from his old blind father, white against the white cushions. He was a deceiver, a thief, a vagrant. Nevertheless, in the darkness above Bethel heaven opened for him and God said: I will go with you, and I will bring you home again.

Joseph sits quietly beside the bed and listens.

He listens to a confession. But would father Jacob have wanted to be without the sin? It has brought him catastrophe but also so many good things. Without the sin he wouldn't be who he is. Through it he has grown in knowledge of himself, knowledge of others and knowledge of God. The deception of his youth still pains him on his death bed, but it also brought him to Bethel and to God's holy angels.

'And after Bethel, father?'

'I had to go a long way, with much loneliness. But far from home I found your mother, and so the days of my exile seemed short to me. Twelve sons were born to me. I became prosperous. I had left Canaan with only a staff in my hand; I returned home with many flocks, rich in blessing. And at the same time poor, since on the way your mother died giving birth to Benjamin. I buried her in the field of Ephrathah, by the wayside, not far from Bethlehem.'

Father Jacob tells of his long life and of the suffering that never diminished. And he ends with the blessing. Jacob is going to die, but the blessing which he received after much struggle will be handed on further by his sons. And by Manasseh and Ephraim. So it will go on, from generation to generation.

Patriarch Jacob, seven and one hundred and forty years old, ends with the blessing. That's how once the old blind Isaac wanted to give the blessing. The youngest then ran off with it...

'Where are the boys, Joseph?'

Israel only sees shapes, not faces.

'Here, father.'

Joseph puts the boys so close that there can be no mistake: he puts Manasseh, the oldest, on his left hand and thus on Israel's right hand, and Ephraim, the youngest, on his right hand and thus on Israel's left hand. The narrator is rather long-winded in describing this, but Joseph wants to exclude any possible misunderstanding; you can't be careful enough in this kind of thing. 'Here, father, here are the boys whom God gave me.'

Israel embraces the boys and kisses them. 'Who would have thought it, Joseph? For years I believed that you were dead and now not only have I been granted the good fortune to see you again; God has also introduced me to your sons.'

Israel stretches out his hands to bless the boys. But strangely, he crosses them as he does so. The old man is confused. He puts his right hand on the head of Ephraim, the youngest, on his left, and his left hand on the head of the boy on his right, the oldest, Manasseh. Israel makes a mistake and Joseph wants to correct it. He takes his father's hands in his own. 'Not like that, father, not like that.'

'I know, my son, I know.'

He doesn't say more. 'I know.'

What does Israel know?

Israel knows that God constantly reverses the roles. Israel knows of God's surprising twists: the smallest shall be the greatest, the last becomes the first. Israel knows that contrary to all human calculation and expectation the Eternal One always takes new ways, breaks down established powers and crosses descent by blood.

46

JACOB AND JOSEPH ARE BURIED

GENESIS 49 AND 50

'Joseph, swear that you won't bury me here in Egypt. I want to go up to the land that God has promised me. Promise me that you will lay me to rest at home, in the field where Abraham and Sarah, Isaac and Rebecca found their last resting place, in the cave of Machpelah, where Leah also lies.'

Joseph promised him.

Jacob was dying. His twelve sons stood around him. Then Jacob also gave them his blessing, a blessing brim full of memory and brim full of promise. 'Wherever I went, there was always a hidden glory on my way. I was often alone, but there was always also this Other. I have been supported all my life by the one who gave me life. Now I shall depart. Be blessed. Be a blessing wherever you go. The Lord bless you and keep you...'

Israel laid his hands on his sons one by one and gave them the blessing.

After that he drew up his feet on the bed again and yielded up his spirit.

Judah and his brothers stood motionless around the bed. Then Joseph bent over his father, kissed him and closed his eyes. He gave the court physicians orders to embalm the body.

When the time of mourning was at an end, Joseph and his brothers prepared to depart. They were to go up to the land of Canaan, as they had promised their father. They were to lay him in the cave of Machpelah, in the hands of the living God, the God who called Abraham, who showed his faithfulness to Isaac and Jacob, and who does not abandon the work that he has begun.

So Jacob was not to be buried in silence. For this faith has to be celebrated. It has to be portrayed in a sad but at the same time festal pilgrimage to the land of promise, where God brings his children home from their captivity. For he doesn't just bring Jacob home; one day, Israel dreams, all this world will come home. Is that why Joseph, the master dreamer, thought that senior Egyptian dignitaries must also take part in the cortege?

Did these Egyptians feel out of place in this cortege, as pallbearers of a Hebrew shepherd? Or did they gradually also become pilgrims? Did they, like Israel, get on the track of the belief that in this one people God has to do with all peoples?

They came to the Threshing Floor of Thorns, on the other side of the Jordan. There they raised a great and very solemn song of lament.

The Threshing Floor of Thorns. What a remarkable name! Is this threshing floor surrounded by thorn bushes? Or are thorns threshed? Can thorns feed a person?

They can. One has to say it hesitantly, but they can. Loss, sorrow, abandonment, death, thorns in the flesh – there can also be a blessing in this curse. You have to hammer it out, though, and that's hard work. But sometimes you can see in a person how suffering has purified, how loss has also led to gain, how what was sown in tears has been reaped in joy.

Something of this joy must have resounded in the laments which the twelve sons of Israel sang at the Threshing Floor of Thorns.

Did the elders of Egypt also hear that joy? And the Canaanites?

Judah and his brothers buried their father in the cave of the field of Machpelah.

More than that isn't said.

More than that needn't be said.

'I wait for your salvation,' said the dying Jacob. He believed that God wouldn't let him wait in vain, and his sons believed that with him.

So they entrusted their father to the God of all mercy. But when they are back in Egypt, doubt creeps over them about Joseph's mercy. Perhaps Joseph has been waiting until father Jacob was dead and buried to avenge himself on his brothers for their wrongdoing.

They're so afraid that they don't even dare to talk to Joseph about it. They hide behind a messenger, and moreover they hide behind their dead father. 'Joseph, before father died, we shared with him our fear that you would take revenge on us. Father then said that we must ask your forgiveness.'

Tears came to Joseph's eyes when he received the message. Was he moved by this confession of guilt? Or rather sad that after so many years they still doubted his forgiveness?

He invited his brothers to the palace. In fear and trembling they prostrated themselves before him: 'Let us be your servants.'

'Do not be afraid. Am I in God's place?'

There was a time when Joseph thought that he was in God's place. But he's changed. So too have his brothers. Reconciliation is now possible. *'Am I in God's place?* Is it for me to judge? Brothers, I myself am dependent upon God's grace. You intended evil against me, but God meant it for good; as a result a great people has remained alive. So why should we still talk of evil; let's rejoice in the good!'

Thus he reassured them and spoke to their hearts.

Years went by: Ephraim and Manasseh grew up and became fathers. Again years went by. Ephraim and Manasseh became grandfathers. Joseph had grandchildren clambering all over him.

'I'm going to die,' said Joseph

Probably you have to be very grown-up to be able to say that in such a childlike way, just like a child going to sleep: 'When at night I go to sleep, fourteen angels watch do keep.'

'The Lord's angels will keep watch over you, too, in the night that is going to come upon you,' says Joseph to his brothers. 'The Keeper of Israel will certainly look after you. One day he will have you go up again from Egypt to Canaan, the land promised to our fathers. And I pray you, at that time take my bones there with you.'

Joseph died. He was one hundred and ten years old.

They embalmed him, and laid him in a coffin.

In Egypt.

47

THEN THERE AROSE A KING...

EXODUS I

'Father, why is isn't this night like all other nights?'

It's Pesach, the Jewish Passover. The family is sitting around the table; it's seder evening. The time has come to tell the story of this night, the story of liberation from the house of bondage, of rescue from death. It's a story passed down from generation to generation. 'Father, why isn't this night like all other nights?'

'I'll tell you, my child. We were slaves of the Pharaoh in Egypt, but God set us free.'

'*We* were...,' says the father. Why does he say that? '*We*' weren't there, were we? After all, this story happened long ago.

Yes, it's a story of long ago, but it's also a story of today. It took place once, and it takes place again and again, whenever a new generation hears the story and it becomes part of their lives. It happened once in a faraway land. And it happened in America when the blacks rose up from their house of bondage: *let my people go*. It happened in the lives of Moses and of Miriam. It happened in the lives of Joan of Arc, of Luther and of Martin Luther King. And it happens in the street in which we live, every time a woman frees herself from the pharaoh who keeps her in bondage; every time a man breaks with his addiction. It happened and it happens. '*We* were...'

So when we talk about Pharaoh, we're not talking so much about that tyrant of those days. And when we speak of Egypt, we're not referring to the Egypt on the map, but to every place of oppression. By Israel, too, we mean more a notion than a nation.* So soon, when we talk about the waters of the Reed Sea, and about the wilderness and the promised land, remember that there's more to this than meets the eye.

'Father, why isn't this night like all other nights?'

'I'll tell you, my child. We were slaves in Egypt. Do you remember how we had ended up there? Joseph, son of Jacob, lived there. Underground at first, in a dark dungeon, and then later above ground, in the palace. Because the Pharaoh had discovered that in the person of this strange Hebrew he had an angel of God in his house, and he brought him into the light and seated him next to himself on the throne. In this way his land became a blessing to all who lived there, and to the strangers who came to satisfy their hunger. Our father Jacob also went to Egypt with his sons, because there was bread there.'

The years had come and gone; Jacob and his sons had died long ago; a family had grown into a people. *Then there arose a king who did not know Joseph...*

Hasn't this king ever heard of Joseph? It's not that; he doesn't want to know him. He detests Joseph, because Joseph was on good terms with God, and in his heart of hearts this king sees himself as God. And look out! Whenever a king arises anywhere in the world who thinks like that, the Hebrews have to scatter and go underground. That's the way these kings are, the kings who don't want to know Joseph and don't want to acknowledge Joseph's God. There arose a king who wanted nothing to do with Joseph, and Joseph's descendants no longer had a life. Death to the Hebrews!

Pharaoh is God's opponent. 'I shall make of you a great people,' God has promised. 'I'll grind you to dust,' Pharaoh promises. He's a terrible person. Or, better said, he represents a terrible human potential. People can live like heathen, or they can live messianically. Pharaoh stands for the first possibility; Joseph for the second. And the choice is up to us. A Joseph arises in every age, and in every age a king arises who refuses to know him.

There arose a king who wanted to banish Joseph and Joseph's God from his life. He tried to silence inner voices which sought to dissuade him from silencing Israel. It's a recipe as old as the world, and as new as today's newspaper. 'The conscience is a Jewish invention,' wrote the Pharaoh of the Third Reich in *Mein Kampf.*

But the Israelites thrived on adversity. *They were fruitful and increased greatly; they multiplied and grew exceedingly numerous, so that the land was filled with them.* Tiresome for the man on the throne.

'*Let us deal wisely with them,*' he says. Unfortunately, his wisdom isn't that of the king who knew Joseph. Pharaoh's wisdom is that of terror:

from early morning to late at night the Israelites have to cut clay and bake bricks. The beating is more frequent than the eating, and many of them die under the strain. I don't need to describe that here; it's been described often enough, and it's indescribable.

But it doesn't work. The Israelites just keep multiplying; more drastic measures must be taken. Two Egyptian midwives are ordered to kill all Hebrew baby boys at birth.

Those midwives are called Shiphrah and Puah. We're never told the name of their lord and master, but these two women, these angels of God, as we shall see, have made a name for themselves with their actions: they're called *Beauty* and *Shining*. And these two women are what one can call wise. They're shrewd. They don't play God, *they feared God*. In the Bible that doesn't mean that they're afraid of the Eternal One; it means that they know the difference between good and evil, that they're full of reverence and holy awe. Just what you'd expect from women like these, whose calling and office it is to help new life be born, not to nip new life in the bud. Every day, these godfearing women witness the great miracle of childbearing, so the godless king's attempts to hire them to help to destroy creation are vain. The women perform an act of civil disobedience; they refuse to hurt a hair of the boys' heads.

'*Why have you done this?*' exclaims the king.

The interesting thing, of course, is that the women haven't done anything at all! '*Your majesty, we could do nothing. These Hebrew women are not like the Egyptian women; they are so strong that they are delivered before the midwife comes to them!*'

The man on the throne says: 'These Hebrews must perish. They're so strange, so different.'

The midwives say: 'As you say, your majesty, they're so strange, these Hebrews, so different. You just can't wipe them out.'

And above, God smiles. For what those two heathen women were doing down below was Beautiful and Shining in his eyes.

That's the way these stories go. There is paganism and there is awe before the Eternal One. There is messianic life and there is non-messianic life. And sometimes it's the pagans who show us what messianic life is, so there's no need for anyone to put on airs. In the stories of Israel, the messianic way of life is often exemplified by women, the non-messianic by men.

God dealt well with the midwives.

Along with Moses' mother and sister and Pharaoh's daughter, they're the ones who protect the mystery of life. Fearing God, they work together to safeguard the future. They're the first to celebrate Passover. In the stories of Israel, women are often the first to understand that, once God has put his hand to something, he will not abandon it.

48

SAVED TO SAVE

EXODUS 2.1-10

In the world's legends and sagas, heroes are often born in a wonderful way. That's also how it is in the stories about the great men of Israel. Sarah, Rebecca, Leah and Rachel, the matriarchs, are barren; they're able to give birth only by the grace of God.

However, the story of the birth of the great Moses is as normal as they come. His mother isn't barren; no angel from heaven forecasts his arrival; no star marks his birth. No, it's quite simple: a man of the house of Levi takes to wife a daughter of Levi; she becomes pregnant and bears a son. One might even ask whether heaven knew anything about his arrival. Wasn't this a man born behind God's back? For the people of Israel are living in wretched conditions and their very existence is gravely threatened. That's what Pharaoh wants, and Pharaoh's word is law: *'Throw all the sons that are born into the Nile.'* The Nile, Egypt's lifeblood, is to become Israel's river of death. The strong assert themselves, the jackboots stamp, the secret police are everywhere and, as always, it's the helpless, the weak, the children, who pay for it. Into the Nile with them.

A Levite mother bends over her child's cradle. Who will banish the tyranny that cuts her to the heart? *She looked at her child and saw that he was good.*

Words from in the beginning, spoken by God the Father, at the birth of the world. *'Let there be light,'* God said, and there was light. *And God saw that it was good.*

These words, spoken by the Eternal One at the birth of the world, are repeated here in a slave's hut by a simple woman at the birth of her child. *She saw that he was good.* It's as though heaven were suddenly back in play, as though she suspects that one day it could be her son who would banish the tyranny that cuts her to the heart. It's as though she had a premonition that, down the centuries, her child would be a comfort to all the outcast of the earth, a shining example to all the oppressed who leave their house of bondage. Rabbis tell that the entire hut lit up when Moses was born. Perhaps it was a miraculous birth after all…

The mother saw what God saw: it was good. So it wouldn't be good if her child died. So she hid the baby Moses. She jumped up to feed him at his slightest cry, afraid that the baby would give himself away. 'Miriam, don't tell anyone you have a new baby brother. Say nothing.'

But after three months she couldn't keep the child hidden any longer. What now?

She took a rush basket, sealed it with pitch, put her child in it and laid it among the reeds on the banks of the Nile, at a place where she knew Pharaoh's daughter came to bathe. Her daughter Miriam would keep watch. 'And do exactly as I tell you, will you?'

A basket made of rushes. An ark. Once again the story matches a story from in the beginning: the story of Noah, who sailed over the waters with the animals in a huge, pitch-smeared coffin, only a thin wall between him and death. 'Into your hands, O God, I commend my spirit, and the spirits of all that lives and sails with me.' Then he reached dry land again. Saved.

The baby's mother laid the little ark of rushes in the reeds along the river. Only a thin wall between her child and death. 'Into your hands I commend his spirit. Save him.'

The princess arrived to bathe and saw the little basket hidden in the reeds. One of her slave girls picked it up and opened it. A baby. A crying baby. And she knew: this was a Hebrew child. She could tell, the rabbis say, because he didn't cry like a baby. He cried like an adult, like a community of adults: his entire people wept in him.

Pharaoh's daughter was moved with compassion. This child mustn't be allowed to drown. He must live. But who could feed him?

Then Miriam appeared. 'Shall I find one of the Hebrew women to nurse him for you?'

'Yes, do that.'

Miriam ran back home. 'Come with me, mother. It all went well. Come with me to the river.'

'Would you nurse this child for me, madam? I'll pay you handsomely for it.'

'Gladly.'

Isn't that a nice twist? For centuries this story has been told with a twinkle in the eye. 'You heard the one about baby Moses? And his mother got paid for it!'

Yes, and later the king saw to the child's education. *When the child was grown, his mother brought him to Pharaoh's daughter, and she adopted him as her son.*

A Hebrew boy in Pharaoh's court. There he learns reading and writing, history and geography, knowledge indispensable to the man he must become. Later, when he reaches adulthood, he will confront Pharaoh with the choice between tyranny and humanity, between salvation and damnation. Two human possibilities. The king has both potentials in him. He can choose. But will he choose wisely?

Only time will tell. For the time being, the boy is still living quietly at court, learning all kinds of things. 'Promise me you'll do your best!,' his mother had said. As if even then she could see what this was 'good' for.

And the princess called his name Moses, for, she said, I drew him out of the water.

That's what Moses means in Hebrew: *drawn out*. Did the princess know Hebrew? No, of course not. The princess gave him the Egyptian name Moses, meaning *son of*. She must have named him something like 'Tut-Moses', the son of Tut, or 'Ra-Mses', the son of Ra. But the Hebrews recognized a Hebrew word in that name, and what better name for their hero? Drawn out of the water. Saved. The Saved One.

Shortly it will become clear that Moses wasn't saved just for the sake of being saved. He was saved to save. He escaped the waters of death so that later he could help his own people to escape from the waters of death.

And God saw that it was good.

49

IN THE WILDERNESS

EXODUS 2.11-22

One day, when Moses had grown big, he went out to his brothers.

But surely Moses was a young Egyptian man at an Egyptian court? How did he know that the Hebrews were his brothers?

Of course the story doesn't take account of such a historical type of question. But if you must have an answer, suppose that he had absorbed this with his mother's milk. Or imagine Miriam becoming a serving girl in the palace and bringing in Hebrew sweets for Moses, wrapped in papyri with Genesis on them.

One day, when Moses had grown big...

He may well be said to have grown big. Big not only in body but also inwardly. Of course he could have remained quietly at court; he was in a good position there. No, he wasn't in a good position there. His mother would never have called it good to live in prosperity while further away his brothers were in need. No, Moses saw that it wasn't good. And he went out to his brothers. There he saw a lot more.

He saw their burdens, their forced labour. He saw that they were beaten until they collapsed.

He saw an Egyptian killing one of his brothers.

And he saw that no one intervened. The people were scared to death and utterly demoralized.

Moses saw it all. '*God will look after you,*' Joseph had said on his deathbed. Was that going to happen now? A servant of God appears on the scene, a messianic figure, who knows that he is called to look after this people. Moses sees the misery of his people. He sees how an Egyptian kills one of his brothers. And he also sees how no one intervenes. Moses is a fiery man; the flames blaze out of him. He takes a lightning look around, sees that no one is watching, strikes the murderer dead and hides him under the sand.

It is later written in scripture that Moses was a gentle man. He must have become that later, for here he's still a provoked, hot-tempered man, who hits out in wild rage. And of course his anger is rooted in his sense of right and justice. However, his violent intervention doesn't lead to any easing of the fate of his threatened people, let alone their liberation. Moses must have been shocked at the devastating power of his urge. Was this violent action the right thing for him, a son of Levi? What did the dying Jacob say of Levi and his brother Simeon when he gave them the blessing? *Their instruments are weapons of violence. Cursed be their anger.*

Soon afterwards it all got even more complicated when Moses saw two Hebrews fighting with each other. 'Who are you to teach me a lesson? Who made you lord and master over us?', exclaimed the man whom Moses saw as the guilty party. 'Are you going to murder me, as you bumped off that Egyptian?'

Moses was afraid. His action had come to light. His brothers knew his weak spot, and if the Pharaoh heard about it... Moses, murderer of a murderer, must get away. He flees into the wilderness, disillusioned, desperate and terrified. Away from his failure.

In the stories of Israel's faith, the wilderness is the place where a person can come to himself and where he can learn to control his urges. The wilderness was the school for all the great figures in Israel. Abraham, Jacob, Joseph, Moses, Elijah, John the Baptist, Jesus, all had to go into the solitude of the desert to attain knowledge of God and knowledge of themselves.

Moses too had to take this way of the wilderness. Utterly alone, he went through the bare hill-country of Midian. He rested by a well. Isn't there someone to look after *him* now?

Lo and behold, the seven daughters of Jethro the priest appear. They come to the well, fill the troughs and let their flocks drink. But look, here come shepherds, also in search of water. The girls are driven away roughly.

The story is as old as the world, but never gets out of date: trouble by the wells of mother earth. And time and again it's the strong who drive away the weak.

'Moses, do you see that? Those seven daughters of Jethro have no brother!'

Moses sees it. And he gets up. He knows what he has to do: he liberates the oppressed and he gets water for their sheep and goats to drink. That's what God has meant this son of Levi to be: a brave fighter, serving with compassion.

The seven shepherdesses are home earlier than usual. 'You're back quickly!,' says father Jethro.

'Yes, there was such a nice man at the well. An Egyptian. He gave the shepherds what for, and after that he even drew water for us and the flock.'

'Where is this man? Why didn't you bring him with you? Go back to him immediately and ask him for a meal.'

Seven guardian angels hasten to the well. So all in all there have been twelve guardian angels in Moses' life: his mother, the midwives Ziphrah and Puah, his sister Miriam, the Pharaoh's daughter, and the seven by the well. The future of the twelve sons of Israel hangs on the one son Moses, who owes his birth and his existence to twelve women, daughters of both Israel and the heathen. They're the ones who literally and figuratively keep the saviour 'above water'.

So Moses came to Jethro's home and so he found his wife: Zipporah, one of Jethro's seven daughters. Zipporah, *little bird*. A creature that unites heaven and earth. The girl of the well, for Moses a well of life. She could help him to deepen and to bring to light what he had in the depths of his soul.

And Moses was shepherd over the flock of Jethro, priest of Midian; and he led the flock deep into the wilderness.

Moses was a gentle man. Here in the wilderness he had become that. He had learned it from the lofty dome of heaven, from the stillness and the stars and the rocks. And at home there was always Zipporah his wife, God's little bird. Not to mention Jethro with his priestly heart, someone who knew the way in the wilderness and who could point out the way to a seeking soul.

And Moses was shepherd over the flock of Jethro.

That's nice. The one who will soon be shepherd and leader of a whole people now leads someone else's flock. Here Moses learned to be a shepherd. One day, the rabbis relate, he went to look for a lost ram at the risk of his own life. He carried it back to the fold on his shoulders.

When Moses was alone with his sheep and his God deep in the wilderness, his thoughts went out to his people who were bowed down under foreign rule over there. Then he saw in his mind their emaciated bodies in the clay pits; he heard the whiplashes of the guards and the bitter cry of his tormented people. And he knew: I must go back, I mustn't remain in safety in Midian, in a foreign land. No, I must be where my fellow-countrymen are. I must make them servants of God instead of Pharaoh's slaves. I must give a voice to those who are smitten with dumbness, help those who have no helper. When Zipporah gave him a son he called his name Gershom. *Sojourner.* 'For I have become a sojourner, Gershom, in a foreign land.'

Zipporah understood.

50

THE BURNING BUSH

EXODUS 2.23-3.15

Moses was shepherd over the flock of Jethro. He led the flock deep into the wilderness and he came to the mountain of God. There the angel of the Lord appeared to him.

He's in the wilderness, deep in the wilderness. Away from home, away from what is familiar and manageable, away from his wife and child. And miles away from his people, who are suffering in Egypt. Mustn't he be with his people? But what can he do? He's a nobody, a puny man all alone in a boundless wilderness, himself also prey to anxiety and despair. What can he do?

It's a hard time for Moses, while he's trailing around with his animals, not knowing what to do with his life. The heat of the day, the cold of the night, the loneliness, the tears, the pain: he feels completely lost. But it's here that Moses is calmed and purged. There, deep in the wilderness, the mountain of God turned out to be. And God called him there.

The angel of the Lord appeared to him in a flame of fire in the midst of a bush. Moses looked, and lo and behold, the bush was burning but was not consumed.

A vision. All that the sheep in his flock could see was the sun, setting fiery red behind the bushes. But Moses suddenly sinks to his knees, for Moses sees more.

His life is on fire and it isn't consumed. The fire which initially consumed him and led him to violence and murder has lost its devastating effect. A bush in the wilderness has neither beauty nor splendour; the wilderness is full of them, and you can't use them for anything – unless the lowliness of this simple creation has been chosen to be the bearer of the fiery splendour of God himself. Will the Eternal One use a nobody like Moses to make himself known in him as warmth and fire?

The bush is also the people of Israel: with great liberators, their personal fate and the fate of their people is always one. It is Israel that may bear the fire of God, right through the wilderness. The flame isn't fed by the wood. Israel doesn't feed the flame; Moses doesn't feed the flame; God feeds the flame. Israel and Moses will bear the flame. One day Moses will stand here again with his people, after the exodus from Egypt. By this thornbush (*seneh*), on this mountain (*Sinai*), God will once again appear in fire. Here the Eternal One will make a covenant with his people.

A vision like this is mysterious. One can get a bit nearer, but never really close.

Moses now thought: 'I shall go and see this marvellous sight.' Then God called to him from the bush: 'Moses, Moses. Do not come near. Take your shoes from your feet, for the place on which you are standing is holy ground.'

Moses took his shoes from his feet. A sign of humility. In bare feet he stood there, like Adam before his creator. And he hid his face. How could a mortal look upon the God of heaven and earth?

'Moses, I have seen the affliction of my people which is in Egypt. I have heard their cries because of their taskmasters. I know their pains. So I have come down to deliver them from the power of the Egyptians and to lead them from this land into a good and broad land, flowing with milk and honey.'

God hears the cry of the oppressed which rises from the earth. God sees the strong who oppress the weak. Those who are hungry and thirsty for food and for righteousness will be filled in the land of God. Their share will be milk and honey: the food of the gods for the slaves. What more peaceable food could there be than milk and honey? No life needs to be taken for it, and no animal needs to shed blood for it. God comes down to rescue his people. But Moses must help in the rescue:

'Now then, go. I am sending you to Pharaoh to lead my people out of Egypt.'

God reveals himself in visions and sights for those who have eyes to see. But there's always an obligation. Acts of liberation go with it. Moses is frightened of this. What a task it is! The mighty Pharaoh will see him coming.

'Lord, who am I that I should go to the Pharaoh and lead the Israelites out of Egypt?'

'Am I not with you?'

Moses asks *'Who am I?,'* and God replies by saying who *he* is: *I am! I am with you, Moses.* That's how God gives Moses courage. Trust in God gives self-confidence.

But confidence must always grow. At the moment, Moses hasn't got there. It's no use going to the Israelites. 'Lead us up out of this house of slavery? How will you manage that? What gave you that idea? Who? God? Who's he?'

'*Lord God, may I make a request? When I come to the Israelites and I say, "The God of your fathers, the God of Abraham, Isaac and Jacob, has sent me to you," and when they ask me "What is his name?", what must I answer?*'

Moses asks God for his name. In doing so he's asking God for his secret. A person's name discloses that person's nature. Thus Moses is called Moses because he's been drawn out of the water and because he's been saved to save. That's why God also calls him twice by his name. It's the name by which he is called – by God. 'Moses, you must be Moses.'

'Mother, what's that?'
   'That's a tree.'
   'And what's that?'
   'That's a baby.'
   'Who made the trees and the babies?'
   'God.'
   'Who's God?'

Now it gets difficult. You can give trees names and you can give children names, but who gives God a name?

'When the Israelites ask me, "What is his name?", what must I then answer? Who can I say there is?'

'*I am who I am, Moses. Just say to the Israelites "I am" has sent me to you, the God of your fathers, of Abraham, Isaac and Jacob.*'

'I am who I am. I shall be who I shall be. I will go with you. Like Abraham, Isaac and Jacob, you will never go anywhere, Moses, where I am not. Be of good courage.'

A mysterious name. A veiling and an unveiling at the same time.

A veiling because we cannot name God. We human beings may not depict God in his image and likeness, nor can we. How could we? God dwells in heaven and we are on earth. There are people who talk about God as if they call each other on the telephone every day. Beware of these people. A great divine wrote fine books about God, but perhaps the finest thing that he wrote was this: 'We know absolutely nothing about who God is.'* A veiling.

The mysterious name is also an unveiling. *I am there for you.* God's name is a promise. 'My being,' says God, 'is being there. Just as I was the God of Abraham, Isaac and Jacob, so I shall be your God. Just as I am who I am, so I shall be there for you. Just believe that, Moses.'

Moses nodded.

He didn't yet know everything.

But he knew enough.

51

MOSES RESISTS

EXODUS 4

'Yes, but what if they do not believe me and will not listen to me?'

Moses has problems again. He's called, but he doesn't want to go yet. He's still hesitating. Why has God chosen him of all people? Why not someone else? Twice already he's resisted, and he still has three more reservations. Moses demurs five times, with a handful of objections. *'But what if they do not believe me?'*

Of course Moses is talking about himself; he doesn't believe it himself. He may just have had that vision, high on God's holy mountain, fire in his dry twigs, but he isn't yet rid of his fear and his doubt. One never gets rid of them just like that. That takes time.

'What do you have in your hand, Moses?'

That's always the question. What do you have in your hands? Without a divine spark, Moses is no more than a useless bush in the wilderness. He's inclined to say, 'I've nothing in my hands. Who am I to have anything in my hands?'

'Why so afraid, Moses? You do have something in your hands. Tell me what you have in your hand.'

'A shepherd's staff.'

A simple piece of equipment for performing a simple task. A staff for the way, a support when you have to go through dark valleys. Although from the outside it looks like a dead piece of wood, it's full of life. It bends, but it doesn't break. 'Do you still have life in you, Moses? What do you have in your hands?'

A staff. You can keep a flock together with it and drive off wild animals. You can preserve life with it and ward off death.

'Throw your staff on the ground, Moses.'

Moses threw his staff on the ground and it became a snake. Moses recoiled from it. Look, it's dangerous to part with one's staff and to stop being a shepherd. That will bring him into great danger.

'Moses, stretch out your hand and pick it up by the tail.'

By the tail? The very place where you mustn't grab a snake if you value your life. A child knows that.

An exercise in trusting God.

Moses overcame his fear, stretched out his hand, gripped the snake by the tail, and it became a staff in his hand.

'Moses, put your hand inside your cloak.'

Moses put his hand inside his cloak and when he took it out again, look, his hand was leprous, white as snow.

Teaching with visual aids. 'Why don't you roll your sleeves up, Moses? Do what has to be done. Put your hand to the plough. Don't make yourself incapable of action because you're trapped in fear. The other hand may wither next. You'll become sick. And a danger to others. Fear is infectious.'

'Put your hand back inside your cloak.'

Moses did so, and when he took his hand out again, look, it was as it had been before.

Moses must look within himself for healing from his fear. 'Trust in your inner strength. Trust in me. I am with you.'

But Moses still hasn't got there. He continues to resist, afraid of what is to come. Who is born messiah?

For the fourth time he begins to object: '*Lord, I am not eloquent. I was not eloquent yesterday or the day before yesterday, nor have I become eloquent since you spoke to your servant. For I am slow of speech and slow of tongue.*'

Can't God get it into his head that Moses is altogether unsuitable for the business that God has in mind for him? His faith is far too small. 'I daren't. You know that I'm no orator and that I never have been. I've never been one for speeches. And honestly, things haven't got better since you called me. In heaven's name, how can you want to speak through my mouth?'

When God called him, why didn't God immediately make him a real hero, inside and out? Moses finds God difficult.

And God finds Moses just as difficult. For the fourth time the Eternal One tries to boost his confidence: '*Moses, you got your mouth from me. You lack nothing. Go now. I shall be with your mouth and you shall say what you must. Go now.*'

But Moses doesn't want to go, and for the fifth time he tries to thwart God's plans. *'O Lord God, please send someone else.'*

Then the anger of the Lord broke forth: 'Very well, I will send you Aaron your brother. He is already on the way. Aaron shall be your mouth. And you shall be God for him. But now you must pick up your staff. And go.'

Moses went. He finally went. Afraid of the consequences of yet another refusal, he overcame his fear, our reluctant hero. He still saw tremendous obstacles in the way; truly he hadn't asked for this; he *was* asked. But he went. He saddled his ass, and together with Zipporah and Gershom, their firstborn, he set out. In the direction of Egypt. In the direction of Pharaoh.

He spent the night in an inn near the frontier. Soon he would be returning to the land that he had left in flight. Did Moses think that night of Jacob, who also returned after many wanderings to the land that he'd left in flight? Be this as it may, as with Jacob, so for him that night was haunted. *The Lord God sought to kill him.*

Apparently a sudden violent fever comes over him. Moses is very ill. But who claims that God is behind it?

That was Zipporah's idea. 'O God,' Zipporah thought, 'he'll die on me.' And she thought, 'How did this come upon us?' And she thought, 'Perhaps God is behind it.' And she thought, 'Perhaps it's *because...*' And when she thought *that,* Zipporah took a stone knife and did what Moses had neglected to do at the time: she circumcised her firstborn son; she cut on Gershom's little staff the sign of the covenant that had been withheld from him.

Moses had dedicated himself to God, but not yet totally. He hadn't yet dedicated his firstborn son to him. Moses' surrender clearly wasn't yet complete. Zipporah knew this and made up for it, in his place. 'Take our life and let it be consecrated, Lord, to thee.' In this way she reminded God of his promise to Moses and his call. Gershom received the sign and seal of the God who wills to be Israel's God from generation to generation.

The sun rose over them. It was the end of a long night, a new day dawned, the fever had broken. Moses arose. His people were waiting over there.

'Come on, Zipporah, let's go.'

52

LET MY PEOPLE GO

EXODUS 5, 6 AND 7

'Father, why isn't this night like all other nights?'

'We were slaves in Egypt, my child, prisoners of a mortal who thought that he was God and had control over life and death. And we would still be there had not Moses returned to us. *'Hear, Israel, the Lord is our God, the Lord alone,'* he cried. These few words said everything; you can find them on the little parchment scroll in the *mezuzah* on the doorpost of our house. It's the core of our faith. Only those who have heard this truth properly will not begin to play God. Only those who have seen this truth clearly will expose any mortal who does. We needn't kneel or bow before any power and any person in the world. God is with us.'

God was with Moses. And with Aaron, whom Moses travelled to meet as soon as he was assured by God that his brother was on the way. God was with them when they told the Israelites about the miracles that had happened to them and the miracles that they might expect. And God was with them when they appeared before the Pharaoh: *'Thus says the Lord, the God of Israel: Let my people go. Let us travel three days' journey into the wilderness to worship our God.'*

The Pharaoh couldn't suppress a small smile. There was something droll about it, these two simple shepherds from the slave people who had just come into his royal palace to tell him that their God wanted their freedom. Where did these strange people get their cheek from? And then three days journey away! Of course they would immediately run off, with considerable damage to his country's economy.

'I do not know this God of yours,' said the Pharaoh.

No, that was quite clear to Moses and Aaron. The man knew neither God nor commandment. 'I don't know your God and I won't let you go. Freedom? Get to work! Bake bricks!'

From then on the Israelites had to gather the straw with which the clay was reinforced by themselves. But the number of bricks that they had to bake remained the same. An impossible task. The forced labourers were beaten harder than ever, and in desperation – as the Pharaoh had foreseen – they turned on Moses: 'You've done more harm than good. You've given the king the sword with which he will kill us.'

And Moses? Moses too was desperate. And in the grip of desperation he turned on God: 'Why are you so hard on this people? Why have you sent me to this people if you yourself do nothing to rescue them?'

'I am the Lord, Moses. I am the God of Abraham, of Isaac and of Jacob. Tell the Israelites not to despair. I shall lead them out of Egypt and bring them to the land that I promised to the fathers. I am the Lord.'

Moses tried to put new courage into his people. 'Don't despair. God will save us. We'll cope.'

But the people no longer dared to hope and didn't listen.

According to a saying of Rabbi Hanokh of Alexander the real captivity of Israel was that they had grown accustomed to it. Only a miracle could save the people now.

'Go to the Pharaoh,' God said to Moses and Aaron, 'and tell him to let the people go. If he will not listen to you, then let Aaron throw his staff on the ground. The staff will become a snake.'

'In the name of our God I tell you: Let my people go!' cried out Moses to the Pharaoh.

'In the name of whom?' asked the Pharaoh.

Aaron threw his staff on the ground and the staff became a snake. However, his gesture didn't make much of an impression: the wise men and magicians of Egypt all threw their staves on the ground, too, and these became snakes.

You can see how the despair of the small Hebrew people is justified: it's an unequal struggle. They can do absolutely nothing against powerful Egypt. When they perform a magic trick with one snake, Egypt over-trumps them with a whole series of tricks.

But look, Aaron's snake swallowed up the snakes of the Egyptians! So they needn't confess themselves beaten so soon. The Hebrews needn't despair of a good outcome. The Pharaoh will now certainly let them go.

But the heart of the Pharaoh was hardened. He didn't listen.

53

PASSOVER

EXODUS 7-12

'Moses,' said God, 'go to the Nile in the morning, at the time when the Pharaoh usually goes there, and tell him: "Thus says the Lord, let my people go!" Then make Aaron stretch out his staff over the water of the river and strike it. It will turn to blood. The fish will die. The Nile will stink.'

So it happened. 'Let my people go!' cried Moses, but the king paid no attention to his words. Aaron stretched his staff over the water and struck it. 'Look, your holy river is red with blood; it stinks here, your majesty, it stinks.'

The Nile, Egypt's lifeline, the land's cash flow, stinks. There's blood in it, the whole land is unclean. But the Pharaoh had no eyes to see it and hardened his heart.

The land had an invasion of frogs. The classic symbols of unclean thoughts and evil spirits. Town and country teemed with the frogs; people even found them in their beds and baking troughs. But when the pestilence disappeared, the ruler persisted in refusing to let the Israelites go.

One catastrophe after another happened, but the king wouldn't yield. An endless struggle. A fight over ten rounds.

A plague of lice tormented human beings and animals. 'This is the finger of God' was the verdict of the government's advisory committee, but the government chose to ignore it and refused to give in.

Swarms of flies struck. 'All right,' the king then said to Moses, 'you may offer your sacrifices to your God. But not too far from here, not three days' journey away.' However, hardly had the flies flown away than the Pharaoh broke his promise.

A cattle plague breaks out. Even the king's servants are infected with boils and sores. Nature gets out of balance: hail and lightning beat down all the vegetation. Trees are felled and animals fall to the ground dead. 'I have sinned,' confesses the Pharaoh. 'God's thunderbolts are too powerful for me. Make this violence cease! You may go.' But as soon as the hail and the thunder stop, the king once again breaks his promise and is just as immovable as before.

It's high time for the eighth plague: whatever vegetation is still left after the hail and the lightning is now consumed by armies of locusts. In a weak moment the Pharaoh is again ready to make a small concession: only the men may go. Isn't worship a man's business?

Now Moses has no ears to hear.

A ninth plague is unavoidable: the powers of darkness seize Egypt, and for three days and three nights the land is shrouded in deep darkness. The king still will not yield. He's really determined to win this battle, for the word of God is an abomination to him and he arms himself against it. To listen to that word would mean the end of his reign. So it was really the word of God that hardened his heart. Moreover that's what the narrator says: *God hardened his heart.*

'Out of my sight, Moses!' he cries. 'And make sure that you never see my face again!'

'I certainly will, your majesty. My people and I, we want to get out of your sight. I shall never see your face again!'

Moses knows that the tenth round will bring the decision. Now blood will flow. Not only has the present been ruined; now the future will be taken away. If the Pharaoh doesn't let Israel, God's firstborn, live, there will be no life for Pharaoh's firstborn. *Thus says the Lord: at midnight every firstborn in Egypt will die, from the firstborn son of the king in the palace to the firstborn of the slave girl behind the mill, and all the firstborn of cattle.*

Without the firstborn, there is no future.

'Aaron,' said Moses, 'tonight's the night. This won't be a night like any other night. Let every family slaughter a lamb and smear the blood on the doorposts and the lintels of the houses, so that the Eternal One passes by those doors when he comes to strike Egypt's firstborn. We shall not go to bed. With loins girded, with shoes on our feet and staves in our hands, we shall stand ready to depart. There will be no time to let the bread rise; we shall eat unleavened bread. And herbs, bitter herbs.'

The blood of a lamb is smeared on doorpost and lintel, so that the Eternal One will pass by that door. *Pesach* in Hebrew. Passover. Thus Moses taught his people a great secret. The innocent lamb who does not resist is the age-old symbol of surrender. By sacrificing the lamb, the Israelites turn their self-surrender into a ritual and submit to God's purposes.

Night falls. They all wait, loins girded, shoes on their feet, staves in their hands. That night death haunted Egypt. The firstborn of the king in the palace died, the firstborn of the slave girl behind the mill died, and the firstborn of the cattle died. One great cry of mourning rose from the land; there was no Egyptian dwelling where no one was mourning to their dead. However, death passed by the houses of the Hebrews.

A gruesome story. Could it be that the Egyptians were killed by God himself because they did evil to his people? The same reprehensible thought lives on to the present day. Tribes of those who see themselves as God's own people – *Dieu le veut, Gott mit uns, with God on our side* – still make short shrift of those who oppose them.

Does the narrator know of cruel men who can only be stopped by violence?

Is this the sweet revenge of which fairy tales tell, and which children, large and small, so shiver at with pleasure, because the wicked get their deserts and the good live happily ever after?

Death haunted Egypt. 'Let the Hebrews go, in heaven's name let them go!,' cried the Pharaoh. He even gave them the country's silver and gold in the hope of gaining the favour of this people and its God.

The doors of the houses and the stables opened and one by one they came out, into the bright light of the full moon: the men, the women, the children and the animals. An odd bunch of people also appeared that night, people who had been just as wretched as the Hebrews and who could come and take refuge under the wings of the God of Israel. It was a colourful band.

'Don't forget to tell your children later about the mystery of this night,' said Moses. 'Sabbath by sabbath initiate them into the mysteries of Passover. Every year you must commemorate this day, with unleavened bread and bitter herbs and fig mousse, which has the reddish-brown colour of the bricks that we had to bake for the Pharaoh when we were still slaves. And then describe above all how brightly the light shone on the night that our freedom beckoned. As in the beginning.'

54

GETTING THROUGH

EXODUS 13-15

And Moses took the bones of Joseph with him.

Joseph had asked for that before he died in exile: 'God will protect you and bring you up out of this land to the land which he promised Abraham, Isaac and Jacob. Then take my bones with you.'

How long has the dead Joseph lain there in his sarcophagus? Generations came, generations went, and he lay there waiting in his vault in the sand of Egypt. For the oppressed people it was as if the stones were speaking: 'God will protect you and bring you up out of this land.'

Now that's happening. Now they will go, the children of Abraham and Isaac, the sons of Jacob. The great journey is beginning. The doors of the vault are opened. Strong hands take up the coffin by the handles and reverently carry the dead man outside. 'Come with us, Joseph, the exile is over, we're going home.'

There they go. Through the night of doubt and sorrow the pilgrim band goes onward, and at the head of this band goes the master dreamer, who as he died dreamed of this future, and who though dead and buried continues to bear witness to it: 'Never forget, we do not live here, we live elsewhere, and one day God will bring us home.'

Moses took the bones of Joseph with him.

Why didn't they go northwards along the coast? In a few days' journey they could have reached the promised land. That would have been rather different from what now awaited them: forty years wandering through the wilderness. Why did God make the people turn round, in the direction of the Sea of Reeds?

'Well,' said Rabbi Joshua ben Levi, 'it's like a king who wanted to give his son his legacy. The son was still small, he couldn't yet even read and write. The king asked himself: if he gave everything to his son now, would he be able to cope with it? Better to wait until he's grown in strength and wisdom. And that's what God also thought. The children of Israel are really still children. First I want the Torah to be easy reading for them, so that they can do anything with the holy teaching. When they've grown up with the Torah, I shall give them the promised land.'

God makes his people turn round, along the way of the wilderness. This way isn't on the map. Our story is about the journey of faith in all times, about a journey which people must constantly undertake afresh, about the way which leads from Egypt to freedom. It's a long way, through inhospitable territory.

It's a while before you dare take the first step, and after that you need time finally to find your destination. First you spend a long time negotiating with the Pharaoh, since you can't just go. And do you want to go anyway? You virtuously ask permission, and you don't get it. Life becomes increasingly hard to bear, but fear holds you captive; you know what you have, but not what you're going to get. You feel too weak to set out, and the king and the queen don't think that's a good thing either. You'd like to go, but preferably not without their consent. You try to find a compromise between the lure of freedom and fear of the people around you. But as long as you keep asking them for their consent and thus acknowledge their power, you don't listen to the Voice that's calling you to go. You know that you must set out, but you still don't have the courage to go. You become a pest to others and a pest to yourself. Then, at long last, the Pharaoh too thinks that it's time for you to go.

You go. At last you can go. Perhaps you breathe a sigh of relief and go out along the Lord's ways with a grateful heart. You're finally rescued from the Pharaoh, and you can only see this as the grace of God. You feel you've got support. A pillar of cloud accompanies you by day, and a pillar of fire by night,

Until you make a shocking discovery. For it seems that you haven't completely escaped the Pharaoh and his minions. They aren't just going to let you go; they're pursuing you with all the means at their disposal. You've barely taken a few steps in your own life than they're out to find you and to bring you back by force: *The Egyptians, all the horses and chariots of the Pharaoh, his cavalry and his army, pursued the Israelites while they were camped by the sea.*

There you are, then. Behind you is the enemy, before you the water.

You're hemmed in on all sides. It's clear that the whole expedition is doomed to failure. You should never have set out. *'Were there no graves in Egypt, Moses, that you have brought us here to die in the wilderness? Look, we have said it already, leave us in peace. Surely it is better to serve the Egyptians than to die in the wilderness.'*

They were trapped. They thought that they were free. Now they're trapped again. They can't go back and they can't go forward. 'O God!'

'Moses, tell the Israelites to go forward.'

Go forward? But the sea's there! So they can go forward only in great confidence that a path will appear where there is no path, and that where we simply see death and destruction the way to life will open before us.

'Moses, go forward. Raise your staff and stretch out your hand over the sea.'

Moses raised his staff, stretched out his hand over the sea, and a strong east wind cleft the water.

That's the breath of God, that wind from the east.

And look, there was a path through the midst of the sea, on dry land! The water of which they had been so afraid became a wall and a protection to them on the left hand and on the right.

So they went forward, behind Moses, step by step. They would never have managed without Moses, the prophet who trusted that if God wills to be the helper of those who have no helper, he will also find ways where there are no ways. 'Come with me,' cried Moses. 'The God who gives the winds their courses and points the clouds their way will also find ways along which your feet can go. Come with me.'

They went. Afterwards the people would say: 'It was a miracle that we went and it was a miracle that we made it. We saw no way out, but we reached the other side safely. We would never have made it in our own strength. God saved the day. And our pursuers? We never saw them again!'

Sunk in oblivion. The Pharaoh and his soldiers, the horses, the chariots, the wheels of all that mighty apparatus of power, got stuck, collapsing under their own weight, and were swallowed up by the waves. Nothing remained of them.

Liberated from the Pharaoh and his armed forces, having escaped death, Moses and the Israelites sang a song:

Praise the Lord, for he is highly exalted,
the horse and its rider he cast into the sea.

and Miriam, Moses' sister, struck the tambourine, while the women followed her in a dance:

Praise the Lord, for he is highly exalted,
the horse and its rider he cast into the sea.

Thus this Passover story ends as it began.

It began with Moses' birth, with Moses' mother and the midwives who respected life. It began with Miriam, who collaborated so bravely, and with Moses' miraculous rescue from the water by Pharaoh's daughter.

And now at the end of the story, now that all the people have gone through the straits and have been born from the water, Miriam strikes her tambourine. In gratitude for this miraculous rescue the women dance and sing their song of freedom.

55

MANNA IN THE WILDERNESS

EXODUS 15 AND 16, NUMBERS 11

Praise the Lord, for he is highly exalted,
the horse and its rider he cast into the sea.

The joy of their regained freedom is short-lived. The song soon falls silent, and new anxieties arise. What now? Liberation doesn't just liberate but also brings burdens. There are no well-trodden roads in the wilderness. Who will show the way? The people hesitate. Go? Where? What do you live on in that barren desert? Can God make meals there? Isn't a house of slavery preferable to death? What can Moses promise this people but toil: blood, sweat and tears?

'I taught Israel to walk,' God would later say through the mouth of a prophet. But it took a long time for Israel to make much progress, since it constantly stumbled, and when things got difficult it wanted to go back, back to the time when it didn't yet need to stand on its own feet.

Israel ends up in *Marah*. The word says it all. It's a *bitter* place, half-way between Egypt and Elim, somewhere between slavery and freedom. It's where human life is often lived: no longer in the slavery of Egypt and not yet in the paradise of Elim. There in Elim are twelve wells of water, one for each of the tribes of Israel, and there are seventy palm trees, giving shade for the seventy peoples of the world. That's still in the future. Or does Elim exist only in the imagination of Moses and his people? There in Marah, that bitter place, where you can choose between dying of thirst and being killed from polluted water, are they only half-way towards being wise?

'Give us a drink, Moses. Give us a drink,' the people cried.

'Give us a drink, God. Give us a drink,' Moses cried.

God showed Moses a piece of wood. Moses picked it up and threw it into the water. The water became sweet.

A nice miracle. Is the narrator speaking of his faith? Does he want to tell us that when life tastes bitter to us and we turn to God, a miracle can happen and life loses its bitterness?

God showed Moses a piece of wood. God showed. Where are they to go in the wilderness unless God shows the way? How do you get from Marah to Elim without God's holy instructions? People can't live in the barren desert without water. In the wilderness of life the word of God gives life.

So the Eternal One taught Israel to walk. And Israel drank God's sweet instruction and sang of this gift in a song: *Your word is as honey in our mouth.**

Until this song, too, fell silent. For gradually the children of Israel lost courage for the umpteenth time; again their faith was in trouble. The journey is lasting so long, so endlessly long. Day after day they drag on. When will they finally get there? And where is God? They begin to fear that God isn't anywhere. And they themselves haven't got anywhere, so they involuntarily think of the past. The life of a slave was truly no fun, but this emptiness and uncertainty are quite unbearable. '*Why do we have to endure all this? Oh, if only we had died when we were in Egypt, in the fleshpots there!*'

The present is so harsh, the future so uncertain, that the people begin to idealize the past: fleshpots! The good old days! In their bizarre imagination even a house of slavery is transformed into a paradise: 'In Egypt we had fish and cucumbers and melons, leeks and onions and garlic, for nothing. Of course things were difficult there, but there were no shortages. Just try to get such things now.'

A well-known scene: the tension between the need of the moment and the uncertain prospect, the eternal clash between the prophet's dedication and the people's need of bread. The wilderness is a long school.

How will it all work out? Perhaps it will take a whole new generation before the period of the Pharaoh can really be closed. So much fear. So much pent-up sorrow. So many wounds that will never heal. The way seems endless. It could take forty years. A whole human life.

'O God,' says Moses, 'if only they had a little trust.'

'As you say,' says God, 'if only they had a little trust. But I will refresh them, Moses, with heavenly gifts, in the heart of the wilderness. Say to the people, in the evening you shall eat meat and in the morning you will be filled with bread.'

That evening quails flew in from on high and covered the camp. That morning the wilderness was covered with something flaky, as fine as frozen dew.

'*Man hu?*' asked the people. '*What is that?*' For they didn't know what it was. '*Man hu?*'

'This is bread from God,' said Moses.

The people called the bread from heaven *manna*. The manna was as sweet as honey.

So their hunger was assuaged and their thirst was quenched.

A prosaic person might ask, 'Where did they get all this from?' And a prosaic person might reply, 'Oh, it's a kind of wood that can neutralize the bitter taste of water. Quails are migratory birds which can easily be caught after a long flight over the sea. Manna is a grain of honey which insects form on the tamarisk.'

But this story isn't about what happened. It's about how this people interpreted what happened. According to Moses and the people, what happened here pointed beyond itself.

'Let's thank God,' said Moses. 'Didn't we receive all this from his hand?'

Moses impressed on the people that they should gather no more than they needed for that day: no less and no more. Then there would be enough for everyone. In this way there would be no needy people in Israel, far less any who were excessively rich. No manna might be kept for the next day.

Of course there were those who couldn't summon up so much trust. By the next day their manna swarmed with maggots and stank, as a judgment on them. Moses was angry. 'Give us today our daily bread. Surely a pilgrim doesn't need any more on the way?'

Moses also added a profound thought: 'In order to become practised in God's service and not to lose sight of what this grace from on high has brought us, on one day of the week we must stop and think about all this. On the sixth day we shall gather a double portion. It will not go bad on the seventh day. On that day we celebrate the sabbath, an oasis in time. Then we shall rest from our work. Then we shall fold our hands on our laps. For man shall not live by bread alone but also by the word that comes forth from this bread. Let God's Torah be our special spiritual food on that day. Like honey in our mouths.'

56

WATER FROM THE ROCKS

EXODUS 17.1-7

> *When Israel came out of Egypt,*
> *Jacob's house from a people with a strange language,*
> *Judah became his sanctuary,*
> *Israel his dominion.*

The author of this song* can see it before his eyes, how Israel went out of Egypt. 'You must get away from there,' God had said . 'It's a land where life isn't good, where the strong oppress the weak. They speak *a strange language* there. Not a language after my heart. Get away from there, Israel! I will teach you a new language.'

So they went, one fine night, the men, women and children of the house of Jacob, together with all kinds of stray people who also had little to lose and who joined them.

> *The sea saw that and fled,*
> *Jordan was driven back,*
> *the mountains leaped like rams,*
> *and the hills like lambs.*

Did you ever see the sea flee? Did you ever see a river flow backwards? Fleeing is something that you will never see the sea doing. Nor will rivers ever flow uphill.

But that's what our poet sees the sea doing. The water, the primal flood, made a way before Israel. And in the years and years of toiling through the sand, hadn't there constantly also been signs of God's goodness, glimpses of up above, which gave them the courage to endure things below? Afterwards the poet can say that no mountain was too high for them, no hill slope too long. The mountains sprang away before them like rams, and the hills like lambs. And when the Israelites had finally reached the promised land, with only the Jordan still before them, the river turned back upon itself.

This is high humour: the poetry of faith in the language of the land. Surrounded by death, our poet in Judah strikes up a Passover song. He knows sorrow and anxiety, but that doesn't prevent him from putting his hand on the strings and striking up a song of liberation. He knows about the sea; he knows how deep the water of death is and how high the mountains are to a small and insignificant human being. But those who do not believe in miracles are no realists, and do an injustice to the God who has also given the children of Israel so many signs of his presence.

The sea and the river, the mountains and the hills, give way before Israel. It's as if they feel that in this strange people which has been raked together, from now on all peoples are moving towards redemption. As if they sense that this is God's own motley crew and that the Eternal One wants to show in this one handful what is happening to the whole human family.

All right, they are and remain cowards. They complain, they murmur, they daren't really believe, they want to go back. The children of Abraham are no people to be proud of. But that doesn't alter the fact that they're the apple of God's eye. And every new generation that's added to them in this procession through time and through the lands may know that they too are God's elect. Every generation must again come out of Egypt. All individuals may know that despite their anxieties and their lack of faith, their failures and their falls, their insignificance in this great universe, they may join in this great journey. And one day they will get home. One day this whole world will get home. Then a new song will be sung in a new language. There will be a new earth.

And the 'old' earth, the sea and the rivers, the hills and the mountains, they know that that is going to happen. They feel that everything will be different.

> Tremble, O earth, at the presence of the Lord,
> at the presence of the God of Jacob,
> who turns the rock into a pool of water,
> the flint into a spring of water.

You can't talk more boldly than that! As if he's God himself, the poet

commands the whole earth: '*Tremble, O earth, at the presence of the Lord!*'
Rivers and seas, hills and mountains, must move before the face of the
Lord, who changes a rock into a pool of water, a flintstone into a spring of
water.

Our poet knows about this. How they went through the wilderness and
got thirsty and there was no water. 'Give us water, Moses, so that we can
drink! Why have you led us out of Egypt? Surely not to let us and our
children and our flocks perish of thirst here? Is the Lord in our midst or
not?' It's one long lament.

It's all right to complain. Isn't the right to complain a sign of freedom?

A Russian Jew emigrated to Israel. 'What was it like in Russia?' people
asked him.

'I couldn't complain,' said the man.

'But what about the housing and the food, then?'

'O, I couldn't complain.'

'Then why have you come here?'

'Here, I can complain.'

'Moses, give us water! Is God in our midst or not?'

Time and again this fearful question. And Moses becomes so desperate
that he in turn begins to complain to God: 'O God, what must I do with
this people? Soon they're going to stone me.'

'Go out before the people, Moses, and take your staff with you. Go to
the rock by the mountain. I shall stand before you. Then strike the rock
with your staff. Water will stream out so that the people can drink.'

And so it happened.

Because that's what God is like. Doesn't he look upon the humiliated and
the oppressed? Don't those who were imprisoned in the shadow of death
see freedom dawning? Doesn't he make a people which is in itself barren
pregnant with salvation?

In other words, from a rock in the wilderness – and what in the world
is as dead as a rock in the wilderness? – he calls living water into existence.
It happens at the foot of the mountain where Moses is to receive the
ten commandments from God's hands. Values and words of life, which
quicken the soul of all those who hunger and thirst for righteousness.
Tremble, O earth, at the presence of the Lord!

A poet from a distant land, an anonymous singer, knows that water can flow from a rock. He dares to raise his voice against fate. He's no longer a slave. He's free. Free from the paganism of Egypt, which firmly believes that poor is poor, slave is slave, death is death. He believes otherwise and sings about it. He bears witness to the raging water and to the rocks of the mountains. He sings about them in a new language.

57

THE FIGHT AGAINST AMALEK

EXODUS 17. 8-16; DEUTERONOMY 25.17-19

Then came Amalek.

The story begins ominously. *Then came Amalek.* This man represents paganism. He's a son of Esau. In other words, the battle which now breaks out is not so much a battle between two generals, nor even a battle between two peoples, but a battle between two ideologies, like the Second World War. It's a life-and-death battle between what Israel stands for and what Amalek stands for. And again, it's about Israel as a notion rather than about Israel as a nation. We're not talking about just one episode from Israel's military history; the story is about a fight of all places and all times, and in Israel's pious fantasy it was also written down at the request of God himself.

When Hitler exclaimed in *Mein Kampf* that the conscience is a Jewish invention and then did everything possible to silence that conscience by silencing that people, Amalek had arisen again. For the narrator of centuries and centuries ago that was no surprise. He already prophesied: *The Lord will have war with Amalek from generation to generation.*

Then came Amalek. Moses has led his people out of the house of slavery. 'Go away from there,' God had said. And they went. With fear and trembling; the future was uncertain. But they went, and sang their song of liberation. Then came Amalek. He abhorred that song. He wanted to silence Israel. The song had to be stopped. He launched a surprise attack.

He attacked precisely where he knew that Israel was weakest, from behind. That's where the old men walk, the cripples, the sick, the mothers with small children. It's the height of cowardice, but that's precisely where he attacked, Amalek, who down the centuries has aimed at the defenceless. He's the embodiment of injustice in the world, godlessness incarnate, paganism in person, brim full of the urge to destroy. Therefore he also reacts immediately, as soon as Israel comes into the neighbourhood. He unfailingly notes that these are dangerous people with a dangerous conscience, whispered into their ears by a dangerous God. If this God has his say, all is up with Amalek's dominion. Therefore this God must be silenced. He must be silenced *in* his people. Then came Amalek.

And Moses said to Joshua: 'Choose for us men, and go out, fight with Amalek, tomorrow. I will stand on the top of the hill with the rod of God in my hand.'

Joshua chose his men and set out. And Moses climbed to the top of the hill with Aaron and Hur. Battle raged below. And when Moses raised his hands to God in faith, Israel had the upper hand. But when his trust in God declined and his self-confidence ebbed, his prayer weakened and his hands sank, Amalek had the upper hand.

Look, there he stands, the prophet who must go before his people upholding God and upholding the divine standard. With his staff in his hand, the staff of the good Shepherd, God's sceptre, he blesses the people. Lift high the banner! For as long as the banner is held high, Israel will survive. But when Moses becomes weary and doubt begins to nag, Amalek becomes stronger, Israel doesn't hold and they risk losing the battle.

How will it end? Moses is exhausted. The journey has lasted so long and the fight has lasted so long and the Amalekites are so numerous and so strong and he is so alone, his troop so small.

But no, he isn't alone. Two men stand by his side in priestly fashion, Aaron and Hur. They bring up a stone for the prophet to sit on. And they support his hands, one his right hand and the other his left, *so that Moses' hands were steady until the going down of the sun.*

High up on the hill top, as mediator between heaven and earth, Moses and his companions held high the banner of the Lord. His hands held firm in faith and the warriors held firm in faith and Amalek was defeated. Thus Israel conquered the paganism which wanted to bar the way to the future. Thank God. Again Israel sang its song of liberation, that old song which is always new.

The story can be read not only as a conflict between two ideologies, two life-styles, but also as an internal battle, for example in the often painful growth to adulthood. Then the battlefield is not somewhere on a map but takes place in one's own soul.

The way to our self-determination is often long and is always fraught with conflicts. We've detached ourselves and fought for some freedom; then suddenly we're attacked from behind by people or forces which seek to bar our way. The battle is exhausting; we begin to despair that all will end well; we're again tempted to give up the battle and return to 'Egypt'. For at least we know the life there, although we weren't free, and who says that we won't be stuck with this present life in the wilderness? Who says that we will ever reach the promised land? Courage sinks, as the arms of Moses sank. But if this side, the side of trust in God and trust in ourselves, let's say this Moses side, gives in, then our other side, our Joshua side, which fights at the front, will collapse impotently. In the battle against Amalek the only thing that helps us is trust that God is calling us as his children to live in freedom.

A Hasidic legend* tells how Rabbi Phinehas of Koretz, overcome by doubt and afraid that he would yield completely to temptation, travelled from Koretz to Medziboz to ask help from the Baal Shem Tov, the Master of the Good Name, there. But the Baal Shem Tov had just travelled to… Koretz. Rabbi Phinehas hastened back and rushed to the inn where the Baal Shem Tov was receiving his disciples. They were occupied in reading, in the Torah, the story of Moses resisting the attack of Amalek with arms outstretched. 'Moses fought through prayer, in prayer,' said the Baal Shem Tov. 'It can happen that someone sees his faith tottering. What is the only thing that he can do then? He turns to heaven, lifts up his arms and prays God to give him back his faith. That is what he does. That is what he must do.'

Rabbi Phinehas of Koretz understood that the Baal Shem Tov had him in mind.

The Lord God said to Moses: *'Write this as a memorial in a book and impress it on Joshua, that I will utterly blot out the remembrance of Amalek from under heaven.'*

That's the way it is. Israel isn't wiped out. Amalek is wiped out. This paganism ultimately has no future. It cannot be and it will not be. If it's up to the narrator, the God who frees the oppressed will never make a deal with the oppressor. The evildoer must repent, otherwise he must disappear. That's the way it is.

But in the meantime he hasn't yet disappeared. Moses called this place *The Lord is my banner* when he built an altar on the hilltop as a thanksgiving for the freedom that had been regained. But he said prophetically: *The Lord will have war with Amalek from generation to generation.*

Amalek hasn't yet disappeared. Time and again he crops up, and time and again his target is the weak: women, children, the sick, all those who are left behind in life. Write it down and stamp it on your mind, for the battle isn't over yet: the tyrant constantly rises from the dead. Then you must go to battle and hold God's banner high. From generation to generation.

58

COVENANT

EXODUS 19 AND 24

Israel pitched its tents over against Mount Sinai.

Once Moses had looked after the flocks of his father-in-law Jethro, priest of Midian, here. Now he is leading his people through the mountainous country. God's flock. Once Moses had received his calling here: *'I am with you, Moses. Lead my people out of Egypt. Then you shall serve me on this mountain.'* And here they are.

Jethro heard that Moses was approaching with his people and ran quickly to Zipporah's tent. Evidently Moses had let her and her two sons return to Midian some time ago. Now they are to be reunited there. 'Come, Zipporah, let's hasten to meet them.'

Moses put his arms around them, Zipporah, Gershom and Eliezer. Father Jethro was delighted at all the good things that God had given Israel; he made a burnt offering to Israel's God, and Aaron and the elders of the people met to have a meal with the priest of Midian before the face of the Lord.

The next day Moses held a session to pronounce law for the people. From early morning until late evening he gave legal judgments, so great was the throng of people who wanted a decision on a dispute. 'That isn't good, Moses,' said Jethro, when he saw how weary Moses was when he returned to his tent that evening. 'It isn't good for you and it isn't good for the people. You must appoint judges, incorruptible people, to pronounce law in the lesser cases. Then people will turn to you for the big and complicated cases.'

Moses took the words of father Jethro to heart, grateful that he had allowed him to share in a settled people's experience of government. The rabbis indicate that this should make the children of Israel modest once and for all: Israel's election doesn't mean that it has more understanding and insight than the rest of the world.

Israel pitched its tents over against the mountain.

A mountain is *the* place for meeting God. There are peak experiences which human beings can describe to some degree only in lofty, exalted imagery. Those who are 'in the clouds' are close to God. A mortal cannot get closer to the Eternal One than on a mountain top.

Israel pitched its tents over against the mountain and Moses climbed up. 'Here I am, Lord, with my people. Your people. We've escaped the tyranny and we're experiencing our deliverance as a gift from you. We don't know how to thank you.'

But God knows what they should do. 'Moses, say to the Israelites: I the Lord have borne you up on eagles' wings. Now, if you heed my voice and keep my covenant, you shall be my possession out of all peoples. Let Israel be a kingdom of priests, a holy people, set apart, hallowed, for the sake of all peoples. The children of Israel could not give me a finer gift.'

Moses went down and told the people what God had said. Then he climbed up again to bring the words of the people to God: 'All that you have said, we shall do.'

'That's good news,' said God. 'Now go down and get the people to prepare themselves, for I shall speak to them. I shall make a covenant with them. With ten words I created heaven and earth. With ten plagues I liberated you from Egypt. Now I shall give you ten words which will point your way to the promised land and which you must carry to the ends of the earth. Go down, Moses, and tell the people to make themselves ready. On the third day we shall make a covenant.'

Moses went down the mountain again. Israel's shepherd. God's own go-between.

No one has ever seen God. How could mortal eyes look on the Eternal One, Creator of heaven and earth? Israel speaks about God only in awe. God is the wholly Other. The Eternal One dwells behind the clouds. When he descends, the mountains quake, the thunder thunders, the lightning lightens. You see smoke, consuming fire. The sound of the heavenly trumpet is echoed a thousandfold by the rocks. What can an insignificant mortal do but keep a respectful distance?

But God isn't unapproachable. The great Moses may go above. The story goes that Moses met God there. God doesn't want to be a God without human beings. Nor does he want human beings to be godless. So he made a covenant with Israel.

On the third day the covenant is made, at the foot of the mountain. Moses built an altar there with twelve stones. Twelve stones, one altar, one God. Twelve tribes, one people. Animals were offered there. Moses sprinkled half the blood, the symbol of life, on the altar. This half of the blood was for God. Moses sprinkled the other half of the blood on the people. From now on God and human beings are bound together by bonds of blood. They are blood relations. And what God and his friend Moses have joined together, let no one put asunder.

Moses again climbed the mountain, now accompanied by the elders of Israel, seventy in number. For there are seventy peoples on earth, and what happens here concerns all of them. The words of God are intended for the whole *erets*. All *goyim* are represented in Israel's elders.

Through the thick clouds, hanging low, they climbed the mountain until suddenly the cloud-cover gave way and they looked upon an azure heaven. And in the glory of this scene they looked upon God himself. It was as if they were seeing the Invisible. *And they saw the God of Israel.*

Usually Israel emphasizes God's invisibility, but not here. *They saw God.* But when they go on to describe *what* they saw, they don't get very far. There isn't a word about the Lord's face, or about his form. They simply stammer something about… his feet. *And it was as though under his feet there was a pavement of sapphire stone, like the very heaven for clearness.*

One could say that in that case they didn't see God. They saw only his feet. They prostrated themselves before God's face in worship and saw no more than the footstool of his throne.

But how else could it be? We never see more of God's glory than the little bit immediately before us. We can't take in more than a fragment even of purely *earthly* rapture. However, for Moses and the seventy this one unearthly fragment bears within it *all* the glory: *like the very heaven for clearness.* They saw only the footstool of his feet, but that was already so majestic, so radiant, so all-embracing a nearness that, as though it were a miracle, something has to be added: *and they remained unharmed.*

Down below the people are waiting. Will the elders be able to tell them what God looks like?

Once they have come down, the elders can only stammer a few lines.

After that words fail. God doesn't correspond to anything that can be found on earth.

> *Who, enthroned so high,*
> *so deep in unfathomable light,*
> *measured neither by time nor eternity,*
> *nor by length nor weight,*
> *exists by himself, no outside support,*
> *but rests upon himself..*
> *Who is it? Can he be named, described,*
> *by the pen of a seraphim,*
> *or do words and voice fail us?**

The elders can say no more than that his feet rest on pure light and that what is dark for us is transparent for him, pure and clear. They also say that no one needs to be afraid of him. God isn't out to destroy frail human beings. They remain unharmed. God wants to deal with human beings as intimately as a mother with her child, as a man with his friend. *They looked upon God and they ate and drank.* They had a meal, as a seal of the covenant.

The Bible often tells of such meals. Jesus and his friends held such a meal, the seal of an old covenant, shortly before his death. *'This cup is the new covenant in my blood.'*

    On the third day, the story goes, it dawned on his friends that God had brought him home. It put his life and death in another light. And they stammered something like, 'We have seen God.' For they believed that they had seen a human being in whom God's feet had rested on earth and in whom the Eternal One had himself walked among human beings.

59

THE TEN WORDS

EXODUS 20; DEUTERONOMY 5

Moses came down from God's mountain, carefully bearing the two stone tablets on which the words of the Eternal One were engraved. Ten words to point the way through inhospitable and unknown territory to the land of promise.

The Torah: a guideline which with a few strokes portrays life and life with God, as God had envisaged it. At least, that's how Israel saw it. Moses and his helpers compiled ten rules to live by, recording as carefully as possible the noblest attainments of their own and other cultures.

Tradition has it that this was a creation from Israel's years in the wilderness. That's by no means a strange idea; after all, the journey through the wilderness is *the* school for a searching soul. And its most important fruit, for then and for all generations to come, is the Torah. You shall, you shall; you shall not, you shall not. That's both an imperative and a future, both command and promise. One day you shall, believe me, arrive in a land where the lie no longer prevails, where death no longer reigns, where parents and children, slaves and free, human beings and animals live together in peace – one day you will experience that. And, on your way there, you shall act accordingly. You have to.

Words for life.

I am the Lord your God who brought you out of the land of Egypt, out of the house of bondage.

That's the heading. The first word speaks of God's liberating love. Sheep won't follow a stranger; they don't recognize his voice. They will follow the shepherd, who knows the sheep and calls them by name. He leads them out and goes before them.

You shall have no other gods before my face. You shall not make for yourself a graven image... you shall not bow down to them or serve them. For I, the Lord your God, am a jealous God, visiting the iniquities of the fathers upon the children to the third or fourth generation of those who hate me, but showing steadfast love to thousands of those who love me and keep my commandments.

I have freed you and borne you up on eagles' wings. I am with you. Trust in me. Stand in freedom. Do not seek refuge in other gods. Stay with your Liberator, don't get entangled again in forms of slavery. You can't serve two masters. I can't bear it when you commit adultery with another god: the god of money, the god of the belly, the god of nationalism. I can't watch you eyeing those gods. Because I love you. I'm a jealous lover.

Never underestimate evil, because it spreads like ripples in a pond. It multiplies for generations; you know that, don't you? Even the child as yet unborn must finally live with the consequences of what you do, and what you leave undone. Love me, and me alone. Do good. Remember, the good you do will multiply a thousandfold. The child as yet unborn will share in that blessing as well.

You shall not take the name of the Lord your God in vain.

No word is so misused as the little word 'God'. Don't misuse God's name. Don't try to involve God in things he doesn't want to be involved in. Don't try to use God for your own ends. Hallowed be his name.

Remember the sabbath day, to keep it holy. Six days you shall labour, but the seventh day is the sabbath of the Lord your God. On it you shall do no work, neither you, nor your son, nor your daughter, nor your slave nor your serving maid, nor your cattle, nor the stranger who is within your gates. For in six days God made heaven and earth, the sea and all that is in it, and he rested the seventh day. Remember also that you were slaves in Egypt, and that the Lord your God delivered you from there by his strong arm.

The sabbath. One of Israel's most original and most precious gifts to humankind. Remember the sabbath. For in the beginning the powers of chaos were conquered, the waters were placed within bounds, space was created in which to live. So celebrate life. Don't live to work, work to live.

Remember the sabbath. Because you were set free from Egypt. Don't let yourself be enslaved again. Be careful not to let yourself be drawn into new bondage. Celebrate your freedom. Let your fellow creatures share in it. The animals, too. Let there be one day on which kings and slaves, citizens and strangers, are all equal. That day belongs to God. Honour that day. Enjoy it.

Honour your father and your mother, that your days may be long in the land which the Lord God shall give you.

Each individual is a precious link in the chain of generations. If parents hand down God's liberating acts, in stories and deeds, and if children take that tradition to heart and pass it along to their own children in turn, then the land where the living is good comes close.

You shall not murder.

Murder was a capital offence in Israel. So we don't read: you shall not kill. Sometimes killing is inevitable. According to a saying of Rabbi Eleazar, a Sanhedrin that passes the death sentence once every seventy years can still rightly be called council of blood.

But far be it from you to take the law into in your own hands. Respect all life. Live carefully. Drive carefully.

You shall not commit adultery.

'Divorce' was allowed in Israel. In other words, in those days, a man was allowed to repudiate his wife. Divorce as a carefully considered decision on the part of two adults was unknown. Breaking into someone else's marriage is another matter. You shall not do that. It tears things apart.

You shall not steal.

You shall not grow rich at the expense of a fellow human being. You shall not treat your neighbours like merchandise. Respect their bodies, their property, their ideas. Blessed are the poor. Own as if you owned nothing. Better to err on the side of generosity than on the side of avarice. You shall give, and keep giving.

You shall not bear false witness against your neighbour.

Be trustworthy. Don't slander. Don't tell lies about others. But if the truth endangers your neighbour, don't tell the truth.

You shall not covet your neighbour's wife, your neighbour's house, or his field, or his manservant, or his maidservant, his ox, his ass, or anything that is your neighbour's.

Rein in your greed. And that applies not only to your actions, but also to your thoughts.

All the people witnessed the thunderings and the lightnings and the sound of the trumpet and the mountain smoking. The people saw it and trembled and stood afar off.
    The people trembled. Just as the flame in a lamp trembles and is in constant movement, so the souls of the children of Israel are set in constant motion by God's words, the holy Torah.

Ten words. Once every year the children of Israel commemorate this gift of God. On *Simchat Torah*: Joy in the Torah. Then they take the scrolls of the law from the ark in the synagogue and dance round with them, like a bridegroom dancing with his beloved. It's a dance with the source of life, with the symbol of eternity. Never believe, little human being, that you're all alone, orphaned and stranded in this boundless universe. This world is God's world.

> *How wonderful is the word of your covenant;*
> *how lovely is the sound of the Torah in our ears.*
> *Yes, it is like honey in my mouth,*
> *I receive insight by listening to it.**

The Torah, the sign of God's presence in our midst. Words given to us to live by, words brim full of promise. When the Messiah comes, he has to come on the day of *Simchat Torah.*

'Remember then, O Israel, how we were freed from Egypt. Remember the gift of God we received on Sinai.'
    We?

Yes, we. For it happened and it happens still. Each individual receives this gift of God in a highly personal way, on Sinai. The Hasidic rabbi Elimelech of Lisensk identified with this so strongly that he said: 'Not only do I still remember how all the Israelites gathered at the foot of the burning mountain, I even remember who was standing next to me.'*

60

CLEAN AND UNCLEAN

EXODUS 21, 22 AND 23; DEUTERONOMY 24 AND 26; LEVITICUS 11 AND 18

Of course ten words are far from sufficient to lay down the rights and the obligations of the people of God. Moreover our story continues with a large number of rules which must be observed in dealings between people. These rules bear the stamp of the time and culture in which they arose; of the *several* cultures in which they arose, for we already see the legislation developing *in* biblical times.

Many rules of that time are now antiquated, just as many present-day rules will soon be antiquated. *Anyone who strikes his elderly father or mother shall indeed be put to death. If an ox gores a man or a woman so that they die, the ox shall indeed be stoned.* We're flabbergasted at these words. The death penalty also applied to homosexuality, so afraid people were in those days of what was then a dark and therefore threatening phenomenon. It was to be centuries before another view of homosexuality developed. We still have the death penalty.

The letter of the law kills, the spirit brings life.* Therefore we must continue to seek the spirit of the law which is handed down to us, and distance ourselves from the laws which in fact simply feed our own anxieties and our bad points.

If you buy a Hebrew slave, he shall serve six years, and in the seventh year he shall depart as a free man, for nothing.

If the first of the Ten Words was about liberation from slavery, the first rule of law is about Hebrew slavery for debt: when someone who has to serve as a slave because of his own debts or those of his parents. But there's a limit to this: just as every seventh day is a day of freedom for free men and women and slaves, so every seventh year shall be a sabbath year in which slaves rediscover their freedom. This regulation applied only to Hebrew slavery for debt in the case of males, but at least it was a beginning, and thus a principle. It is incomprehensible and an eternal sin that it took so long for this principle to be generally recognized in the world.

But one mustn't deal arbitrarily with women, girls and slave-girls either. Special care is to be taken of widows and orphans. If you lend money to a poor man, don't charge him any interest. You mustn't hand over a foreign runaway slave to his master. A creditor may not enter the house of a debtor to take away a pledge. He must stand outside and wait for the pledge to be brought to him. If you take the garment of a poor man as a pledge, you must return it before sunset, so that he can sleep in it. You must also respect the foreigner within your gates. Weren't you yourselves foreigners in Egypt? Well, you know how that feels!

The poor, the weak, the least are precious in God's eyes. Just as the earth isn't yours, for the earth is the Lord's, so too no person belongs to you. Every human being belongs to the Lord. *And anyone who saves one person, saves the world.**

So break through the circle of evil in which you're imprisoned. Restrain vengeance! What did Lamech, that vengeful avenger, once say? He would wreak bloody vengeance seventy-seven times: he would kill a man *even if that man had only wounded him*; he would kill a child *just for a blow*.

'Let it not be like that with you,' said God: '*You shall give an eye for an eye, a tooth for a tooth, a wound for a wound, a blow for a blow, but no more.*' You may not take unlimited revenge for a past injustice. Even a criminal has a right to protection. Of course the guilty must make good the damage that they've done. But the punishment must be in proportion to the suffering inflicted. So don't give two blows in retaliation for one blow, or take two eyes for one eye, two tongues for one tongue. No, it must be an eye for an eye, a tooth for a tooth. Only then will the disturbed balance be restored. Only then can there be peace again. The Hebrew word for recompense, *shillam*, comes from the same family as the word *shalom*. If it's good, recompense brings peace to both parties.

No person may be oppressed, no animal maltreated. You must also treat your field and your vineyard with respect. *The earth is the Lord's.* Let the whole of creation share in the holy rhythms. You may cultivate your land for six years, but on the seventh year grant your fields a sabbath rest. The crops that grow on the fallow ground shall be for the poor and for the beasts of the field.

The earth is the Lord's and all its fullness. As a sign of that, bring the firstfruits of the harvest to the sanctuary. Give the basket of firstfruits to the priest and say: '*A wandering Aramaean was my father. He went down into Egypt and sojourned there, few in number; and there he became a people, great and mighty. When the Egyptians oppressed us, God saw our misery and oppression and led us out of Egypt with a strong hand. He gave us this land, flowing with milk and honey. And now, look, I bring the first produce of the fruit of the land which you, Lord, have given me.*'

And above all, my people, don't forget that there's a difference between clean and unclean. Only animals with split hoofs which chew the cud are clean. For in this life you must distinguish carefully, always choosing between good and evil. There's a dividing line between clean and unclean. Animals which don't chew the cud are unclean. You must never just swallow what's in front of you, whether it's been put there by someone else or you've put it there yourself. You must always reflect on things and take in what has been given to you by God. If you want to keep the words of God, then always ponder them in your heart.

You may eat the fish in the seas and rivers which have fins and scales. Keep off the fish without fins and scales, which are like snakes.

As for the birds, keep off those which fly around at night. Look out also for the birds which hover high in the bright sunlight, suddenly to swoop unexpectedly on their defenceless prey. Keep off the buzzard, it's hovering for its prey. Always remember that the high flight of human idealism can suddenly turn into abuse of power and cruel violence.

However, we must be careful about finding a rational explanation for the food laws and the laws about the holy times of feasts and fasts. These explanations are highly speculative and overlook the significance of the regulations. At the deepest level the laws serve only one purpose: they aim to keep people's attention on God from sunrise to sunset. They seek to remind people from hour to hour that they must not just live, but that limits are imposed on them; that they're only stewards on earth and that there's a difference between clean and unclean.

That has never been put more attractively than by Abel Herzberg* in a story about Labi, a schoolmaster from Benghazi, in North Africa. The Germans had transported him to Bergen-Belsen. He looked as if he'd been carried off from devastated Jerusalem by the general Titus in AD 70. Labi and his fellow-countrymen wore the same kind of clothes as their forefathers, had the same manners and customs, and literally the same faith.

And that faith prescribed for them that they might not eat particular kinds of food. So is it surprising that Labi, their schoolmaster, who was a young and very pious man, scorned the soup in the camp? In the soup from time to time there was a piece of horsemeat, and the eating of horsemeat is forbidden.

Of course the prohibitions are general, and never apply in circumstances when their observance endangers life or health. Naturally there were such circumstances in the camp, so all the food laws were abolished. Indeed it was forbidden to observe them for religious reasons, precisely because of the danger that they posed to life.

That applied to Europe, it applied to Africa, but it did not apply to a schoolmaster who had just come from burning Jerusalem. Labi lived by the law and would not budge an inch. Whether or not he died, he would not eat horsemeat.

Now of course one person will be prepared to give him a laurel wreath because of the heroism that he showed. A second, who comes from a more rationalistic world, will say: This is not heroism; this is fear or at least superstition, a taboo. A third will say: It's an obsession. We know from experience that people have to eat to live, but Labi is one of those people who set experience aside and believe that by *not* eating something they can mollify the deity and by doing precisely that will live. And a fourth will ask, 'What does Labi say?'

They ask him. For Labi is very fragile and graceful, and it would be a great sin if the horses also came to get Labi.

'Labi, why don't you eat any soup?'

But Labi refuses.

'Labi, if you don't eat, the horses will come and get you.'

And then Labi whispers, with an infinite melancholy and seriousness, as a confession to himself: 'Because there is a difference between clean and unclean!'

Now however stubborn an opponent of Labi and his stubbornness one may be, one cannot pass over such a statement in silence. For taboo or no taboo, obsession or trust in God, courage or superstition, Goebbels and his propaganda cannot say anything like that, and least of all the Führer of all the Germans.

There is a difference between clean and unclean, and we know, although perhaps Labi did not, that it is not about soup or horsemeat, which even Labi rejects only as a last symbol, but about the first principle of human civilization. It is about the recognition that some things are permissible and some are not.

And because of this first principle, which was once expressed by the Jewish people, or at least also because of it, Adolf Hitler hated the Jews and persecuted them and killed them. He was not the first here, and he will not be the last.

There are no clean and unclean people – of course, in principle. There are no chosen peoples. But there are those who know of a dividing line between what is permitted and what is not, and people who not only do not know that but do not want to know it.

There is no peace between them.

61

THE TABERNACLE

EXODUS 20.24-26; 25.1-9; 26; 27.1-9; 30.17-21; 38.8; LEVITICUS 1; 8; 6-13

And they looked upon God and they ate and drank.

A scene from paradise, high on God's holy mountain. But how do you hold on to such a vision when you're back on the flat, on the treadmill of everyday life?

The Lord said to Moses: 'Tell the Israelites to make a collection. And let each give what his heart dictates: gold, silver, copper, purple and scarlet, fine linen, rams' skins, acacia wood, oil for the lamps, spices for the incense, onyx stones. They shall make me a sanctuary and I shall dwell in their midst. You shall make it precisely as I show you, the tabernacle and all its equipment.'

The children of Israel are going to build a sanctuary for God, as a copy of what they have seen and experienced on high: *God is in our midst.* We don't live unnoticed and unloved in a terrifying and silent universe. No, above, behind, under this world dwells the Invisible One, and it is his creation. There is a warmly beating heart behind and in our reality.

It's this faith that Moses and his people want to depict, preserve and celebrate in the dwelling that they build. There's a detailed description of the colours and materials, the precious stones and precious metals, of which the sanctuary is to be made. No number is random, no measure arbitrary, no image unconsidered. The beauty of creation must be confessed, depicted and celebrated here. That calls for scrupulous care over every detail; it calls for dedicated love, even for the smallest and simplest detail, by virtue of which the whole object exists. Isn't it the creation of the one whose glory fills the whole earth?

But how is it that this impoverished slave people is carrying all these valuables with them? No, they weren't rich, nor did they have sufficient knowledge in those days to work all these materials. Moreover this is a story from much later, from the time of the Babylonian exile.

In the wilderness the slave people will have had a simple tabernacle, a tent for God, a portable sanctuary. Later, once they had settled in Canaan, they built their temple in Jerusalem. Still later this temple was destroyed and the people was deported. Only then, by the rivers of Babylon, where the priests were pondering on then and now and a little while ago, was this story born. Far from home, the children of Israel think back, full of nostalgia, to the days of old. To the tabernacle in the wilderness, the temple in Jerusalem. They dream of it. They muse on how it was and how it could be again if God brings them home from their exile. Then they will build a new sanctuary, a new temple in which to meet God. For although the Invisible One doesn't dwell in a house made by human hands, and although God and human beings can meet one another everywhere, a holy place is quite indispensable for silence and prayer and for the holy times of the feasts of the faith. It's a place here below for holding fast the vision from on high.

Let each give what his heart dictates.

The tabernacle rose. Not on the rocky ground of the wilderness, but by the rivers of Babylon, in the spirit, in an attractive mixture of the fantasy of faith, precious memory and dreams of the future. It's one of Israel's most beautiful and most mysterious creations. And the deeper we penetrate into the sanctuary, the more beautiful and more mysterious it becomes.

First we enter the broad forecourt, one hundred cubits by fifty, marked out by wooden pillars with bronze bases and curtains of woven fine linen between them. At the end of the forecourt stands the tabernacle, and behind a curtain the holy place; behind another curtain there's a second space: the holy of holies with the ark, a wooden chest, in which the two stone tablets of the Torah were kept. In the holy of holies one is so to speak closest to God.

On top, these holy spaces are covered with canopies of goats' hair, tanned ram's skins and fine leather. The curtains and these coverings bear witness to Israel's reluctance to bring the Exalted One, praised be His name, too far into our reality. God is the Hidden One. He is the Invisible One. But they also bear witness to Israel's faith that the Hidden One has revealed himself and that the Invisible One wants to dwell among us human beings.

The forecourt. Look, a farmer is bringing the firstfruits of the harvest to the priest. Next to him, with an equally grateful heart, stand a father and a mother with their newborn child. Over there, at the entrance of the tent of meeting, a man is waiting. A disfiguring skin disease had driven him from the community, but now he is healed and he asks the priest to receive him back again into the midst of the people. A criminal is grasping one of the four horns of the great altar of burnt offering. The people want to kill him. He seeks support from God, and until his guilt is demonstrated, not a hair of him will be harmed.

In the middle of the forecourt stands the altar of burnt offering, five cubits long, five cubits broad. It's a colossal cube, and is clearly in the way of anyone walking straight from his own tent to the tent of God. It's a constant block. It blocks the way to God. First a sacrifice must be made.

An altar of earth you shall make for me and on it offer your burnt offerings and your peace offerings. It must be a simple altar of earth. Serve God with both feet on the ground. *You shall not go up by steps to my altar, so that your shame is not seen.* You don't need to climb to heaven to meet God. Don't build any temple towers or such Babels. Beware of vaunting yourself.

Look, someone has come with his whole family. The man is bringing a sacrificial animal with him. This animal stands for them all. In offering this animal he's offering himself and his family. First he puts his hands on the animal's head. He is thus loading on this animal as it were the whole burden of their existence and also their burden of guilt. The animal is to die that they may live. He puts on the altar the front legs, the back legs, the eyes, the ears, the heart. In so doing he is saying: 'Take our life, Lord. Take my hands, make them strong, loyal and worthy of your work. Set my feet on the ways of your Law. Take all my actions, all that I have and hold.' He puts yet other parts of the animal, the symbolism of which now escapes us, on the altar before God's holy face: the gall, the sexual parts, the heart and kidneys, the entrails. 'Take our life and let it be consecrated, Lord, to thee.'

This is an exercise in the art of giving and in the art of surrender, a religious exercise in the art of possessing as though one possessed nothing, in the art of letting go and dying. The ritual also creates community; it's a feast of reconciliation and peace: the people's burden of guilt goes up in smoke and they eat a meal sitting at long tables.

On our way to the holy place we encounter yet another special object: the bronze basin for washing. Who can wash his hands in innocence? But with God there is forgiveness. He makes sins go up in smoke. He cleanses us of all unrighteousness. Purified by water and fire, a person may boldly approach the throne of grace.

The basin was made of the mirrors of polished bronze which the women gave. A precious gift and a precious thought. Really the women were giving themselves.

62

THE HOLY PLACE

EXODUS 25.23-40; 26.31-37; 27.20, 21; 30.1-10; 34-38; LEVITICUS 24.1-9

We leave the forecourt. Not without awe we move aside the curtain which gives access to the holy place. There stands the table of the showbread.

Moses had been on the mountain for forty days and forty nights. Once more he had begun to sense that the Eternal One, blessed be His holy name, wills to be a God of human beings. 'I am the Lord, *your* God.' After that Moses came down, to make everything below as he had seen it above. 'God must have a table,' he said to the carpenter. The God who is enthroned in the holy of holies between the cherubim, with the Ten Words in the ark, must also have a table. Moses says that the table must be made of the same wood as the ark: the word of God brings people together,

Where shall Moses put the table? Not in the holy of holies. There are limits. The table must be closer to people. But again not too far from the holy of holies. Then Moses knows: the table will be put in the holy place, close to the holy of holies but not too far from the forecourt. In this way Moses seeks a balance between the reverence that wants God to be God and the love that wants to have him close.

Twelve loaves of the showbread lie on the table, *bread before God's presence.* Each loaf weighs twice as much as the daily ration of manna that the children of Israel received in the wilderness. Thus in the tabernacle the table is laid for two. Table fellowship with the Eternal One must be maintained by all twelve tribes of Israel. Just as the Eternal One is enthroned on Israel's songs of praise, so he is fed by the showbread. God would starve otherwise, just as human beings would starve without God and without God's gift of daily bread.

Here in the holy place Israel wants to celebrate and feed its communion with God day and night. So opposite the table stands the lampstand.

Light shines in the holy place. The light shines *between the two settings,* from the setting of the sun to the setting of the moon: light for God and light for human beings. The lampstand is *of one piece*, a tree whose roots reach deep into the underworld and whose crown reaches to heaven, the tree of life from the heart of paradise. The lampstand bears seven lamps. Between the two settings, when darkness covers the earth, the light must be kindled. The Keeper of Israel neither slumbers nor sleeps. In bearing witness to this, Israel is the light of the world.

Moses said that God must have light, just as God must have a table. The oil for the lamps must be carefully got from olives and be pure, so that the lampstand doesn't smoke and burns brightly.

In the midst of the night of the world, Israel will bear witness to the divine light. Therefore motifs from the almond tree are appropriate on the lampstand. This tree is called *the early waker. The waking tree.* When all the trees are still sleeping their winter sleep, in January the almond tree already begins to blossom. It's the first. And it will also be the first to bear fruit.

We see yet a third object in the holy place: the altar of incense, the altar of worship. It isn't large, made of wood covered with gold, and on top of it is the golden container in which the priest lights the incense. The incense has to be collected with great care from balsam, onyx, myrrh and frankincense.

The incense represents people's prayer. In this house, praise and thanksgiving is offered to God in smells and colours. '*Let our prayer be counted as incense before your face.*'*

We're close to the holy of holies, where God is enthroned between the cherubim, on the other side of the curtain. No wall divides God from human beings, no wooden partition, but simply a curtain. No one has ever seen the Invisible One; no mortal has ever looked upon the Eternal One. But God isn't far away. Don't we receive a sign from heaven from time to time? Don't we sometimes sense God's presence? Isn't it only a covering of clouds that divides heaven from earth?

You must make a curtain, Moses said. For that's what he had seen above, and that's what the children of Israel must make below, of blue, purple, scarlet and woven fine linen. With pious imagination they project skilfully woven cherubim and other mythical forms and creatures of paradise on the curtain.

No human being has ever seen God. A curtain hangs in front of him.

That's why prayer is sometimes so difficult. Then the sorry suspicion creeps over us that there's nothing behind the curtain and that in our prayer we're simply talking to empty space. And sometimes prayer isn't difficult. Then we've received so many signs from the other side, glimpses of God through the curtain, that we believe that nothing will be able to separate us from God's love.

In the holy of holies is the ark, the holy chest containing the two stone tablets. On either side of this ark are two carrying poles. They're a bit too long for the holy of holies. The two poles make the curtain bulge slightly. We can't see God's glory on this side of the curtain. But we can see something of it. God's glory isn't completely hidden from our eyes: in two places the curtain bulges a little. Just as, in the words of a playful rabbi, the breasts of a woman make her garment bulge. The rabbi can't see these breasts. But he can have some idea of the glory which the garment is hiding beneath it.

63

THE HOLY OF HOLIES

EXODUS 25.10-22; LEVITICUS 16; NUMBERS 6.22-27

The holy of holies. This is where God dwells, in light inaccessible. No human being may enter this space. Who shall see God and live?

No, that's not quite right. Once a year a human being may move aside the curtain and enter the holy of holies, the high priest on the Day of Atonement. But before he does that, he must first lift up a bit of the curtain and send before him a cloud of holy incense with the thurible. He won't look upon God eye to eye.

There's only one object in this holy of holies, the ark of the covenant. It's a chest of acacia wood, two and a half cubits long, a cubit and a half wide and a cubit and a half high.

Just as in the synagogue the Torah is kept in an ark, a chest, a box, so too in the tabernacle the Torah is kept in an ark. From olden days in Israel an ark has been *the* place for preserving things. Moses, the personification of the Torah, was preserved in an ark of rushes and so was saved. And in Noah's ark the whole creation is preserved and saved.

You shall overlay the ark with pure gold. And you shall cast four rings of gold for it and put them on its four feet, two rings on the one side of it and two rings on the other side of it. You shall make poles of acacia wood and overlay them with gold. And you shall put the poles into the rings on the sides of the ark, to carry the ark by them. The poles shall remain in the rings of the ark; they shall not be taken from it.

Two cherubs with terrifying eagles' wings adorn the cover of the ark. They're mixed figures who represent heaven on earth: their bodies are formed by parts of different animals, and their head is a human head. Thus they're the epitome of speed, power and discernment, beings especially suited to protect the ark with their golden wings. The ark is God's footstool, the seat of the Eternal One, enthroned on the cherubim.

The ark is a sign and pledge of God's liberating and protective presence and of Israel's election to service.

No image of God adorns the ark. *You shall make no graven images.* Nothing can be seen between the cherubim. Only those with eyes to see know that the depiction is of a great mystery.

The ark must be provided with two carrying poles. Precautions must be taken at all times for the holy shrine not to be touched by human hands. Keep off!

The carrying poles have to be stuck into four rings. These poles may never be removed from the rings. If they are, the people will get lost. Before they know it, they will have lost the sense that God can never, ever be fixed: in any land, any people, any tabernacle, any church, any book or any human being. We may never make God a static God, a God on a pedestal, an unchangeable, immovable, unmoved God. Israel's God isn't like this. Israel's God is a God of journeys. He travels with us through time and through countries, always ready to set off. With this God we're constantly on the move: nothing is fixed, nothing is firm. He is the God of pilgrims who similarly have no fixed dwelling or resting place.

On the ark lies the mercy seat. *'And you shall put the mercy seat on the ark, of pure gold. There I shall meet with you, and from above the mercy seat, between the two cherubim on the ark of testimony, I shall speak with you of all that I shall command the Israelites.'*

Everything can be spoken of in the holy of holies. Once a year, on the Day of Atonement, the high priest enters here. He does so in the name of all. He carries a bowl of blood. That blood is the image of all life. In the holy of holies a person doesn't give *something* of himself; he gives himself. Here everything is involved. Seven times the high priest sprinkles the blood on the mercy seat. 'Lord, take our life; take the burden of our life, the burden of our guilt, all the sighs of creation. Lord, take it all.'

After that, the high priest returns to the people in the forecourt. There a goat is ready. The high priest lays his hands on the goat. In this way he loads the animal with his sins and with the sins of his people. Then the scapegoat is driven into the wilderness.

Finally the priest turns to the people to give them the blessing. Probably this is an old saying from some sun ritual, but in the mouth of the high priest it has become a blessing, which in a threefold way bears witness to

God's love and warmth. In it you hear the sun of God's grace shining as it rises over the people and over the land.

> The Lord bless you and keep you,
> the Lord make his countenance shine upon you and be gracious to you,
> the Lord lift up his countenance upon you and give you peace.

64

THE HIGH PRIEST

EXODUS 28

We're given a detailed description of the curtains hung between pillars which mark out the forecourt, together with the curtains in front of the holy place and the holy of holies and their threefold covering. These are veils which bear witness that God can be spoken of only in veiled terms, but they equally bear witness that God wills to dwell among men and women.

The servants of God also wear their coverings. In the temple they don't serve in their own clothes, for there they don't stand for themselves. They represent God to human beings and human beings to God. They hold an office. They wear official dress.

The high priest is clothed in a royal mantle. His garment is multi-coloured, made of precious material and decorated with gold braid and precious stones. It's a garment of heavenly stature.

He wears a covering over his shoulders, the *ephod*, made of the same material and in the same colours as the curtain in front of the tabernacle. God and his servant have the same garment. It's as if the priest may wear God's mantle. Whoever has seen the priest has caught a glimpse of God.

God always travels incognito. He veils himself: in a person, king or beggar, in a book, in a lily of the field, in water, in bread and in wine, in the voice of the priestly person who proclaims forgiveness to you and lays hands upon you.

On the shoulder pieces of the ephod there are two onyx stones in golden settings. The names of the twelve tribes of Israel are engraved on them. We also find these on the ephod twelve names on the twelve stones which decorate the breastplate. It's a square breastplate, and in four rows of three stones the priest bears his people on his heart. Israel's high priest will never appear before God unless he takes *everyone* with him to speak with the Eternal One about *everything*.

There are twelve precious stones: sardius, topaz and carbuncle; emerald, sapphire and diamond; jacinth, agate and amethyst; beryl, onyx and jasper. In the splendour of shining colours they bear witness to the beauty of the light created by God. The children of Israel are as precious as these stones. They are called to be the reflection of God's light on earth.

The upper garment of the priest is a heavenly blue. Golden bells are fastened to the hem, little bells with little clappers, which tinkle as he walks. Wherever the high priest sets his feet, the evil spirits are driven away, and the powers of death yield.

There are also cotton pomegranates on the hem of his garment. Alternately a bell and a pomegranate. The pomegranate is a luxurious fruit: juicy, tasty, a warm red and rich in seed. It's a symbol of love, of fertility and happiness. 'How beautiful you are, my beloved! Your garden is a paradise of pomegranates.'*

On his head the high priest wears a linen turban with a plate of pure gold on his forehead, a diadem. On it is engraved *holy to the Lord*. Set apart for God. The high priest is chosen for service, just like his people. Moreover, the turban has to be worn always. Ceaselessly the children of Israel must be a kingdom of priests, *holy to the Lord*.

Centuries later, a certain John, in exile on Patmos, dreams of a new heaven and a new earth. In a vision he sees a new Jerusalem descending from on high at the end of time. In his imagination the new Jerusalem is a square.* Is it an enlargement of the square on the breast of the high priest? But what then has become of the twelve precious stones?

They form the foundation of the new city. The stones which are now carried by the high priest will one day be the ones that carry.

65

THE GOLDEN CALF

EXODUS 32

For forty days and forty nights Moses was on the mountain. God spoke with him as one friend to another. God gave him the Ten Words, words which point the way to the promised land. Signposts for life.

Forty days and forty nights, and all this time the people stayed at the foot of the mountain. Waiting. Waiting. Waiting. Moses was out of sight and gradually he also got out of mind. What were they to do with their strange prophet, who was now staying I don't know how long in higher spheres? At least, if he was still there. Perhaps he was dead. 'The Invisible One goes before us,' Moses kept explaining, but was that really so? There was so desperately little to *see.*

The people in the valley got tired of waiting. After all, what were they to make of this God of Moses? Wouldn't they be able to expect more salvation from a new leader and a tangible God? *'Aaron, make us a God whom we can see, a God like the others have.'*

What's Aaron to do? Aaron is a priest. He's moved by this wandering people. They're weary and burdened, like sheep without a shepherd. And they so want something concrete to hold on to in this world, something visible. Is that surprising, and is there much harm in it? Would Moses think differently about it? Probably Moses would agree with him: after all, they're brothers; they come from the same stock. Of course Moses is more of a prophet; he stands closer to God, but that means that he stands further away from the people. Moses is often sitting up there. Aaron is more a priestly man, close to the people, and that's quite something. Aaron knows the people, sympathizes with them, feels with them.

'Aaron, here's our gold. We want you to make a god from our gold, a god just like the peoples have, a god whom we can see and where we can feel something. A golden bull.'

It's always like that. No sooner have people liberated themselves from the fetters which held them prisoner and stand on their own feet than the temptation arises to see salvation completely and totally in their own power. 'Do it yourself!' Under the spell of their own fertility and power, human beings are inclined to put themselves on the throne. They're autonomous and free, brim full of the power of life. God has become a thing of the past, from the time when they were still small and dependent and didn't dare trust in their own power. But that's now past. Now they take their lives into their own hands. Really they put themselves on a pedestal. A golden bull.

'Aaron, here is our gold.'

Aaron made a bull out of it, at their request. But as a reassurance that this hadn't changed their faith essentially, he gave the beast the name of *God. He who has brought you up out of Egypt.*

Aaron is engaged in a good deal of to-ing and fro-ing. Of course the golden calf must be unveiled in a great and impressive ritual; pagan blood is now creeping in where it shouldn't. But because he would regret it if the whole people departed from God completely, he has notices put up: *Tomorrow is a feast of the Lord.*

Tomorrow. Does Aaron hope that Moses will be back before then?

The feast gets going, but it isn't *a feast of the Lord.* The children of Israel dance in ecstasy round the golden idol. Aaron has given the people the play they so wanted and from which they expect salvation and blessing.

The festival is in full swing, and all are enjoying themselves, when Moses comes down the mountain with the stone tablets in his hand, brim full of God. Already from a distance he hears strange sounds, a hellish racket. What do his ears hear? What do his eyes see? Flames blaze from him, he's snorting with fury. God Almighty! Moses immediately understands what they're at. He also senses that this worship of their own vital force irrevocably leads people into slavery and takes them back to 'Egypt'. For this paganism is a prison. It makes people judge their own lives and the lives of others only in terms of power and beauty, success and ability. Moses is furious. That this could have happened! He's aware in every vessel of his prophetic body that he has the mystery of life and blessing in his hands: the Ten Words which God himself has engraved on the stone tablets, the God who dwells on high and thus may never be identified with a bull.

Moses sees and hears the pagan hubbub down below. What a come-down after the exalted vision that he's just been granted on high! Then he raises God's tablets to heaven and throws them on the ground with all his might, so that they smash to smithereens. What can he do down here on the flat with the words of the Eternal One?

Isn't Moses making a bit much of it? Isn't Aaron, his brother right in making allowances? 'You mustn't ask too many questions, Moses. The people wanted it so much, and after all, our neighbours also have a god like this! And why were you away so long? We had to do something in the meantime. So we melted some gold and then out came this bull calf. It happened more or less by itself. And the calf is called God, so that can't be the point. Of course I understand you, Moses. After all, you're my brother. But put yourself in my position. You were sitting all that time with your head in the clouds and I was sitting here all by myself with all those people. Honestly, I admire you, Moses; your idealism is splendid, but there's also something called everyday reality. A person must also take into account things as they are.'

What a fascinating conversation the two brothers are having here! It's the kind of role play that is constantly there in the Bible: Cain and Abel, Abraham and Lot, Jacob and Esau, David and Saul. There's always a royal figure and there's always his counterpart, a contrast figure. There's always tension between these two. For whom shall we opt?

I've a weakness for Aaron. Moses is so great. He prompts admiration, and keeps people at a distance.

But what a seer! He sees more than his brother. He sees further. He sees where the worship of this bull can lead, and he's afraid of a disaster. He sees a religion in prospect which proclaims and legitimates the right of the strongest. The prophet fears the glorification of blood and soil. The seer foresees a world in which the high commandment of justice and love lies in fragments. Moses smells disaster. Moses sees mass graves.

And then this cowardly evasion: 'It came out by itself, Moses, the molten gold happened to take the form of a bull.' As if that's by chance! As if paganism could ever make a lamb by chance!

That's why Moses is so beside himself! That's why his trembling hands once again grasp God's holy Torah. That's why he calls for the golden calf to be broken into pieces and the ashes scattered on the water. That's why he forces the people to drink this water with ashes in it. The children of Israel must swallow their own brew and then deposit the remains of their god where this god belongs: on the dunghill. That's also why blood now flows: the instigators of this idolatry are put to death.

Is this the story of a barbaric happening in barbarous times? Does this story express a pernicious notion, of a cruel God who destroys what he doesn't like? Or is it a parable which is being played out here on the stage of the Exodus Theatre to illustrate how deadly serious what is happening here is: a matter of life and death?

How are things going to go on between God and this people? Is it now all over between them? Is everything now in smithereens? For ever?

The next day Moses climbs the mountain again. Again he speaks with God as one friend to another.

'Moses, I'm bitterly disappointed in your people,' says God.

'So am I,' says Moses. 'But why do you speak about *your* people? Hasn't it struck you, Lord God, that when the people observe the Torah you always say *my* people, but when they're disobedient, you immediately speak of *your* people?'*

'It's my anger that makes me speak like this, Moses.'

'Yes, I know,' says Moses, 'but you shouldn't get so bothered about it! How does that help? Even if in your anger you were to destroy heaven and earth, your people would still survive. You've promised. Why are you making yourself so cross unnecessarily? Moreover, surely you know how long this people has lived in the midst of all kinds of idolatry? The temptations are great, and people can easily fall. Put your hand on your heart and forgive this people its sins.'

Moses the mediator. Before his people he stands on God's side. Before God he stands on his people's side. He even manages to present a bold ultimatum to God: *'Here's the alternative: either you forgive the Israelites the evil that they have committed, or you blot my name out of the book that you have written.'*

God may choose.

66

THERE IS A PLACE BY ME

EXODUS 33

'Forgive this people, O Lord. If not, then blot my name out of the book that you have written.'

God finds it difficult to choose. Moses, the good Moses, is certainly the last person he would want to blot out of his book. But to forgive this people? However, they are going to have to go on further together; Moses is right there. God is in a dilemma.

'Moses, depart. My angel shall go before you. However, it seems better if I myself do not go with you; the people is slow to learn and if I become angry again...'

God's anger hasn't yet abated, as we can hear. That's not surprising when you think how much he loves this people. God finds it hard to swallow that Israel, his beloved, committed adultery with this God of the pagans in an unguarded moment. The Eternal One is disillusioned and insulted. It's because his love is so deep that his anger is also so deep. Even with God, something like that isn't over in a moment, our correspondent in the wilderness reports.

Of course they have to go on. God himself wants to go on. He loves this people despite everything. But he also needs to keep them at a distance. He doesn't want to lose sight of the children of Israel, but for the moment he doesn't want to see them either. *'My angel will go before you.'*

The Israelites heard the bad news: God himself won't be going with them. God is dropping out. Sorrow descended on the camp. They felt rejected. They repented. *No one put on their ornaments.* (Surprising that they still had any, after the collection for the golden calf!).

Moses pitched a tent outside the place where they were camped, a tent for God. It wasn't a tabernacle, far from it, but it was something. Moses pitched this tent outside the camp, for some distance could do no harm. The prophet had understood that clearly. God and his beloved needed some time apart. But the prophet also understood that they must remain on speaking terms with each other. Therefore Moses, too, could always be found in the tent. And when he went there, the people saw him off. The children of Israel would appear in the openings of their tents and follow Moses with their eyes until he got to God's dwelling. Then a pillar of cloud descended and stood by the entrance. Everyone knew that God was there. Then they knelt, while God and Moses spoke together.

'Lord, you say that we must depart from here. But you haven't let us know whom you will send with us. So make your ways known to me. Surely this people is your people?'

'Must my face go with you, Moses, to give you rest?'

'What I would pray you, Lord, is that if your face doesn't go with us, don't make us go from here. How else will we know that we've found grace in your eyes unless your face goes with us? After all, that's why you've separated us from the peoples, so that we may bear witness to your faithfulness. Now...'

'You're right, Moses. I love you. I also love your people. My people. That's why I was so beside myself when they turned their face from me. But you're right. So I may not yet turn my face from them, faithful or not. Let's continue our journey, Moses. I will go with you.'

Moses can't restrain his joy. He had hesitated whether to say what he had just said. Now he's glad that he did so. Does he now also dare to ask that other question? It's been on his mind for so long. Does he still dare to ask?

'Lord God, there's something else that I so want to ask you. Let me... let me see your glory.'

Even Moses, the great Moses, has difficulty with an invisible God. The prophet, too, finds it difficult to entrust himself blindly to God. 'O God, I would so much like to see the top of the carpet, and not just the underneath, with all that tangle of threads and knots, where I can't make anything out. How does the world look from your viewpoint? I would like to be a bit more certain of my calling and the way I must go. Please don't be offended, but I would so like to have a bit more than simply a vulnerable and shaky faith. I also ask this for the sake of my people. Lord God, let me see your glory.'

Moses shouldn't have asked. He feels this immediately. He's asked too much. He's gone beyond human bounds. How could a mortal see God's glory? He can't even look at the sun. The fuses would blow.

But the Eternal One isn't sure how to answer Moses. No human being can see God's glory and live. But how can a human being live if God's glory remains hidden from him? In revealing himself, God must remain the Hidden One, but while remaining hidden he must reveal himself. What answer must God give to his friend?

Then a smile plays on God's mouth. 'Listen to my words, Moses. I shall make my splendour pass by you. I shall be gracious to you and have mercy on you. However, my face you cannot see. Who I am at my most profound depth shall pass you by; no human being will ever see me and live. But there is a place by me where you can stand in a cleft of the rock. When my glory passes by, I shall cover this cleft in the rock with my hand until I have passed by. Then I shall take away my hand. Then you will be able to see me from behind. However, my face you shall not see.'

The prophet isn't granted the direct sight of God. In living and dying, even Moses has to make do with a faith *as seeing the Invisible*.* Moses spoke with God as one friend speaks with another, but he might not see God's glory. No mortal can say 'I have seen God.' Only afterwards, when he has gone past, can one say 'God was in this place.' But those who have seen God when he has gone past have seen enough.

To look on God's glory is not given to a human being in this life. However, the evangelist John believed all his days that he had seen God's glory.* He had encountered Jesus of Nazareth, and afterwards, when Jesus had gone by, he believed that in this human being God himself had tabernacled among us: *'We have seen his glory,'* he said.

67

A NEW BEGINNING

EXODUS 34 AND 39

'Moses.'

'Here I am, Lord.'

'Moses, I want to ask you to come above again. But first you must hew out two stone tablets, just like the first. Then I shall give you the Ten Words again. Be ready early in the morning to climb to the top of the mountain. I want to make a new beginning.'

Moses hewed out two new stone tablets and climbed the mountain, early in the morning. And the Lord descended in a cloud and placed himself there. *'Lord, Lord,' cried the Lord. 'I am a God who is merciful and gracious, long-suffering and faithful.'*

Twice the Lord cried out his name. 'I was the Lord. I shall be the Lord. With me is forgiveness.'

That's how the story is in the Bible; otherwise you could never have told it like this, says a rabbi: full of wonder and grateful at God's loving-kindness and for this new beginning. It's rather different from Voltaire's contemptuous saying, *'pardonner, c'est son métier'* – forgiveness is God's job.

God extends his loving-kindness to thousands. But he visits the un-righteousness of the fathers on the children and the children's children, to the third and fourth generations.

What's this? How in heaven's name can this be reconciled with the grace and loving-kindness of God that has just been mentioned? Is that long-suffering? Is that forgiveness? What kind of an image of God underlies *this*? Are we suddenly hearing the words of another narrator? We're inclined to say that the story should never have been in the Bible in this form; it should never have been told like this.

This much is clear: evil isn't being trivialized here. In God is forgiveness, but that doesn't mean that sin is no longer being taken seriously. The author doesn't think that God's job is to turn a blind eye to everything. The good bears fruit, but so does evil – let there be no mistake about that. Sin continues and leaves long traces. Surely we know that. Those who look carefully can see with their own eyes how children and grandchildren are still bowed down under deeds done by their ancestors. For example, when is a war over? Not earlier than a century after people first thought that it was over. One can't live too carefully.

Moses, too, is shocked by God's strictness. He quickly kneels down, prostrates himself and says humbly but persistently, 'O God, go with us. I know that we're a stubborn people. But by your leave, that's precisely why you must go with us. You're greater than our heart. Forgive us our trespasses. Make us your possession.'

Then God again made a covenant with Moses and the people: '*I will do marvels such as have never been performed anywhere by anyone. Keep my commandments. I shall drive out the Amorite and the Canaanite and the Hittite and the Perizzite and the Hivite and the Jebusite before you.*'

What do we have now? The mind boggles! Are these the words of a loving and tender God? Must we take these words literally? Is Israel here giving vent to nationalistic feelings of superiority in a hawklike way? In that case this story should never have been told like this and would be better out of the Bible. Or need we not take this literally? After all, in reality Israel lived for centuries with the Amorite and the Canaanite and the Hittite and the Perizzite and the Hivite and the Jebusite. It incorporated into its own culture the best of what its neighbours had to offer. There's something to be said for supposing that in these stories the Amorites and their allies represent God's enemies, the opposing powers which want to divert a people on their way to the promised land. The 'amoral Amorite' is then the embodiment of the voice which wants to lead us astray into idolatry. The narrator could have said, '*I shall drive out the devil from before you*', if the devil had been invented in Moses' days.

Up above on the mountain God and Moses have made a new covenant. But in the meantime the affair of the golden calf has taught them that such a covenant can't be guarded carefully enough. For isn't it true that the Hivite and the Hittite and the Perizzite lurk everywhere, the devil and damnation. Strange gods are ogling on all sides. Therefore in concluding this new covenant the children of Israel are made to swear an oath that from now on they will respect the sabbath. The covenant must be renewed every seventh day, even when things are busy on the land, even at the time of ploughing and the time of harvest. The rot must never set in, otherwise we shall go wrong again. Before you know it, once again you've made gold your god, and ten to one it again 'comes out' as a bull. Those who forget that they're God's creatures and God's stewards on earth, those who no longer have grateful wonder and awe of the Lord, will cease to believe that the earth is his. They will live accordingly. The consequences are well known.

The earth is God's. As a sign of this, and as a constant reminder of it, a reverent creature of God must hallow every seventh day, set it apart, and as a good steward must return the first produce of the fruit of this earth to the good Giver.

And then there is something else: *you must not seethe a kid in its mother's milk.*

With this commandment, is Israel indicating opposition to a Canaanite fertility rite? Be this as it may, there's something abominable about seething a kid in its mother's milk. That's not how you deal with creation. The milk is given by God to make that vulnerable kid grow and live!

'*Write down these words, Moses. They are the words of our covenant.*'

Moses wrote down the words and came down from the mountain, full of God, full of light. Moses shone. The glory of the Lord shone from his face with such blinding splendour and radiance that Aaron and the rest of the Israelites didn't dare to approach him. They were sore afraid, like the shepherds later in Bethlehem. This heavenly glow was more than they could bear. Moses had to cover his face with a veil.

Moses showed them the sketches of the tabernacle. 'A sanctuary for God,' he said. 'That's how it must be.'

The craftsmen got down to work and in complete accord with the heavenly plan the tabernacle arose, as it has already been described here. After months the work was ready. *And Moses saw all the work, and look, they had made it just as the Lord had commanded them.*

Where have we heard these words before? They're like words from the story of *In the beginning: And God saw all that he had made, and look, it was very good.*

Just as *in the beginning* we heard seven times that God saw that it was good, so now, in this new beginning, we hear seven times that all is done *as the Lord had commanded.*

It doesn't say that Moses saw that it was good. Moses isn't God. When Moses sees the tabernacle, that piece of heaven on earth, he can't go further than to say that the work done is *as the Lord had commanded.*

Anyhow it's a new beginning.

And Moses stretched his hands over the children of Israel and gave them the blessing.

68

WAITING FOR MIRIAM

NUMBERS 12

The laborious wanderings through the wilderness are almost at an end. Over there in the distance the hills of Canaan already glimmer and the fragrance of the land wafts out to meet the children of Israel.

But there's some delay. *And the people did not set out.* The people are waiting for Miriam, Moses' sister, who has to spend a few days in quarantine. Why?

It's a tragic story.

It began when Miriam was opposed to Moses also marrying a black woman, an Ethiopian, after his marriage to Zipporah. She was probably one of the colourful group of the rejected of the earth who had seen their chance at the time of the Exodus and had fled with Israel out of Egypt. Did Moses marry this woman for love? Or did he want in this way, close to the land of promise, to teach his followers that those who had fled with them might also share in God's benefits? But in that case, too, it was a marriage for love.

Miriam the prophetess was against it. Did she see her own position as Moses' confidante weakened by it? Did she think a marriage with a black woman undesirable? Didn't she want soon to have to share the milk and honey with all the non-Hebrews?

Miriam talked about it to Aaron. They had already said that Moses was very conceited. As if he were more a prophet than they were. As if he had a separate line of communication with God. And now this! It wasn't very nice of Moses to regard himself as a servant of God set above everyone else, but at the same time to get involved with such a stray black girl from Africa.

The Eternal One heard it.

Moses also heard it, but he didn't say anything. *Moses was a very gentle man, more than anyone on the earth.* Moses said nothing.

But the Eternal One did. '*Go outside, the three of you, to the tent of meeting.*'

They went.

And the Lord descended in a cloud, stood at the entrance of the tent and called Miriam and Aaron. 'Hear my words. With prophets in your midst I speak through dreams and visions. Not with Moses. With Moses I speak face to face, clearly and not in riddles; he is entrusted with all my house.'

Miriam and Aaron got the point: there are different kinds of prophets. With ordinary prophets God speaks in roundabout ways. But Moses is something else. The Eternal One speaks with him with a special trust, as with someone who has the run of the house. Why don't Miriam and Aaron delight in the greatness of their brother? Why do they harbour so much disapproval in their hearts?

That's what the Eternal One said, and then he left the scene. He didn't want to see those two for a while. Exit God. Exit cloud.

When the cloud had disappeared from above the tent, look, Miriam was leprous, as white as snow.

Not black as soot, like the Ethiopian woman; no, she was white as snow, a leper. Unclean! Unclean! That's what she would truly have to call out when she wanted to approach the world where others lived. Unclean!

The story doesn't tell us why only Miriam had to repent and not also Aaron. But Aaron takes up the pitiful fate of his sister: '*O Moses, do not impute to us the sin that we committed in our folly. Let her not be as a dead person, whose flesh has already half perished!*'

What is Moses, the gentle man, to do? What will this friend of God say?

'*Father, forgive them, they did not know what they were doing in their folly. O God, I want Miriam to be healed.*'

Miriam was healed.

After seven days' quarantine she will again be accepted into the community. *And the people did not set out.* The people waited for her.

On the seventh day they went on, with Miriam and with the Ethiopian woman.

Out together, home together.

69

A DISPUTE OVER A CENSER

NUMBERS 16

'*You shall be to me a kingdom of priests,*' God has said.

That means that in Israel every person is called to live a priestly life. But one tribe in particular is called to keep this sense alive: the tribe of Levi. Every day the Levites do service in the tabernacle. They represent God to human beings and they represent human beings to God. They show what priestly life is.

A priest is a treasurer. The stories of the faith are entrusted to him, the images, symbols and rituals for good and bad days. He gives little people a place in a great history. In hours of despair a priest maintains hope. He knows where the green pastures are; his prayer restores life, his commandment brings light, and his rod and his staff bring comfort. There's no reason why a priest shouldn't also be a priestess, but in the Israel of those days this wasn't yet possible.

Moses and Aaron, shoots of the stem of Levi, have aroused the wrath of a number of fellow Levites, Korah and his followers, auxiliary priests, servants of the chief priests and of the high priest. Korah refuses to be content with a subordinate role any longer: 'Aren't we all holy? You've even said that God's word that we must be a kingdom of priests, a holy people, doesn't apply to us. Why don't you take your own words seriously? Why do you think yourself holier than anyone else? Why do you take all power to yourself and threaten the community?'

Moses is alarmed. He prostrates himself on the ground and prays.

This alarm is to his credit. Is Korah right? If he's right, Moses and Aaron must mend their ways immediately.

The priesthood is a dangerous profession. Constant self-examination is needed. Before you know it, you're in fact thinking a lot of yourself. A servant then becomes a master; he comes to stand between God and human beings so that he obstructs the sight of the Eternal One. How many priests begin to play God, and build walls, and charge for admission, and bless weapons, and dine in great houses? Holiness can easily degenerate into sanctimoniousness, and those who have to conserve become ultra-conservative. 'Why do you set yourself above us? Are you more than us? Aren't we all priests?'

Moses is alarmed.

Is Korah's criticism justified? Are his motives pure? Or is Korah stirring the people up so that he can seize power himself? Is he preaching democracy but with a view to secret anarchy? Or is he angry with God and is he projecting all his frustrations on Moses? *'You have taken us away from a land of milk and honey.'*

But that's a falsification of history. Fundamentalists and cultural pessimists are prone to this: 'If only we lived in the good old days. It all used to be better, and now everything's going downhill.' Not true. A lie. Egypt didn't give its slaves a drop of milk, or a taste of honey!

'What has become of your promises, Moses? You promised us fields and vineyards. But what do we get? Wilderness and yet more wilderness!'

Have Korah and his followers lost their trust in God, and are they there-fore ceasing to trust in Moses and Aaron? *'Away with our leaders, away with our high priest, we are all priests.'* But what precisely do they intend? What's their aim?

God will know. God is the only one who knows. So he may decide. A divine judgment will indicate what God thinks about it: *'You, Korah and your followers, and you, Aaron, shall appear tomorrow before the face of the Lord. Bring your censers, with fire and with incense, and offer your censer to the Lord God. The one whom God shall choose will be the holy one.'*

Moses provokes a divine judgment. Korah and his followers will offer incense in the tabernacle together with Aaron. That will prove who enjoys God's favour.

A warning is probably appropriate here: this story doesn't have a happy ending. God will immediately make short shrift of Korah and his fol-lowers; he will strike them with lightning. What kind of story is this? Perhaps it's a much later conflict in disguise, a life-and-death conflict between rebellious country priests in Canaan and the high-up Levites in Jerusalem. Perhaps it's the same conflict as that in our day between the Bishop of Rome and the worker priests in the slums. And perhaps that's at the same time an explanation of the harsh conclusion: in such conflicts simple priests always come off worst; the chief pastor settles the matter. That's God's will, he claims, and woe to you if you think differently!

Korah and his followers gathered with their censers at the entrance to the tent of meeting. And God said to Moses and Aaron: 'Separate yourselves from the people, that I may consume them in a moment.'

Moses and Aaron prostrated themselves a second time: 'O God, Lord of all life, will you be angry with all for the sin of one person?'

It's priestly of the two to pray like this. And stubborn of God not to give in: fire comes down from heaven and swallows up the rebels.

Fear strikes at the heart of the children of Israel. Perhaps it will happen to *them* tomorrow.

Yes, and if it is up to the Eternal One, perhaps even today, since God is clearly out to strike the rebellious people with a disaster: 'Moses and Aaron, stand back quickly, so that you too are not struck.' For the third time Moses prostrates himself on the ground and begs God to withhold his catastrophe. He cries out to Aaron to go immediately and stand with his censer among the poor people and swing the holy incense: 'Quickly, for the plague has already begun.'

Aaron runs to the altar with his censer, takes fire, puts the incense on it and returns to the people. Inspired by a love which will not let him go, he stands there like one possessed, swinging his censer round and round, begging and praying that the disaster may depart.

Thus Aaron stood between the living and the dead.

And the plague ceased.

Meanwhile fourteen thousand seven hundred people had died. The narrator is playing with the holy number seven, but it's a dark game and you could hardly call this story holy.

Be this as it may, it's impossible to forget the solitary figure of Aaron the priest who, instead of getting away, went to stand among the threatened people, praying fervently for mercy and deliverance from need. In hours of despair he held out hope.

70

THE STAFF THAT BLOSSOMED

NUMBERS 17

People are quick to forget. And slow to learn. So history repeats itself. Again there is murmuring in the camp, and again Aaron the Levite has caused it: is he more a priest than anyone else? Aren't all priests? Surely it's true that not just the tribe of Levi is called to priestly service?

God gets tired of the murmuring: *'Take from each tribe the staff of the leader and write on each staff the name of the tribe. Write the name of Aaron on the staff of the tribe of Levi. Then lay down the staves before the ark of testimony. The man whom I choose, his staff shall blossom.'*

A shepherd has such a staff for driving off wild animals and keeping his flock together. A bishop has such a pastoral staff, but his is gilded. A king holds the sceptre in his kingdom, a marshal the baton in his army, a magician uses his wand for spells.

The staff is a symbol of our knowledge and ability, as in the song which the children of Israel sang* when on their wanderings they arrived at the well of Beer:

> Spring up, O well, sing to it in a refrain,
> the well which princes dug,
> which nobles of the people delved,
> with the sceptre, with their staves.

Here the praise of the ancestors is sung. Long live the man with the staff! This man can cast spells. He imposes his will on nature. With his hand and his staff he creates chances of life for himself in a world threatened by death. He knows how to bore wells in dry lands. The blessing of the staff!

But as well as the blessing there is also the curse of the staff, for misuse is also made of it. Then the staff becomes a stick for beating with. And whether the staff remains a shoot of the tree of life or becomes a dangerous weapon entirely depends on the disposition of the one who carries it.

Who shall lead the tribes of Israel? Who shall guide the people to the wells of life? Whose staff will bring salvation and awaken life? *'The man whom I choose, his staff shall blossom.'*

It's evening. The twelve staves of the twelve tribes of Israel are put in the holy of holies next to the ark. Before returning to their tents the leaders walk a while to and fro across the forecourt. They clearly find it difficult to conceal their embarrassment. What's a man without his staff? The leaders are somewhat put out and unmanned. Chiefs without staves. The signs of their dignity, the symbols of their power and might, are now with God.

That night they also sleep somewhat restlessly. How will their staves fare before the face of the Lord? If only nothing happens to them!

Happily nothing has happened to them. The next day they all receive their staves back undamaged. But something has changed. One staff has come to life. *Look, Aaron's staff blossomed. It had put forth buds, produced blossoms, and borne ripe almonds.*

We already met the almond tree earlier: the tree in Israel which always shoots in the winter. The waking tree, which awakens when all the rest are still asleep. *Look, Aaron's staff blossomed.*

Aaron is a priest after God's heart. Is that because he knows the secret of sacrifice, as this is described to us in the next chapter?* Be that as it may, it's Aaron's staff which is loaded with the power of life. It is his staff which blossoms and bears fruit and promises new life to all.

The staves of the other leaders of the tribes are as they were before.

But everything is different now.

The rulers get their staves back. With his staff, each can be a shepherd in his place, and a king and a judge. But they must be so with a truly priestly heart. They must be so in the way of that one in their midst who points towards the One. Serving. Wakeful.

71

THE BRASS SNAKE

NUMBERS 21.4-9

The end still isn't in sight. The tedious wandering is lasting much longer than they'd expected, they're getting sick to death of the manna, and when on top of everything else they still have to make a detour round the land of Edom, something snaps in the people. They mutter and murmur and resist: 'Moses, why have you... if only we... it would have been better... if you hadn't.' All those nagging questions and sneaky insinuations, all that venom which pollutes and poisons the atmosphere, the death blow to the last remnant of faith. Something like a plague of snakes.

And they know it. For when in fact a plague of snakes torments the people, they themselves make the connection between the brood of adders and their own recalcitrance: 'This must be the finger of God. Wasn't our moaning and our complaining to Moses essentially directed towards God? And as a result we've clearly brought down the wrath of the Eternal One upon us. The Lord truly has a grudge against us. The Lord is truly venomous. Those snakes don't come from just anywhere, they come from God.'

Is this primitive thought? Or is it primitive to think that? Is it naive to look to see whether there can be a connection between our way of living and the misfortune that strikes us? Or is it naive not to look for a connection and tacitly assume that whatever happens to us is always chance?

'Moses, we've sinned. We've murmured against God and against you. We've messed things up; we've poisoned ourselves and one another. We're sorry. Please ask God to forgive us. Ask him to take the snakes away from us. Please, Moses, ask. They know you at court. Will you plead for us?'

Then the good Moses prayed for the people. And the good God gave Moses the answer: '*Make a fiery snake and put it high on a pole. Every one who looks at it if he is bitten will remain alive.*'

The snake. Sneaking out of the underworld, suddenly shooting out from its dark hole, hissing with a double tongue. Its paralysing gaze and deadly bite betray the evil powers who are housed in it. For Israel it's the embodiment of evil.

'Make a snake and put it high on a pole.'

This wasn't an unknown phenomenon in those days: the image of the snake as a magic means of warding off evil. That was the teaching of ancient magic: like is healed by like. So magicians made you drink a potion of the herbs of the field in which misfortune befell you. The wisdom that lies hidden in this therapy is that the power to heal again lies *in* the powers which caused the sickness.

Another piece of wisdom is that we can bring the power of a dangerous being under control by making an image of it. The doctor who investigates a sick body or a sick spirit must first form an image of the hostile invader before he can begin a counter-attack. No therapy without diagnosis. The servant of Aesculapius can only crush the snake's head when he has first diagnosed where the monster is. Only when the beast has a name can he try to spear it with a fork, bring it to light and render it harmless.

'Moses, you must make a fiery snake and put it on a pole. Everyone who is bitten and looks at the image of the snake shall live.'

Moses made a brass snake and put it on a pole. Anyone who was bitten and looked at the brass snake was healed.

A view of the sin heals. Insight into the source of evil can be the source of healing.

The snake on the pole: a breathtaking image. Once seen, never forgotten. The snake as a symbol of sin, a visible sign of human failure. But brought to light and put up in the air as a staff of Aesculapius, at the same time it's a sign of healing and salvation.

72

BALAAM'S ASS

NUMBERS 22, 23 AND 24

The Israelites are approaching the promised land. The Moabites see them approaching and are very frightened: *'They will devour our whole land, as an ox devours the grass of the fields.'*

    King Balak desperately seeks his salvation with the prophet Balaam, a soothsayer whose words are laden with miraculous power. 'Come to Moab and curse this people, so that it perishes before we perish! Curse it! Whoever you bless is blessed and whoever you curse is cursed. Curse this people.'

We no longer recognize the curse as a deadly ray, but it isn't such a primitive idea as all that. Sometimes we hesitate to utter a loaded word: 'Don't say it aloud; don't mention it. Once it's said...' A word once spoken can never be taken back. It's been said. We can be afraid of a word that just slips out: touch wood, you never know... Words have power: they can do lifelong damage and bring lifelong comfort. They can be a blessing and a curse.

'Curse this people' was the request with which the king's messengers from Moab came to Balaam.

    Balaam is a pagan, but he nevertheless knows of Israel's God and he knows deep down inside him that this God's word cannot be gainsaid. How could he, Balaam, curse a people that this God has blessed?.

    Or perhaps...? The king's messengers said that he would be recompensed royally for it, and that put the matter in another light. Yes, light – that altered things.

    'Let me sleep on it,' said Balaam. 'Tonight I hope to hear from God whether or not I can accede to your request.'

'What are they asking?', asked God.

'They're asking whether I will curse Israel, Lord.'

'But that's not on, Balaam. It's my people. It's blessed. And you can't curse a people that is blessed. That's not on. At least, not as long as I'm God. In a word, it's not on.'

'And?,' asked the king's messengers.

'I'm sorry, gentlemen, but you must tell the king that it's not on.'

Empty-handed, the delegation returns to king Balak. 'In my view, he said no but he meant yes,' said one of the ambassadors. 'Indeed,' remarked another, 'it didn't sound very convincing to me either.'

'Perhaps Balaam thought my delegation was at too low a diplomatic level,' thought Balak. 'Or perhaps he thought that I wasn't offering him enough.'

More senior diplomats are sent to make a more princely offer in the name of the ruler.

'Gentlemen,' said Balaam, raising his voice – perhaps a bit too much to sound really convincing – 'gentlemen, even if Balak offered me his palace full of silver and gold, I would find it impossible to go against the will of the God of Israel.'

You could see the disappointment on the faces of the king's ambassadors. But also on Balaam's face. What a pity! What a waste of all that silver and gold!

'Will you spend the night? It's possible that tonight I shall hear from God whether he still has anything to add.'

'You called, Balaam?'

'Yes, Lord, I asked myself whether you couldn't think of something. Those men from Balak have come again. And I thought that to be sure I would ask you again whether...'

'Go, Balaam. Go to Moab. On one condition: you shall say only the words that I inspire in you.'

Balaam is delighted. What a good thing that he asked God once again! And it was nice that God said what he said. Or had he put words into God's mouth? No, that was nonsense. Clearly God had slept on it for another night and now it was all right. What a piece of luck! 'Gentlemen, I'm going with you. Gold be with us. I mean, God be with us. Let's go.'

Balaam mounted his ass. When he grasped the reins he saw that his hands were trembling. Nonsense! His hands didn't tremble. Why should they? No, the ass was trembling. The ass's whole body was trembling. Indeed, the animal was playing up; he reared and suddenly went left off the road, into the fields, as if he wanted to make a wide detour round something. Balaam raised his stick and whipped his mount back on to the road.

'Brother ass' is what St Francis called his body. It took him everywhere and served him faithfully along the ways of the Lord.

Balaam's brother ass refused to serve him; he reared up, he wanted to warn Balaam of the disaster which threatened. But Balaam chose not to see it. He wouldn't listen to what brother ass wanted to say to him.

Often the body sends out signals which people refuse to notice. A pain in your back, in your head, in your stomach, your hands tremble: 'You aren't going the right way,' says brother ass, but its rider doesn't listen.

Balaam won't listen. He won't see. Who really has the say here? His body must be obedient, he has to go on, he has to go through with it, and if need be he will flog brother ass harshly.

Yes, until the animal drops...

How did it go on, Balaam? You got that capricious animal back on the road and then?

'Then it went well for a while. Oh, I suppose it didn't go all that well, but at least we were on our way. Until we got to the vineyards, with the rough stone walls alongside them, you know it. There the beast suddenly had a fit. It was just as if he was afraid of something, but there was absolutely nothing to be afraid of. He squeezed against one of the walls in panic, and accidentally squashed my foot. I screamed out, tugged at the reins, gave him a bit of a beating, but the animal just wouldn't budge.

And further on, where the road got narrow and you couldn't go either to the left or to the right, he stopped completely and lay down. I rolled off his back, had a bruised foot which suddenly hurt; I stumbled, I started to beat him again, I even wanted to kick him, but that didn't work, of course, and then that beast suddenly turned his head and I looked him in the eyes, those great big eyes. 'Why have I deserved this of you, Balaam?' the ass asked. 'Have I ever beaten or kicked you? I've served you for I don't know how long, gone with you everywhere, carried your burdens – why do you strike me?'

Then it happened. Was it because of his desperate eyes? Was it the sorrow in his voice? I don't know. But I do know that suddenly my eyes were opened, and in the middle of the road, right in front of us, I saw an angel standing, dazzlingly white, with a drawn sword. And I understood. *'Why have you struck your ass three times? You were going to your downfall until three times brother ass turned aside before me – had he not turned aside, I would have killed you and left him alive.'*

The next moment the angel had gone. We were together again, the ass and I. 'I'm sorry,' I said to the good animal. 'I'm sorry. God knows I'm sorry. I've been disobedient to his voice. The blows that I deserved have come down on your back. Forgive me, in God's name forgive me. Come, let's go from here. We're going back home, my dear ass. Lord God, will you forgive me? I've behaved in a really despicable way. Thank you for intervening. Message received and understood.'

'No, wait a minute, Balaam. I would like you to go to Balak. If I remember rightly, we had agreed that there you would say the words to which I inspired you.'

'All right, Lord, I'll go. And you speak the words that I must say.'

King Balak saw Balaam approaching from afar. 'You've kept me waiting a long time, Mr Balaam.'

'I'm sorry, your majesty, but I was delayed on the way. I had some difficulties with my ass. I mean, my ass had some difficulties with me.'

'I don't understand what you mean. But don't let's lose any more time. Let's go quickly to the hill over there; it's high time that you cursed Israel.'

Balaam climbed the hilltop, had Balak build seven altars and sacrifice seven bulls and seven rams, opened his mouth and said:

> *This is the saying of Balaam,*
> *the man with the open eye,*
> *the man who hears the words of God...*

The open eye? His ass saw more than he did!

The man who hears the words of God... But didn't brother ass have some difficulty in making him listen?

> *This is the saying of Balaam,*
> *a star shall come forth from Jacob,*
> *a royal sceptre shall rise in Israel.*

'Take back those words!' cried Balak. 'that's not a curse, that's a blessing! Those words immediately begin to lead a life of their own. Curse this people, Balaam, you must curse this people!'

'How can I, sire? How can I curse those who are blessed? It's the people of God, your majesty! *God is not a man that he should lie, nor a son of man that he should repent of anything. Should he say and not do, speak and not accomplish?*'

In an all-out attempt to make the best of this hopeless situation, Balak took Balaam from hill to hill, built seven altars on each hill top and sacrificed there seven bulls and seven rams, always in the fervent hope that from another place other words would descend on Israel. His hope was vain. Balaam could speak only what God gave him to speak.

> *How good are your tents, O Jacob,*
> *how good are your dwellings, O Israel.*

The daily prayer of Jews still opens today with these words of Balaam.
Even the broadcasts of Radio Israel begin every day with this old saying.
The blessing of a pagan.

73

THE TWELVE SPIES

NUMBERS 13 AND 14, DEUTERONOMY 1

Now the journey is almost at an end. The Israelites are only a few days' journey from the promised land. Where are they to cross the frontier and where are they to settle?

Moses sends out spies, twelve in number, one from each tribe: '*See whether the land is good or bad and whether the people who dwell in it are strong or weak and whether they dwell in tents or in fortresses. Be bold and take of the fruit of the land.*'

Among those chosen is Hosea the son of Nun. He may bask in Moses' special favour, since he is his crown prince. The prophet also gives him a new name: Joshua, *God saves*. With this name he receives his calling: 'Joshua, all your life I want you to bear witness to the God who saves.'

The spies spy out the land as Moses has commanded them. After forty days they return. With good news and with bad news.

They need hardly report the good news, since everyone can see it with their own eyes: two men carrying an enormous bunch of grapes on a stick: '*We surveyed the land and we saw that it is fertile land, overflowing with milk and honey. This is its fruit.*'

However, the bad news immediately puts a damper on their joy: '*The people of the land is very strong, the cities are great and their walls reach to heaven; children of Anak dwell there, sons of Long Neck.*'

The sons of Israel have a terrible fright. It's a catastrophe. They're almost there; just a little way and all their suffering will be over. And then everything seems to have been in vain. Their world collapses. They're nowhere. They're finished.

It's an old story: the future looks attractive, but there's also nagging fear. Aren't we too small, too weak, too inexperienced? The people over there are big and strong; it's no use approaching them. Why ever did we set out on this journey? Wouldn't we have done better to stay where we were? After all, things went well for us there.

Joshua sees that matters are getting out of hand. He exclaims once again *that the land, the* erets, *is good, indeed very good*: precisely what God said at the beginning when he had created the *erets*. And the spy Caleb had clearly looked with other eyes than the rest: according to him they can go up in confidence; the land truly isn't an impregnable fortress. But the people will no longer see reason because they're so afraid, so disillusioned, so empty. And to make matters worse, the other spies add their bit: '*It is a land that devours its inhabitants; no ordinary people dwell there but giants; we were like grasshoppers, in our eyes and in theirs.*'

Yes, that's usually the case: those who are insects in their own eyes think that they're also insects in the eyes of others.

The people wept that night, and for the umpteenth time rebellion broke out: '*If only we had died in Egypt or in the wilderness! Why has God brought us here, to be killed by the sword, while our women and children are taken captive? Let us return. Let us choose a new Moses who will bring us safe and well back to Egypt.*'

It's the eternal struggle between fear and longing.

Longing gets us moving. We set out from the land or the house which we've outgrown. We long for freedom. But at the same time we're afraid, since we're treading unknown ground. Who will we encounter there? Shall we find what we're looking for? We shrink from it. Our fear can even be so great that we daren't take another step. Hadn't we better go back? *Giants and man-eaters live there! Let's go back!*

Fear and longing determine how we perceive the world and people. They also colour our attitude to God.

Fear depicts God as an almighty, a threatening God. In that case God is no companion, no friend, no caring father or mother, no good shepherd. He's a terrifying God, inexorable, vengeful. A sinful person can hardly breathe in the shadow of this God. Faithfulness, reverence and gratitude are obligations, not the spontaneous expression of someone who is free and happy.

But there is also a fear of the Lord which feeds human desires and makes people grow in confidence and a zest for living. The true fear of the Lord finally leads them to a God who loves men and women, who goes with them and who bears them up on his wings lest they fall. That is the God of Moses and Aaron, of Joshua and Caleb, the God in whom they gradually gain so much trust that they overcome their fears.

> *Those who trust in the Lord renew their strength,*
> *they stretch out their wings like eagles,*
> *they run, but do not become weary;*
> *they walk, but do not become faint.**

The people is weary and faint. 'Have trust,' exclaims Moses, 'believe me, you aren't grasshoppers, you're children of God. Truly, there are no giants in that land who will swallow you up. Be of good courage.'

But the people can't and won't listen to him any more. If Moses says another word, they'll stone him and silence him for ever.

Moses seeks refuge in the tent of God: 'What am I to do with this rebellious people? They want to stone me! All the blessings that you sent, all your loving and caring looks, seem to mean nothing to them.'

'Yes indeed, Moses, what am I to do with this rebellious people? When will they trust me just a little bit? Never, I suspect. I made such a mistake with them. Wouldn't it be better if I sent the plague so that none of them remained alive? Then I can make a new beginning with you.'

Moses is alarmed. Can he believe his ears? 'I can give them the plague,' said God. Are they words for God? For a human being to toy with such a vengeful thought in an upsurge of anger – well, nothing human is alien to him. But for God now also to react in this way... In his retort, Moses becomes a little bit godlike: 'Lord, with all due respect, you can't do this. After all, you're God. I mean, on your holy mountain you promised that you wouldn't let go of this people. Just think what they'll say about you in Egypt! 'This God of Israel promises more than he can really deliver,' they will mock; I can already hear them scoffing! No, truly you mustn't abandon the work that your hand has begun. Forgive this people. After all, you're slow to anger and long-suffering. So put your hand on your heart. Don't let go of the children of Israel.'

That's how Moses spoke with God that night, and in the end God indeed put his hand on his heart and granted his people forgiveness. Except that God thought it far too good for them that they should go on as usual and enter the land as though nothing had happened. He thought it better that for the moment the children of Israel shouldn't enter the promised land.

So both Moses and God repeat their moves. And the Israelites don't really know what they want: a moment ago they wanted to go back to Egypt; now they want to invade the land immediately at all costs. It seems to be a flight forward. Moses has to dissuade them forcefully; in his view an unplanned attack is just as bad as an unplanned retreat. Hadn't they better wait, give themselves time, sort themselves out with one another and with God?

The children of Israel don't listen. They can't and won't. They set out – without the ark of the covenant accompanying them. Moses doesn't accompany them either. They lose the battle.

It's remarkable that they wrote all this down. Israel's epic is truly no heroic saga. Or is it heroic to look back in exile and regard your defeat as the consequence of your eternal rebellion? And is it brave, after examining yourselves, to repent so honestly and to bear witness so openly to your fear and your disputes, to the long painful way from slavery to freedom and to your laborious quest for God?

74

THE DEATH OF MOSES

DEUTERONOMY 34

Then Moses died.

He died as he had lived: in great solitude and close to God.

All alone he had lain in a little basket of reeds, surrounded by the waters of death.

Alone he had lived at Pharaoh's court, a little Jewish boy far from home.

Alone he had fled to Midian, where he tended Jethro's herd as an exile.

Alone he had stood before God, who spoke to him from the burning bush.

Alone he had fought the struggle of faith, until he finally found courage and accepted his calling.

Alone he confronted Egypt's Pharaoh face to face, and alone he walked out before his people on that wondrous night, so different from all other nights.

Alone he led the long column of fugitives through the sea and through the wilderness, with no idea where the next day would find them. A journey without end, with constantly receding horizons, ever new enemies and hardships, continually endangered by the wavering faith of his followers.

Alone he spoke with God on top of the holy mountain. He spoke with God as one friend speaking to another, in a gratifying intimacy which at the same time threatened to estrange him from his people. He had never been lonelier than when, coming down from the mountain, he saw in the valley below how his beloved Israel had turned from God and were dancing in cheap adulation round a tawdry god of their own making.

It had been an exhausting existence. *But Moses' eye was not dim, nor did his natural force abate.* That must mean that right up to the bitter end, he never lost his vision. And that's exactly the way the story is told: God allows his faithful servant to see the promised land from a mountain top.

How sweetly it lies, on the far bank of the river!

Will Moses, after all his wanderings, finally be allowed to cross the river and enter the land he's longed for all his life?

No, he won't.

And no one knows exactly why.

One story* has it that Moses was denied entry because he'd blundered by striking a rock, rather than commanding that rock to give water to a thirsty people. But what precisely Moses' transgression was remains unclear, as do God's reasons for finding it so serious that he couldn't forgive his old friend. Another story* makes a connection with Moses' extreme old age; in that case it isn't so much a matter of guilt as of tragic destiny. Yet another source* would have it that Moses acted in solidarity, even in death, with the many who had passed through the wilderness with him and died before entering the land of their dreams.

Thus from time immemorial there have been many thoughts about the end of Moses' life, and in our day too his death continues to fire the imagination. Goethe toyed with the idea that Moses may have been murdered, and Freud followed him here: in the course of their exodus, the Israelites had gradually grown to hate their leader so much that they finally disposed of him. A case of parricide.

But is it really all that complicated? By dying in the wilderness Moses remains the man of the Torah. He's completed his task. It's up to others, to Joshua and his men, to tread the holy ground of Canaan and there give form to the Torah.

And where Moses died, just this side of the border separating us from the promised land, isn't that the place where all mortals die? Does anyone ever see the final fruits of their labour? None of us sees the harvesting of what we've sown. That's up to other people. We've heard of a land on the other side; it's been promised to us and we've dreamed of it on the way. We've even caught a glimpse of it, from a distance. But we can't enter it; it lies on the far shore of the river of death. *Abraham, Isaac, Jacob, Sarah, all these died in faith, not having received the promise, but having seen it and greeted it from afar, and having acknowledged that they were strangers and exiles on earth.**

God let Moses see the land from a distance. His eye was not dim, nor his natural force abated. There was a vision, a distant prospect which he kept constantly in view. Perhaps Moses, now that he was about to die, saw more clearly than ever.

Moses went up the mountain. He sat on a rock. And while he was sitting there, on the edge of timelessness, where distant prospects open up, the children of Israel came to bid him farewell.* One by one, they passed behind him in single file: not in front of him, for then they would have obstructed the old man's view of the land. No, they passed behind him, one by one, and one by one they laid a hand upon his shoulder. And every time Moses felt a hand upon his shoulder, he laid his own hand upon it, as a final farewell. Until, yes, until finally the moment came when no more hands rested on his shoulder. Moses kept feeling, but there were no more hands. They had all passed by. Even the last of them had passed by. Moses was alone.

That's how we all die. We can't hold on to each other. We have to let each other go. A person has to die alone. The others go on.

No one was there when Moses died.

Moses, the man of God, died in the land of Moab, according to the word of the Lord. And God buried him.

God did him the last honour. He buried his friend with his own hands. He covered him, as a mother covers her child.

God buried him in a valley in the land of Moab, opposite the sanctuary of Baal*, and no one knows his tomb, to the present day.

It should be possible, you might say, to find that place opposite the sanctuary of the god of the Moabites. But it's not a place on the map. Nowhere can Moses be shown to be dead. Those who seek him don't seek him in a tomb. Those who want to honour the dead man honour the living word he brought down from on high. It's a word opposing all idolatry, and that word isn't dead: from that place in the land of Moab, opposite Baal, it resounds down to the present day. Each new generation that wishes to enter the land must hear it.

And the people of Israel wept for Moses in the plains of Moab for thirty days; then the days of weeping and mourning for Moses were ended.

The days of mourning, even mourning for great men, come to an end. The workers come and go. The work goes on.

And Joshua, the son of Nun, was...

To be continued.

ABOUT THE BIBLE

The Bible (from the Greek *biblia*, meaning 'books') is a library in itself, comprising a varied collection of books – sixty-six in all – written during a period of more than a thousand years (900 BC – AD 130). Often the texts underwent a long development, and in the form in which we know them today they are the result of an age-old process of growth. The book consists of two main sections.

Christians call the first section the Old Testament; it comprises the thirty-nine sacred books of the Jewish faith, written in Hebrew. The second section is called the New Testament, and comprises the twenty-seven sacred books of Christianity, written in Greek.

The First, or Old, Testament is referred to by Jews as the 'TeNaKh', an acronym consisting of the T of Torah (Law), the N of Nebi'im (Prophets) and the K of Kethubhim (Writings), the main divisions of the book.

The *Torah* (called 'Pentateuch' in Greek) comprises the first five books of the Bible and describes, primarily in narrative form, the way to live. *Instruction, guidance*, is a better translation of the word Torah than law. Because Moses was thought to be the author, these books are also called *the books of Moses*.

In the *Nebi'im*, the prophetic writings, the people of God are summoned to follow the Torah. The *Nebi'im* are subdivided into the 'Former Prophets' (Joshua, Judges, Samuel, Kings) and the 'Latter Prophets' (Isaiah, Jeremiah, Ezekiel and the twelve minor prophets). In an unguarded moment, Christianity called the 'Former Prophets' 'the historical books', thereby wrongly giving the impression that these stories are historical and not prophetic in character. It is especially because of this that in my retelling of the Old Testament I have preferred to follow the division of the TeNaKh.

In the *Kethubhim* we find a more individual reflection on the Torah. These writings offer a richly varied collection of prose and poetry (including Psalms, Job and Proverbs), as well as the five *megilloth*, the scrolls read publicly in the synagogue during Jewish days of remembrance (Ruth, Song of Songs, Ecclesiastes, Lamentations, Esther).

The Second or 'New' Testament consists of four Gospels (Matthew, Mark, Luke and John), the Acts of the Apostles, a number of letters and the Book of Revelation. The Gospels and Acts were written some time after Jesus' death (between AD 70 and AD 100), and bear witness to the faith of the first Christian community. They are not 'historical' texts in our sense. The letters, written by various authors, are among the oldest books of the New Testament. The Book of Revelation was written as a work of the Christian resistance, intended to offer comfort to persecuted believers in a language accessible only to the initiated.

TRANSLATOR'S ACKNOWLEDGMENT

Translating Nico ter Linden's remarkable books have presented enormous problems. In retelling the stories of the Bible he uses a special kind of Dutch, at times colloquial, at times archaic, and often reflecting the original Hebrew. This interplay of various levels of Dutch is one of the appeals of the books, but is sometimes all but impossible to reproduce in English. In addition, he makes use of Dutch hymns and children's hymns, Dutch traditional songs and other indirect allusions, which again cannot be translated directly; sometimes it is possible to introduce English equivalents to retain the effect, sometimes this cannot be done.

I wish to acknowledge here the interest and concern shown in the English translation by Nico ter Linden himself, but more particularly the painstaking work and the help of Dr Henk Aertsen, Senior Lecturer in the English Department of the Free University of Amsterdam, who has checked out the translation and has been a sure guide through the minefield of sub-meanings as well as correcting errors and misunderstandings. Without him the translation would have been much inferior, and he deserves my deepest gratitude. Any errors that remain are mine.

John Bowden

BIBLIOGRAPHY

This retelling is often based on sermons that I have given over the years. Where I can discover the sources that I consulted for these sermons I have mentioned them.

For this book as a whole I am much indebted to the work of Dr F. H. Breukelman and Professor Dr K. A. Deurloo. I have also sometimes made grateful use of the sermons of my teacher Dr J. A. Kwint, who died in 1964. My debt to the well-known commentaries will be evident.

A list of the other Dutch works which I have used can be found at the back of the Dutch original of this volume. Here I list simply those works which are available in other languages:

Martin Buber, *Moses*, Heidelberg 1966

Karel A. Deurloo and Nico Bouhuys, *Lesen, was geschrieben steht. Zur Bedeutung biblischen Redens und Erzählens*, Offenbach 1988

Karel A. Deurloo and Nico Bouhuys, *Näher zum Anfang. Die Bedeutung der ersten Erzählungen der Bibel*, Offenbach 1989

Karel A. Deurloo, 'Narrative Geography in the Abraham Cycle', *Oud Testamentische Studiën* 26, Leiden, etc. 1990, 48-62

Bernd Jorg Diebner and Karel A. Deurloo (eds), *YHWH – Kyrios – Antitheism*, Amsterdam 1996

Eugen Drewermann, *Den eigenen Weg gehen*, Munich 1995

Eugen Drewermann, *Ich lasse Dich nicht*, Düsseldorf 1994

Eugen Drewermann, *Leben, das dem Tod entwächst*, Düsseldorf 1991

Eugen Drewermann, *Strukturen des Bösen*, Paderborn 1988

Eugen Drewermann, *Tiefenpsychologie und Exegese* I and II, Olten 1984 and 1989

Eugen Drewermann, *Voller Erbarmen rettet Er uns*, Freiburg 1985

Edmond Fleg, *Moses*, Munich nd

Joannes P. Fokkelman, *Narrative Art in Genesis*, Assen, Amsterdam 1975

Martin Kessler (ed. and trans.), *Voices from Amsterdam. A Modern Tradition of Reading Biblical Narrative*, Atlanta 1994

Helen M. Luke, *The Inner Story. Myth and Symbol in the Bible and Literature*, New York 1982

J. Sandford, *The Man who Wrestled with God*, New York 1974

Meir Shalev, *Tanach achshav*, Tel Aviv 1985 (German: *Der Sündenfall – ein Glücksfall? Alte Geschichte aus der Bibel neu erzählt. Aus dem Hebräischen von Ruth Melcer*, Zurich 1997)

Phyllis Trible, *Texts of Terror*, Philadelphia 1984 and London 1985

NOTES

Chapter 1

p. 4   H.M. Kuitert, *I Have my Doubts*, London 1993
p. 5   M. Buber, *Tales of the Hasidim*, New York 1947

Chapter 2

p. 7   Revelation 21.1

Chapter 3

p. 12   M. Buber, *Tales of the Hasidim*

Chapter 4

M. Bal, *En Sara in haar tent lachte*, Utrecht 1984
p. 20   M. Buber, *Tales of the Hasidim*

Chapter 5

K. H. Kroon, in *Phoenix Bibelpocket* 2, Zeist 1962
C. Meves, *Psychologische kijk op de bijbel*, Freiburg 1973
Related by H. van Praag, in *Phoenix Bibelpocket* 1, Zeist 1962

Chapter 6

K. A. Deurloo, in *Amsterdamse Cahiers* 6, Kampen 1985
p. 25   Gerrit Achterberg

Chapter 7

p. 29   J. J. Buskes, *In nacht en stormgebruis*, Utrecht 1941
p. 30   Matthew 18.21-22

Chapter 8

F. H. Breukelman, in *Amsterdamse Cahiers* 1, Kampen 1980
T. J. M. Naastepad, *Onder het gericht*, Amsterdam 1968
W. Janssen, *Hij zei: Noach maak een ark*, Zoetermeer 1995
p. 32   A. Koolhaas, *Noach*, Amsterdam 1970
p. 33   Matthew 24.38, 39

Chapter 9

M. Vervenne, in *Schrift* 153, Heilig Landstichting 1994

Chapter 10

J. M. de Jong, *Bijbelse knooppunten*, The Hague 1952
K. H. Kroon, in *Phoenix Bibelpocket* 2, Zeist 1962

Chapter 12

B. Becking (ed.), *Een patriarchale leugen*, Baarn 1989

Chapter 14

E.L. Smelik, *Vrije postille*, The Hague 1962
A. Wessels, *En allen die geloven zijn Abrahams geslacht*, Baarn 1989
p. 53   Hebrews 7.1-3

Chapter 15

p. 57   Hélène Swarth

Chapter 16

J. W. Mazurel in R. Abma (ed.), *Nog dichter bij Genesis*, Baarn 1995

Chapter 17

B. Siertsema, in *Werkschrift juni 1987*, Amsterdam 1987
P. Trible, *Texts of Terror*, Philadelphia 1984 and London 1985
p. 64   Luke 1.7

Chapter 19

p. 71   Muus Jacobse, *Het oneindige verlangen*, Nijkerk 1982
p. 72   Psalm 113
p. 74   Luke 1.46-49

Chapter 20

M. A. Beek, *Wegen en voetspoeren*, Delft 1957

Chapter 21

M. A. Beek, *Wegen en voetspoeren*, Delft 1957
R. Zuurmond, in *Amsterdamse Cahiers* 5, Kampen 1984
p. 82   Matthew 10.15
p. 84   Luke 9.62

Chapter 23

K. A. Deurloo, in *Amsterdamse Cahiers* 5, Kampen 1984
E. Drewermann, *Leben, das dem Tod entwächst*, Düsseldorf 1991
p. 92   Hebrews 11.18,19

Chapter 24

p. 94   *Hymns Ancient and Modern Revised* 292, *English Hymnal* 503

Chapter 25

p. 99   Psalms 42.6; 103.2

Chapter 26

p. 104   Mark 12.18-27
p. 105   Edmond Fleg. I have the text only as a cutting

Chapter 27

T. J. M. Naastepad, *Onder het gericht*, Amsterdam 1968

Chapter 28

Probably this is the scene that we find in Rembrandt's painting 'The Jewish Bride'. The part of the canvas which depicted King Abimelech has been lost.

p. 110   W. Barnard

Chapter 29

p. 113   F. H. Breukelman's fantasy
p. 117   Psalm 133

Chapter 30

K. A. Deurloo, in *Schrift, November 1989*, Heilig Landstichting 1994

Chapter 31

M. A. Beek, *Wegen en voetsporen*, Delft 1957
F. H. Breuklemna, *Bijbelse theologie* I 1, Kampen 1980
M. Shalev, *Tanach achshav*, Tel Aviv 1985

Chapter 32

E. Drewermann, *Ich lasse Dich nicht*, Düsseldorf 1994
B. Siertsema, in *Werkschrift juni 1987*, Amsterdam 1987

Chapter 34

K.H. Miskotte, *Uitkomst*, Amsterdam 1958
A. Uleyn, in *Schrift* 80, Heilig Landstichting 1982

Chapter 35

T.J.M. Naastepad, *Het scharlaken snoer*, Hilversum 1961

Chapter 36

O. Jager, *Daglicht*, Kampen 1970
p. 143   Genesis 49.4
p. 143   Genesis 34

Chapter 37

F. van Dijk, in *Schrift* 112, Heilig Landstichting 1987
G. van Broekhuizen, in *Schrift* 158, Heilig Landstichting 1982
A. H. van den Heuvel, in *Werkschrift juni 1987*, Amsterdam 1987
p. 152 Psalm 92.13

Chapter 38

F. H. Breukelman, in *Om het levende woord* 5, Kampen 1995
p. 157   Deuteronomy 23.24

Chapter 39
J. Smit and H. Stroeken, *Lotgevallen*, Amsterdam 1993

Chapter 40
J. Smit and H. Stroeken, *Lotgevallen*, Amsterdam 1993
p.165   Felix Timmermans

Chapter 47
p. 192   W. Barnard

Chapter 48
R. Zuurmond, in *Mededelingen Van der Leeuwstichting* 41, Amsterdam 1970

Chapter 49
J. Siebert-Hommes, *Laat de dochters leven*, Kampen 1993
J. Witkam, *Spiegelbeeld*, Hilversum 1977

Chapter 50
p. 206   Thomas Aquinas

Chapter 54
H. A. Visser, *Ik gedenk u uit het land der Jordaan*, Nijkerk 1961

Chapter 55
P. Kevers, in *Schrift* 133, Heilig Landstichting 1982
p. 220   Psalm 119.39

Chapter 56
K. A. Deurloo, *Wat heb je, zee, dat je vlucht?*, Baarn 1986
p. 222   Psalm 114

Chapter 57
p. 228   Elie Wiesel, *De wanhoop verdreven*, Hilversum 1986

Chapter 58
p. 233   Vondel, *Lucifer*, Amsterdam 1937

Chapter 59
J. Soetendorp, *Symboliek der Joodse religie*, Hilversum 1966
J. J. Buskes, *Kort en goed*, Wageningen 1973
p. 237   Psalm 119 (which sings the glory of the Torah) v.39
p. 238   M. Buber, *Tales of the Hasidim*

Chapter 60
P. A. H.de Boer, in *Phoenix Bibelpocket* 6, Zeist 1963
p. 239   II Corinthians 3.6
p. 240   Talmud
p. 241   Abel Herzberg, *Amor fati*, Amsterdam 1946

Chapter 61

D. E. Hofstra and D. Monshouwer, *Exodus*, Zoetermeer 1995
W. ten Boom, *Bloed en Vuur*, Amsterdam 1946

Chapter 62

p. 249   Psalm 141.2

Chapter 63

B. Diebner, in K. A. Deurloo (ed.), *YHWH – Kyrios – Antitheism*, Amsterdam 1996

Chapter 64

p. 255   Song of Songs 4.3, 13
p. 255   Revelation 21.9-22

Chapter 65

p. 259   Elie Wiesel, *Messengers of God*, New York 1976

Chapter 66

p. 262   Hebrews 11.27
p. 262   John 1.14

Chapter 67

J. P. Boendermaker, in F. G. van Binsbergen, *Grensgebieden*, Kampen 1985

Chapter 70

p. 272 Numbers 21.17, 18
p. 273 Numbers 18

Chapter 72

E. Drewermann, *Voller Erbarmen rettet Er uns*, Freiburg 1985.

Chapter 73

H. Andriessen, in *Speling september 1981*, Nijmegen 1981
p. 283   Isaiah 40.31

Chapter 74

p. 286   Numbers 20.2-13
p. 286   Deuteronomy 31.2
p. 286   Deuteronomy 1.37; 3.26; 4.21
p. 286   Hebrews 11.13
p. 287   The image is taken from the film *Green Pastures*.
p. 287   Deuteronomy 4.3